LES PAUL

IN HIS OWN WORDS

CENTENNIAL EDITION

Les Paul and Michael Cochran

Foreword by Paul McCartney

Photographed by Wolf Hoffmann

T0346202

Backbeat
Books

An Imprint of Hal Leonard Corporation

Centennial Edition, 2016

Backbeat Books
An Imprint of Hal Leonard Corporation
7777 West Bluemound Road
Milwaukee, WI 53213

Trade Book Division Editorial Offices
33 Plymouth St., Montclair, NJ 07042

Published by Backbeat Books in 2016

Previously published by Gemstone Publishing, Inc., in 2008 and The Russ Cochran Company in 2005

Printed in the United States of America

Book design by Michael Kronenberg

Library of Congress Cataloging-in-Publication Data is available upon request.

ISBN 978-1-4950-4739-8

www.backbeatbooks.com

Contents

Acknowledgments from the First Edition

The publisher wishes to thank the many individuals and institutions who contributed to this book. By providing important photographs or information, they enrich our enjoyment of the life story of one of the most fascinating characters in the history of Twentieth-Century America.

Foremost among these is Les Paul himself, who opened his home and his heart to us. Most of the visual images and historic data in this book come from his extensive archives of photographs, clippings, instruments, recordings and memorabilia. The vast amount of information generated by his 75-year career is managed and organized by Les's oldest son "Rusty" (Lester George Paul). We are especially indebted to Rusty for the many hours he spent looking for photographs and scanning them for this book, Rusty also helped immensely by locating each of Les's guitars for photography. Les's friends, Ralph De Liz, Elliott Liggett, and Chris Lentz (www.redhotred.com), assisted Rusty by scanning and sending photos in response to our specific requests. Arlene Palmer was always there to offer her support.

Sue Baker of the Waukesha County Historical Society and Museum provided important early photographs and historic information about Waukesha. The Museum is building a permanent exhibit devoted to Waukesha's favorite son, Les Paul. Thanks to Gibson historian Walter Carter, who proofed the text and corrected some of our errors.

Peter Kiefer, Coordinator of the Fred Waring's America Collection at Pennsylvania State University, supplied great photos from the 1938-1941 era. Other photos were provided by Marty Winter, and by Les's sideman of over 20 years, Lou Pallo.

To meet the challenge of contacting Sir Paul McCartney directly to request his foreword, we called on two old Nashville friends, Harry Warner and David Conrad. Our troubadour guitarist brother Tommy Emmanuel had an important role in helping point us in the right direction, and we are indebted also to John Dillon, Larry Lee, Mike Henderson, Jim Photoglo and Bernie Boyle for helping us in this effort. We offer our sincere thanks to Sir Paul, who responded instantly on Les's behalf upon receipt of our request.

Tom Doyle, who has done sound for Les at the Iridium Jazz Club and driven him to the show every Monday night for twenty years, was a constant source of help and support. Tom vouched for us in helping establish our first connection with Les, for which we will be ever grateful.

Thanks to Victor's House of Music in Paramus, New Jersey, who loaned us guitar stands used in Wolf Hoffman's photography for this book.

Most of all, thanks to Les Paul for allowing us into his life and making this book possible. Over a period of three years and many visits to his New Jersey home, Mike and I always found a warm welcome and willingness to keep going with stories old and new. With over a hundred hours of tape-recorded interviews and innumerable telephone conversations, we feel we have portrayed the essence of the man, "in his own words."

—Russ Cochran

Preface

Born in the bustling little city of Waukesha, Wisconsin in 1915, Lester William Polfuss came of age in an era ripe with opportunity and brimming with the new technology of life-altering inventions by Tesla, Edison and Marconi. Stoked by the surging spirit of adventurous self-reliance personified by Tom Swift, the Hardy Boys and the Boy Scouts, the post-war Twenties roared with rapidly changing social mores, artistic creativity and pre-Depression optimism.

The grandson of immigrants, young Lester soon exhibited an inborn Germanic talent for analytical thinking and an insatiable curiosity about the world around him. Coupling a relentless dedication to accomplishing his goals with a natural flair for showmanship, his scientific and musical abilities merged with the advent of electronics and the birth of jazz to launch and maintain a spectacular career that now spans three-quarters of a century.

The guitar techniques perfected during his playing prime introduced innovations universally copied but seldom equaled. His contributions to audio recording and the electronic processing of sound blazed new trails that have become superhighways in his wake, and his public persona as an irrepressible, devil-may-care rascal of rapier wit infused authentic spontaneity into the scripted world of entertainment.

Always an aggressive and fearless daredevil in the face of change, he began his professional career at 13 as Red Hot Red, evolving into Rhubarb Red and achieving wide success as a country performer while still in his teens. Inspired by jazz greats of the day, he introduced Les Paul as a new persona and became the primary force in popularizing the electric guitar. Jazz purists accused him of selling out when he turned from that genre to pursue success in popular music, but theirs was a self-serving complaint. Possessing the courage and determination to repeatedly re-invent himself, Les was just doing what he wanted to do.

We had never met Les before we knocked on his door for the first time in June 2002. By reputation, we expected an unpredictable combination of genius, prankster, and storyteller. Now, three years and many intimate conversations later, we know the real Les Paul is all of the above, and much more. In receiving the honor of his trust, we've realized that all aspects of this complex man emanate from a single source: a formidable intellect and one of the most

Michael Cochran, Les Paul, and Russ Cochran.

perceptive minds you will ever encounter.

To illustrate, consider the day we were with him in his Mahwah home observing his good friend, Ralph De Liz, scanning pictures at a computer. Absorbed in thought, Les suddenly said, "You know, the body is analog, but the mind is digital." The profound simplicity of this revelation illustrates an integral aspect of his genius: the innate ability to see directly into the heart of the matter, and then to express that insight in terms anyone can understand.

We doubt any single individual should be credited as the sole originator of any of the multiple pursuits to which Les has applied himself. The history of how breakthroughs in audio technology and the advent of electric guitar impacted the evolution of popular music includes the noteworthy contributions of many people, and to be overly concerned with who did or did not invent this or that misses the point of this man's individual greatness.

What Les Paul has always done is take everything available outside his mind and integrate it with his own ideas to produce unique innovations. And what his creative tinkering brought forth was an audio charisma not heard before, a sound that made everyone else stop and listen. Taken together, the enduring influence of his singular contributions to recording technology, instrument design, and American popular music are unsurpassed by any other single individual.

We are privileged and proud to present the Les Paul story as he himself wants it to be told. We've verified facts where possible, but make no claim of infallibility. We will say that, time after time, when we were in doubt about something Les told us, new information from other, unbiased sources proved him right.

Michael spent many long days interviewing Les.

In his own introduction, Les makes the point that right answers start with right questions. As you read his story, you'll see that Les has been asking the right questions all his life, compelled by the desire to know that bedevils him to this day. Wherever his ideas have taken him, he's been a Cadillac barreling down a dirt road at 90 miles per hour,

Russ sits in during one of Les's Monday night shows at Manhattan's Iridium Jazz Club.

leaving everyone along the way to contemplate his dust. The challenges have been many, the triumphs are forever woven into the tapestry of modern history, and the truth can now be told: his greatest invention is himself.

Russ Cochran *Michael Cochran*

Foreword

Les Paul is one of those guitar players who is every other guitar player's hero. From his earliest recordings, he stamped his incredible energetic identity on everything he did. Having long been an admirer of his, I have seen him more recently at a small club in New York and the magic is still there. The innovations that he brought to the electric guitar are astounding and it is not surprising that the guitar named after him by Gibson is one of the best on the market.

When I was a kid, John Lennon and I were staying at my cousin's pub in the South of England and had been encouraged to play a small gig on our guitars one Saturday evening. While we were considering what our opening number might be, we suggested 'Be-Bop-A-Lula' to my cousin but he said 'no, go for something faster and instrumental to get you onstage, then sing 'Be-Bop-A-Lula'. The song we decided to play instrumentally was 'How High the Moon' based on our love of Les and Mary's record.

Seeing that this gig was before the Beatles, you could say that Lennon/McCartney's first live gig opened with a tribute to Les Paul…and if that is so, it sounds like a great idea to me, for Les is truly one of the greats.

Paul McCartney

9

Introduction

For all the interviews I've done for books about the history of the electric guitar and audio recording, and the countless articles generated by my work as a musician and entertainer, whoever was doing it would talk to me and then write what they thought. Looking back, I can see where each one made a wrong turn, and then it wasn't my story anymore. My Mother would go into a rage over these things. She'd read something, and say, "This is not true, Lester. It's wrong! Why can't they ever get it right?" And I'd say, "Ma, you've got to allow for shrinkage. Maybe you get 50 percent, maybe you get 75 percent, but nobody gets everything."

And then came the wonderful accident to have these two fellows from Missouri come into my life. Not only was I familiar by my own experience with their background, but when we first met, I felt right at home. I had that great warm feeling that comes from dealing with the kind of people I prefer to have as friends, people I can trust who have their act together. Their talents are as important as my own, so it was easy for us to establish the personal connection and mutual respect that had to exist for this book to be created.

If the right questions are asked, I'm glad to give the right answers. And the great thing about this book is the fact that the right questions were asked, including the tough ones. The answers acknowledge that some of what I did hurt people I loved, that I'm a workaholic and a little hard to get along with sometimes, or very hard to get along with, depending on the situation. And I'm glad it's included because I don't want any blame to go to the people who worked so hard to help me get where I was going. The good side was the tremendous success we achieved, and the down side was that nobody could run as hard as I did, and when they one by one fell by the wayside, I just kept going that much harder. And in Mary's case, it was things she never bargained for in the first place.

Mike took what I said over a three year time period and put it on paper with better clarity than I could ever have done myself. I've gone over it with a fine-toothed comb, and the thing that impresses me is that the very thought I'd be about to add was already written in the very next line. All I had to do was read a little further, and the thought was there without me having to say it. And Russ has done a fantastic job heading up the whole thing, arranging for Wolf to do the incredible photography and putting the written story together with the pictures in such a beautiful way.

It's very difficult to find people as talented as these two guys are, who

Ma and me on her 100th birthday.

also understand how to get the job done right. Everyone is talented in some way, but to have the smarts and dedication to take that talent and put it into an exacting form like this book, that's the rare thing.

When it comes to a dedication, I couldn't pick one person any more than if I had eleven kids and was asked to pick my favorite. I've been terribly lucky to have many great friends in my life, and they weren't hard to come by. Friends are what I live for, and to all of them, new and old, this book is dedicated.

I love this book. It's honest, it captures all my thoughts and verbalizes how I feel about so many things I never anticipated putting on record. I think it's fantastic in every way, and it's too bad my Mother won't have the opportunity to read it. I know she would be very proud of it, just as I am. I can just hear her saying, "Lester, I think they got it right this time."

Les Paul

CHAPTER ONE

Waukesha Childhood

I remember listening to my Mother play the piano when I was still crawling on the floor. When she needed time to herself, she would just say, "Now you go in the kitchen and play with your pots and pans." So I'd go pull out everything I could reach and spread it around on the kitchen floor and form an imaginary orchestra while she sat and played the piano in the living room. She was getting a divorce during that time, with two young boys to raise, and was going through some very rough times a little kid wouldn't know anything about.

We moved into this house at 320 West St. Paul Avenue when I was 2 years old.

Mother's Blues

It was mostly old German songs she loved to play. They took her back to her childhood, her young, young days when she was a kid herself. She would play mournfully and cry because of what she was thinking. She didn't know, but I was listening and watching. I recognized the soul Mother had by the tears in her eyes and by the fact that when she played, she was talking with her hands, saying she was very unhappy. Everything she was going through was all expressed very clearly, without any words. This was the blues, and I felt and understood it long before I knew where it came from or what caused it. I saw something very strong and deep in my Mother then, and the great thing is that she very soon saw the same in me. She was the biggest single influence of my life, and we were close in a way that never diminished till the day she died at the age of 101 and a half.

13

I was born upstairs over my Dad's Garage on June 9, 1915.

George Polfuss

I loved my Dad, too. He was good man, a great rascal and storyteller, but he just didn't pay much attention to family matters and was never around. He was the first to call me Red, and always called me by that name. After they got divorced, he stayed in Waukesha and ran a garage business, George's Garage. He was well known around Waukesha, and usually off on the road or trying to catch a nurse somewhere. If you wanted to find him, you had to find the nurse, or the crap game.

When he was gambling and running around, my Dad was in with a pack of local high rollers in a regular crap game, and he would win all kinds of strange things. He came home one winter night, drunk as a skunk, with a trombone he'd won. I woke up enough to hear him blow one note. He opened the bedroom window, blew the note, then threw the slide out the window into the snow, and the rest of the trombone after it. And that was the end of the trombone. Another time, he came home with a violin. He

14

said it was too small for his fingers, and it went out the window too.

Another time, he won a taxicab company, which he owned until he lost it back in another crap game. He also won a trucking company, and a hotel. The Schlitz Hotel was located at Five Points, the Times Square of Waukesha where five streets meet in the center of town, and he only owned it a short time before losing it on another gamble.

Every week he came home with something he'd won from gambling. For years, I wore a ring my Dad won in a crap game, and I've still got a couple of statues of tur-baned Arabs he won the same way. He was something else, a real trip.

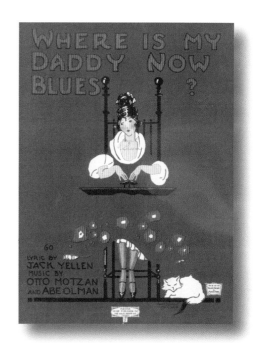

Dad won the Schlitz Hotel in a crap game, and then lost it in a later one.

My older brother Ralph and me, around 1919. Mother made our outfits.

Brother Ralph

My older brother and I were close. Ralph was a wonderful, outgoing guy, handsome and popular, and definitely took after our Dad. He was seven years older than me and I looked up to him, but we were worlds apart. For one thing, he didn't have an ear for music. Our parents got him a saxophone because Mother was set on him becoming a musician. Obie O'Brien had a saxophone too, and the two of them went to the same teacher. My brother's was a C melody sax, and Obie had the E-flat alto. The two of them would put a piece of sheet music on the piano and play it together, one playing in C and the other in E-flat. They'd be going at it like everything's fine, and I'd go to Mother and say, "There's something wrong with those two guys in the living room. What they're doing doesn't sound right. It's bad." They were playing in different keys at the same time, but she didn't recognize it, and neither did they.

I remember sitting with Ralph on the front lawn when there was going to be a parade. All the bands would gather a couple of blocks from our house where the parade started, and you could hear them coming. I'd say, "Here comes the reform school band." And Ralph would say, "How do you know it's the reform school band, wise guy? We can't see 'em yet." I would explain, "You don't see them, you hear them." The reform school band was composed of mostly black people, and their rhythm was much more precise and definite than anyone else's. They had a pulse and cadence that was lacking in the other bands. I could hear it, most people could hear it, but not Ralph. He just didn't have an ear for music.

Mother planned on Ralph becoming a musician, but it didn't take. He just wasn't interested, wasn't driven to do anything. I was just the opposite, and that was what Mother wanted to see. I did a lot of crazy, stupid things when I was a kid, but rather than scold me, she always took pride in the fact that I was thinking creatively and had the initiative to do something. She always said don't look at the negative, look at the positive, and you can do it. And she shoved me out on stage the same way. "Go out and get 'em, Lester. Go out and get 'em."

But that doesn't mean she was easy on me. If I didn't mow the lawn or make the bed just right, if I didn't do what I was supposed to do, there was a consequence to be paid for it. Either you don't get to go out and hear that orchestra, or you don't get to listen to the radio, or you don't get the crank to the phonograph. She had that German strictness and made the rules so they were impressive and didn't cut any slack when it came to enforcing them. That taught me a lot right there.

Waukesha was a bustling town of 17,000 in the early 1930s.

Curiosity

Another way Ralph and I differed was curiosity. If he walked into a room and threw a switch and the light came on, well, it's supposed to come on and that's the end of it. When I threw the switch, I wanted to know what happened between the switch and the bulb that made it come on. I knew there was something going on there and I wanted to know in detail what the hell it was. And Ralph would say, "What for, who cares?" Well, I didn't know what for, I just had to know. I think if you're born with this inquisitive trait, you always have it. It's called curiosity and I got a double dose of it. I've never stopped trying to figure out what makes things work or how to make things work better.

Curiosity led me into the two most important parts of my life and career:

music and electronics. I got my first musical instrument, a harmonica, because of it. Workmen were digging up the street in front of our house, and during the lunch hour, one of them pulled out a harmonica and started playing. When I heard it, I went and stood there and expressed my interest by staring at him. When this sewer digger saw me hawking him, he offered it to me and said, "Here kid, you try it."

I didn't know she was there, but when he offered the harmonica to me, my Mother's hand suddenly reached out from behind me and took it. And she said, "You're not playing this thing till I boil it." When she took it in the house to do the boiling, the ditch digger recognized the intensity of my interest by saying, "I think you want it worse than I do, so tell your mother I said you could keep it." So he kindly gave it to me, and I started learning to play it.

I thought the sound was beautiful and immediately began wondering what it was that vibrated when I blew into it. I took the metal side covers off and took it apart as far as I could to figure out how it worked. Then I put it back together again and began driving my Mother and brother crazy imitating what I was hearing on the radio. And I realized from that experience that when you soak the harmonica, it's easier to play blues on it. So the joke I tell is that I've been boiling my guitars ever since.

Around this same time, when I was 10 or 11 years old, I had my first electronics mentor, a kid named Harry Tice. We both had a newspaper route, and we used to sit on the Indian mounds at Cutler Park there in Waukesha and supplement papers. Supplementing meant taking a green ad sheet and physically inserting it in the newspaper. So you'd stuff 'em, roll 'em, put 'em in your bag, and then you're ready to get on your bike and sling 'em. And this guy next to me was quick. He could roll them faster than I could, he could do everything better than I could. So I'm still folding and rolling, and he's already finished and busy working on an oatmeal box. He's got an oatmeal box and he's winding wire around it and counting the turns. So I said, "What are you doing, Harry?" He said, "I'm making a crystal set." "What the hell's a crystal set?" "Oh," he said, "It's a radio that doesn't take batteries, and you can pick up stations with it."

Radio had only been around a few years and was just becoming the big thing, so I naturally had to build my own crystal set. And when I did, oh, my God Almighty, I was hooked. I've got the radio bug now and I have to carry it further than Harry does. I couldn't be satisfied with just hearing the voices on the radio station. I wanted to hear the clock ticking on the studio wall; I wanted to hear the hum in the transmitter. When Harry made his crystal set, he was probably content just to hear whatever he got, but I wanted to hear the fingers on the strings, I wanted to hear the papers rattling, I wanted to hear everything.

The desire to make sure my little radio receiver wasn't missing anything took me to my next mentor. One of the early radio stations in the area was WTMJ, which was owned by the *Milwaukee Journal*. The broadcast studios were in the *Journal* building in Milwaukee, but the transmitter and tower were located in the country outside Waukesha. It just so happened that once a week, I bicycled out to that neighborhood to take piano lessons. So I would bundle up my homemade radio and pedal out there on my bike and park underneath the transmitter tower to make sure I was getting everything. The first time I went there, it was raining, so it wasn't long before I was knocking on the station door and introducing myself to the engineer, a guy named Bill. He was very kind and said, "Come on, get out of the rain. Come on in."

So I tell him about building the crystal set and coming out for the piano lessons and wanting to get the clearest possible signal. And he said, "So, you weren't knocking on my door just to get out of the rain?" And I said, "No, I knocked because I'm curious about how all this works. Someone sings into a microphone somewhere, and from there, where does it go and how does it get into my head?" And Bill said, "Well, I'll teach you something today, and then you can come back again for another lesson." So I had just inherited a teacher who was glad to help a kid interested in learning. He sits out there all alone at the transmitter shack doing his thing, and to have someone come up and ask some of the simplest, most obvious questions was enjoyable to him. It's where you have to start if you want to learn, and he knew that. And he asked, "Well, will you be here next Sunday at this same time?" And I said yes, I would be there. And then I went down the road to my friend who played the piano and took a piano lesson.

Getting inside that station was a wonderful break. It meant I could pump out there on my bike every Sunday and right in the same neighborhood take my piano lessons and also get the radio instruction from Bill, who answered my questions with great care and patience. I'm just a young kid and I'm on fire learning about the two things that are going to mean the most to me in my life. Having the opportunity to learn about music and electronics at the same time was terribly important because it led me to the marriage between the guitar and the amplifier.

Living Room Laboratory

I was a lucky kid to grow up the way I did because my Mother was so supportive, and everything I needed to try out my ideas was provided. We had the whole world in our living room. Against one wall was a Kimball player piano, my Mother's pride and joy. Right beside it was a big crank phonograph, and next to that a cabinet radio and next to the radio the telephone. And there's me. And I didn't have to leave that living room because everything was there. Everything that I could imagine was right there to build everything I have today.

When that big player piano came into the house, Mother gave me the strictest orders not to tamper with it, but there was no way I could leave it alone. I took it apart and put it back together so many times I knew how it worked better than the guy who sold it to her.

When I saw those keys going down and heard that wonderful music coming out, the first thing I wanted to know was, what if I put a piece of tape over a hole, will that key go down? Well, it didn't go down. So the next step was, I started punching my own holes in the paper, and in no time at all I was making multiple piano rolls. At the very beginning of each roll there was always a stretch of blank paper for threading the roller and aligning it so it would play properly. And I used every bit of that blank space right up to where you hook it on, poking my own holes by trial and error. If something sounded okay, I left it, but if it sounded out of tune, I'd put tape over the holes to get rid of the wrong notes and then try something else. At first, Mother was getting mad because there were a lot of wrong notes and an awful lot of tape plastered on those rolls, but she changed her mind when she saw how intent and interested I was. And it was right there that the idea came upon me for multiple music tracks. I didn't know how I was going to do it, but I knew I was to going to have to figure it out.

There was something else that bothered me that came from the things in our living room. It was the fact that if you slowed down the piano roll, it didn't change key. You could push the tempo lever on the piano and slow the music down but the pitch didn't change, it just took longer to get there. But with the phonograph, I'd wind it up and start playing a record, and when I put my finger on it and slowed it down, the music went lower. So I said, "Ma, we got a problem." And then I had to find out why these two mechanical things made the music behave differently.

So Mother says, "Well, Lester, I'll take you over to the junior high school

23

and we'll talk to the science teacher." We talk to the teacher and end up at the library, and that's where I get my answer. With a little help from the teacher, I find out the player piano is basically digital, and the phonograph record is analog. And again, it's the curiosity, the fascination with the way things work, that got me there, and it all came out of a simple observation that one thing does this and the other does something else and wanting to know why.

So here I am, a babe in the woods with all these bits of information adding up in my head. Mother sees my wheels turning and says, "Now what are you up to?" I said, "Well, I have to get my voice and guitar and harmonica into those holes," and I was talking about the ideas of recording and multiple tracks. That's what I knew I wanted to do, that's what had to be done, but I didn't want it to go through any damn pump blowing air. It wasn't the air, it was the hole, and I had to figure out how to do what the hole does. But how to get there, that's what was bothering me. And this was the crude beginning of the multiple world. It wasn't until years later, when I was in Chicago with Jimmy Atkins and Ernie Newton in the trio, that I finally began to figure out how to do it.

Deford Bailey

I loved the country music shows on the radio, and there were several performers who impressed me. One was an old harmonica player I would hear on WSM, a black man named Deford Bailey. *The Lost Train* and *The Fox Chase* were two specialty numbers I heard him play on the radio. I loved his sound and made up my mind I was going to play just like him and be the best harmonica player in Waukesha. Once I learned those two songs, I took my little act around town and started making pocket money from tips. That just made me practice all the more, so I was hooked again.

Along in the late '20s, Mother took me all the way down to Nashville to see and meet Deford Bailey. He was very much a gentleman, and after he heard me play his songs, nice enough to invite me on his show and let me take his place in the program where he would do one of those numbers, which was a big thrill for me.

The Power Of The Airwaves

It's hard for someone now to understand what a powerful thing radio was then. Our radio was the most important thing in the house, the most awesome device. It was like the Internet today because it connected you with things that were going on all over the country. You heard the shows and the music with your ears but you saw it with your imagination. After I had the little crystal set and discovered the best reception was late at night, I'd use the springs in my bed for an antenna and stay up all hours listening to whatever I could find. Then we got the console radio in the living room, which let me hear the daily programs from Chicago, Milwaukee, St. Louis, Memphis and Nashville. Then I'd listen at one or two o'clock in the morning to the East Coast broadcasts from places like Pennsylvania Hotel, the Grand Terrace Ballroom and the Waldorf. I didn't care if I got any sleep or not, and that was the beginning of the nightlife for little Lester.

Pie Plant Pete

Another radio performer who influenced me was known as Pie Plant Pete, a regular on WLS who sang comedy songs and accompanied himself on guitar and harmonica. Mother liked him too, and when the WLS show came to the Auditorium Theatre in Waukesha she took me to see him. The theme of the show was *Showboat*, and all the performers, including Pete, were dressed like sailors. It was a big thrill for me when we got to meet him backstage after the show and he let me hold his guitar. It wasn't long after that I got my first guitar and started figuring out what he was doing. Mother knew I idolized him, so she made me a sailor suit similar to his, which I wore for my first publicity photograph. When people see that old picture, they always ask, "Why a sailor suit?" The only reason for it was that I wanted to be like Pie Plant Pete, and if he wore one, I was going to wear one too.

My first publicity photo, taken in Waukesha at the studio owned by Obie O'Brien's family.

First Guitar

I got my first guitar in 1927 at the age of 11. It was a little Troubadour flat top from Sears and Roebuck, a cheap little bow-wow that cost less than five dollars. The guitar came with a regular nut, a raised nut, a capo, a thumb pick and a booklet. The raised nut was for playing lap style, so you could go either way with it. The strings that came with it were made for Hawaiian style playing to accommodate the raised nut and included a plain G string, not a wound G. This was unheard of for regular guitar players then, but that's what I started with and I've stayed with it all these years. I couldn't reach across all six strings, so I took the last string off, the low E, rather than let not being able to reach it slow me down. So, at first, I was playing on just five strings. I was so proud of that little guitar and spent most of my spare time playing it, using the chord book I got with it to learn the simplest basic chords.

To sound like Pie Plant Pete, I had to be able to strum the guitar and play the harmonica at the same time. There were harmonica holders being made commercially then, but they couldn't change keys. You clamped the harmonica into them and you couldn't change keys unless you took one harmonica out and put another one in. That wasn't going to work for me because by now I had a good German harmonica that played on both sides. So I made my own harmonica holder out of coat hanger wire and wood, and mounted my harmonica on pivot points so I could flip it over with my chin. On one side, if you blow, you're in C; if you draw, you're in G. On the other side, you blow in D, and draw in A. So that gave me four different keys I could play in with just the one harmonica, by flipping it over when I needed to. That buffaloed everybody, and it was a lot of fun. I've still got the harmonica and the original holder I made when I was 12, and it's never changed. It was my first invention. I'm giving them to the Waukesha County Historical Society & Museum for its permanent Les Paul exhibit.

Red Hot Red

Once I had the guitar and harmonica thing going, I got bolder and started playing anywhere somebody would listen. It's about this time Mother gave me

27

the name Red Hot Red. Everybody in town soon knew me by that name and I seemed to draw a crowd wherever I showed up. I got a little group together and we billed ourselves as "Red Hot Red" with the slogan "Music So Rotten It's Good" supplied by my Mother. We played for tips or free, wherever we could get in the door. At the age of 13, at the Schroeder Hotel in Milwaukee, I played my first job where the amount of payment was pre-arranged. After that, I proudly considered myself to be a professional entertainer.

From day one, I was always comfortable in front of an audience. Playing the guitar and entertaining was easy and fun for me, and the people could feel it. I knew I was where I belonged because it made me happy and it made them happy too.

I played all around town, and became a regular attraction at Beekman's Barbecue Stand, a hot spot located at a crossroads near Waukesha. I was playing for tips, and my first night there, I did pretty well. I figured if the people sitting in cars parked further away could hear me too, I'd do even better. So the next time I played there, I took the mouthpiece from a telephone, stuck it on a broom handle and then ran it through my Mother's radio speaker to amplify my voice. And it worked, more or less. But then a fellow sitting in a rumble seat sent up a note that said, "Red, your voice and harmonica are fine, but your guitar's not loud enough." So then I had to figure out a way to make my guitar heard too, and this led to my first experiments in trying to amplify the guitar strings.

I tried using the microphone from a telephone by attaching it to the top of the guitar and running it through the radio, but the feedback problem was terrible. So I took my Dad's radio-phono player out there and took the tone arm off the phonograph and just jammed the needle right down into the guitar's bridge and taped it in place. Then I turned up the volume and played through the amplified speaker. It wasn't that good and there were still feedback problems, but it got me more notice and I started making more money. So now I'm performing there with a sort of stereo thing going, using the two radios I could borrow, my Mom's and my Dad's. With my homemade microphone, I ran my voice and harmonica through my Mother's radio, and the guitar through my

Dad's phonograph. But I could only do this on certain nights because there were restrictions. Saturday night was when Mother listened faithfully to the country music shows on WLS and WSM, so I couldn't have her radio then, and if the fights were on, I couldn't take my Dad's.

The barbeque stand was just a summer thing for the Beekmans. When the seasons changed, they'd shut the place down, go to Florida for the winter, and then come back and open up again in the spring. So when the weather turned cool that fall, they headed south and that was the end of my performing there.

This Waukesha photo was taken when I was around 14. That's my old pal Warren Downey holding the banjo. Warren later played bass for Mary and I on our first gigs.

Electric Beginnings

What I did at Beekman's was the beginning of my interest in the electric guitar and in finding a way to get a better, more controlled sound. Using a short length of steel railroad rail and two railroad spikes, I invented a device that could give me a consistent reference point for my experiments. I took a guitar string and fastened it at each end of the steel rail, using the spikes like a bridge and nut to raise the string so it could be plucked. Then I took a telephone microphone, wired it into Mom's radio for amplification, and placed it on the rail under the string. I soon figured out that the tremendous solidity of the rail allowed the string's vibration to sustain for a longer time, and there was no feedback.

Pressing the phonograph needle directly into the bridge increased the guitar volume, but feedback was still my number one problem. You can't get away from feedback when you're working with crystal material, which is what the phonograph cartridge was. Applying pressure to it, as I was doing, actually worsened the problem because the pressure captures and intensifies the feedback properties. When I would turn the volume up, the speaker would squeal and I would feel the top of my little round-hole guitar vibrating. But despite the problems I had, I loved the way my guitar sounded coming out of the speaker, so I started trying different things to deaden the vibration and stop the feedback. I tried filling the guitar up with tablecloths and shorts and socks to muffle the sound, anything to clog it up so it wouldn't feed back. That was a step in the right direction, but not the solution. So then I poured it full of Plaster of Paris, and finally destroyed it. That turned out to be bad surgery, but I was trying everything to solve the feedback problem that was bugging me when I performed.

After the Plaster of Paris experiment, the Troubadour was no longer playable, so I just gave it to a friend rather than throw it away. I don't really

MAY TIME

CHARMING FOX TROT SONG

WARINGS PENNSYLVANIANS

FRED WARING
Director

know what became of it. Then, in 1931, I sent to Sears and got a Dobro. I got the Dobro because it didn't have a sound hole in it and I thought it wouldn't feed back on me like the Troubadour had. It had the metal resonator in it, and acoustically it sounded more in the direction of an electric guitar. This is the direction I was craving to go, based on what I had learned from my experiments with the piece of railroad track. I didn't know it yet, but I was on my way to the solid body electric guitar.

First Radio Station

At the same time I was learning guitar and harmonica, I built my own little broadcasting station there in our home. This was back when I first got the Troubadour guitar and before the railroad track experiment. I built a little one-tube radio transmitter and lengthened the antenna up to the roof so you could hear it all over the block. People would listen to it around the neighborhood and then come over to the house and talk about it.

I noticed in listening to the radio that Jimmy Rodgers sounded like he was singing in just a blank room that had very hard walls, like a hall, and it echoed too much to suit me. Most radio stations in those days were just flat dead sounding, or they were using an empty room and the sound would ring around in there forever and it was awful. I wanted to sound somewhere in between the two, and in broadcasting on my own little radio station, playing my guitar and harmonica and singing, I learned that if I sang in the bathroom, there was too much echo, and if I sang in the bedroom, it was too dead. So I would position the chair halfway between the bathroom and the bedroom, and I'd place the mic in a certain place to get just enough echo so I'd get the equalized sound, the ambient sound of the room. It was a lot of fun. I was really into the radio thing then, music and electronics equally.

First Recording Machine

As soon as I had an understanding of how the radio signal was amplified, the first thing I did was to take the guitar and get it into the radio's amplifier. That's what I did at Beekman's, and once I did that, I wanted to do it all the time so I kept it wired up at home. When Mother heard the guitar coming through the radio speaker, she said, "You sound great, that sounds wonderful." And I said, "Yeah, but I can't judge it while I'm playing it. I want to listen to it without having to play it at the same time. I want to record it so I can listen to it and study it." And that led to my first recording machine.

The chief mechanic at my Dad's garage was a guy named Hooks, another person that liked to help a kid. So I went to Hooks and told him I wanted to be able to record something and then be able to play it back so I could hear it. He said, "Well, to do that you either gouge a signal into a groove, or you emboss it." He happened to know about these things and was good enough to explain it. After I got the picture, I said, "Well, we're going to need a balanced turntable to do this," and the next thing you know we're out in the alley taking the flywheel out of an old motor. And that was my turntable.

But this thing didn't get built overnight. The next step was I went to my dentist, and his drilling equipment was powered by those old endless belts they used to use. So he's there cleaning and shining my teeth and I'm looking out of the corner of my eye at the way his tools are powered, and I ask, "Hey, Doc, where do you get those endless belts?" He says, "Why? What do you want with those belts?" I said, "Well, I'm building a machine and I think they would be useful but I need them in different lengths."

He said he could get them any length I wanted and he ordered

them for me. So I get my belts and go back to Hooks and we finally get this thing put together.

Embossing was the method I used to make my first recording. That's the technique of pressing the groove into a soft material, which in my case happened to be an aluminum disk.

My very first recording was cut with a nail and didn't amount to anything more than just strumming a couple of chords on the guitar to see if it would work, and it did. My Mother saved that disk for many years, but it was lost when our house was torn down. This was years later when I was too far away to do anything about it and they came in with a bulldozer and flattened the place and destroyed a world of stuff that was left in the house.

I think it was around 1929 when we first built that machine, and I continued to experiment with it and make improvements to it. By the time I went down to St. Louis to go to work at KMOX, I had it set up at home so Mother could use it to record my performances off the radio. She did record several things, and I still have those disks. They're rough, but that old sound is there and it will sure take you back. When I look back on how all these things came about, I'm just amazed. If it hadn't been for my friends, I wouldn't have gotten anywhere. It's always your mentor, somebody who appreciates your interest in learning, and who makes such a difference in your life.

My first disk recording machine no longer exists, but I was always building new ones, trying to improve the result. I made this one in California.

The studio at WTMJ where I performed when I was 16.

CHAPTER TWO

Red Hot Red

I kept going as Red Hot Red with my guitar and harmonica, copying things I heard on the radio to build my repertoire. Pie Plant Pete was the biggest influence, but I had also discovered Eddie Lang, and I was drawn to piano too. If I wasn't out playing music half the night, I was up dialing the radio searching out the jazz that came through in the wee hours.

The first radio station I ever performed on was WRJN, a tiny little station

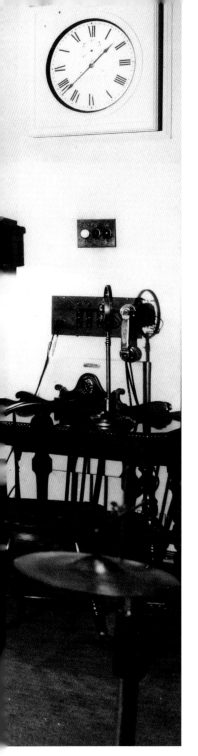

in Racine, Wisconsin, and the next was WISN, owned by the *Milwaukee Sentinel*. The third station was WHAD, located at Marquette University. I went to the dental school there and said, "I'm willing to negotiate with you." The idea was for Red Hot Red to perform on their station in exchange for getting my teeth cleaned. So a dental student cleaned my teeth, and then I sat on a bed and did my two songs on WHAD, which is now a big public radio station in Madison and Delafield.

The fourth station I performed on was WTMJ, owned by the *Milwaukee Journal*. It was the biggie in Milwaukee, and it was Bill, the transmitter engineer, who opened the door. The station's transmitter and tower were near Beekman's Barbecue Stand, and when I performed there using the radios as amplifiers, Bill would come over to see how I was doing. He put in a good word for me at the station, and Mother then arranged for me to perform there. So I got to sing into the same microphone in the same studio I had been listening to when Bill let me come in out of the rain. The number I did, *Don't Send My Boy To Prison*, was the first performance my Mother recorded off the air, using the cutting machine Hooks and I built.

There were two Milwaukee theatres which featured live performers, the Uptown Theatre and the Downtown Theatre. I appeared as Red Hot Red at both places and had a different piano player for each engagement. The first time I ever appeared on a stage in Milwaukee was at the Uptown, and my piano player was Al Buettner, a musical star on WTMJ. Then I performed at the Downtown Theatre, and my piano player was Liberace. He was very young, just starting out, and I'm not sure what name he was using then, but it was him.

Through The Window

By now, all my friends knew I was obsessed with learning to play guitar and piano, and that I would stay up all night in order to not miss anything. When I did go to bed, I didn't want to be disturbed unnecessarily, so I'd tie a string to my big toe and throw the ball of twine out my bedroom window. And I told all my buddies, don't yank the string unless it's something urgent.

So one summer morning I'm in the sack, and somebody yanks the string. I stick my head out the upstairs window, and it's Harold Vinger, an older school buddy, and he's got news. He says, "Hey Red, wake up and get down

35

here. There's something you gotta know." So I go out to see what the buzz is, and Harold says, "Rube Tronson's playing out in Genesee, and it's unbelievable. He's got a guitar player who plays above the fifth fret and all the way up the neck!"

This was big news because, till that moment, I thought the upper frets were just markers, for looks. I didn't even know they were frets. The thought that you could do anything with them had never occurred to me. So this is something I've got to see, but there's a problem because I'm too young to get in. And Harold says, "Don't worry about it. We'll go out there this evening, I'll go in by myself and then let you in through the bathroom window."

So that night, Harold pulls me through the lavatory window of this Genesee roadhouse, and I'm suddenly in a strange new world. Everything's going fine, but I've never been in a place like this before and I'm wide-eyed. I'm just a kid looking at all these people having a high time on a Saturday night, and they all seemed so old, so far beyond from where I was. This was during Prohibition, and to see all these men and women drinking bootleg beer out of thunder mugs and carrying on to the music was a wonder to me. The band was Rube Tronson and His Texas Cowboys. I liked them on the WLS National Barn Dance radio show, but seeing them live with a dancing, happy crowd made a deep impression on me.

Meeting Sunny Joe

I planted myself close to the stage to take it all in and couldn't stop staring at the guitar player, a skinny little fellow named Joe Wolverton. Actually, his name was Ralph Wolverton, but he was known as Sunny Joe, and yes, he was playing above the fifth fret and doing one amazing thing after another. And he did more than just play guitar. He also played mandolin, violin and banjo, so I was terribly impressed.

When they take a break, he sees me hawking him and says, "Hey, kid, you seem to be awfully interested. Do you play the guitar?" And I said, "Well, I thought I did. I'm trying to learn." He holds out his guitar, a beautiful Gibson L-5, and says, "Do you want to try this?" So I take it and awkwardly play a couple of things and he says, "Hey, you may show some promise. Why don't I show you a few things to learn and then we'll see how you're doing when we're back this way." So he showed me the harmonics, the grand barré F chord and a couple of other things, and told me to come see him in two weeks in Calhoun, which was about halfway between Waukesha and Milwaukee.

I went back home and started practicing. The harmonics were easy, but the barred F chord seemed impossible. I worked until my fingers were just killing

Sunny Joe Wolverton, Al Simons, Al Mee, Rube Tronson, and Red Blanchard.

me because I wanted to have everything he'd shown me down by the time they came back to the area. I also was able to figure out some things I saw Joe do on stage which he didn't show me directly, and I practiced those too.

Two weeks later, I'm in a Calhoun joint to see Joe, and this time I go right in the door. I'm not climbing through the men's room window anymore; I'm on my way. Ol' Joe says, "Well, let's see what you got." So I played everything just like he showed me, and then I played some things he hadn't shown me, and that impressed him. He showed me several more things and we agreed to meet again in another two weeks. So that night, I'm pedaling my bicycle back home with no hands because I'm practicing air guitar while I ride to make sure I don't forget anything.

Another two weeks go by and the Texas Cowboys are back in Genesee and I go to see Joe for the third time. This time they let me come right on in with my Dobro and harmonica. And again, I've got everything he showed me

37

down solid, plus more. So Joe calls Rube Tronson over and tells him, "You know, this kid is pretty good. He works hard and learns real fast. Maybe we should let him play something." So Rube says, "You want to get up and do something, kid?" And I say, "Sure!"

So during the show, they call me up and I take my harmonica and guitar and sing *Don't Try It 'Cause It Can't Be Done* and I wow 'em, more or less.

Mom posing with her flowers.

It's my hometown, the people know who I am, some of them have seen me do my thing elsewhere, so everything is on my side. The band is behind me, everybody's behind me, and when I finish, all the people are clapping and whistling and cheering and I feel like I'm floating off the ground. Joe gives me a grin and a wink, and I know right then I've got a friend for life.

The crowd reaction was an enormous thrill, but I didn't realize how successful it was until I got word Rube Tronson wanted to talk to me out in the parking lot. So I meet him out behind his big car, and in between swigs he asks if I would like a job with the band. I say, "Gee, I'm still in school. I'm making beds for my mother. I'm dusting the floors. I got chores to do at home." He sees me hesitating and says, "I'll tell you what I'll do, I'll offer you $8." I thought about it and said, "Well, gee, I do that good right here in Waukesha." And he says, "You do?" And I say, "Yeah, I do..." and I'm thinking how I might scare up that much playing at Beekman's and elsewhere in a week's time. So he says, "Well, you think about it."

Mother's Blessing

So I go to my Mom and tell her about sneaking into the dance hall, meeting Joe and that whole thing, and then the offer from Rube. She says, "You should've told me what you were doing, I'd have helped you get in." That's the kind of gal she was. I was always doing something any other kid would've gotten scolded for, but I wasn't because it was usually something she would've done herself. She loved it every time I came home with news of another adventurous episode and was proud of me being that way. She'd tell her friends, "Lester doesn't wait for things to happen, he makes 'em happen."

So we talk over the offer from Rube, and she's telling me what a rough lot traveling musicians have, how it's not fit for a kid my age, but at the same time, she knows what an amazing opportunity it is to learn and gain experience. So finally, she says, "Well, you need to finish school, you need to get your education, but if you want to do it during your summer vacation, it'll be all right." So I had Mother's blessing. This was at the beginning of summer, school was months away, and I was climbing trees at the prospect of being a part of Rube's band and getting to play with Sunny Joe and learn from him.

So Rube finally calls and says, "Have you made a decision?" And I say, "Well I talked it over with my Mother and she is very concerned." And he says, "I'll tell you what. I'll make it $10." I said, "Well, that would make it a little more comfortable." So we had an agreement with the understanding that it would just be for the rest of the summer, until school started.

First Professional Job

Right away, Rube's brother picks me up with a truck and we're heading north for Escanaba, Michigan where I'm to get some cowboy gear and other odd stuff to get ready to join the band. That night, we're getting ready to start the show and I ask, "Well, where is Joc?" And they say, "Well, don't you know? He was let go, and you're taking his place." So they fired the very guy who helped me get the job, the guy I joined the group to study with and my new friend that I admired so much. I was very disappointed and felt terrible about it, but that's the way it was and I couldn't change it.

So that first night we're playing there at Escanaba, and for the first time, I hear myself introduced on a real stage as Red Hot Red. I'm mostly playing piano on the band's numbers, but for my solo stuff, I'm playing my Dobro, singing and blowing the jug, playing harmonica, the whole nine yards. There's six, seven of us in the band, and there aren't enough cowboy hats to go around. So as soon as a guy finished his solo, he'd go to the back and lay the hat down on the piano. I'd grab it, quickly stuff the crown with paper so it wouldn't come down over my eyes, jam it on my head and do my thing.

It's a wild night, and after the job is over, Rube comes and pays me $10. And I say, "You pay for the whole week on the first night?" "No, no," he says, "This is just for tonight." So I called Ma and said, "You won't believe this. It's not $10 a week, it's $10 a *night*!" This was at a time when my brother was working 60 hours a week to make $18.

That first night on the road was quite an experience. I was on my own for the first time, a boy among grown men, and things happened that were shocking to me. I was put in a room with a champion hoedown fiddle player named Brusso. He had a couple of suitcases he carried wherever he went and never let out of his sight. And when I got into the room with him, I found out what was in them. They were full of trophies, all the awards he'd won for being the greatest hoedown fiddle player. He'd take them all out and carefully arrange them on the dresser and tabletops, so when he went to bed at night the room was full of trophies. We'd lie down for a few hours sleep, then he's up putting them all back into his suitcases, and we're gone to the next town.

Brusso wasn't the only one in the group who was peculiar. Every guy in the band was odd in some way or other. Booger Fields was a guitar player from Texas who took me under his wing. He was involved with a beast of a gal who was traveling with him, a big, fat Texas gal. She was rough and tough and would try to scratch his eyes out whenever they got into it. And I asked him, "What in the world's happening with you two and why do you put up with that?" And he says, "Well, when you get a little older you'll know. It's called sex."

40

We were in Chicago when Booger said, "I'm going out tonight, and you're coming with me." And he took me to a burlesque house on State Street. If you were going to see a real burlesque show, especially your first one, this was the best one in the whole world to see. I sat there gawking in amazement at the glamorous women with their risqué routines, the raunchy comedy skits, the pit band, and just the feel of the whole thing. It was my first glimpse into that wonderful world.

If The Shoe Fits

One night, Rube took me aside and asked a favor. He wanted me to go to a particular shoe store and buy shoes for him. We're playing in West Allis, so I'll have to take a lot of streetcars to get all the way to this downtown Milwaukee shoe store. And I say, "What shoes do you want me to get?" He gives me the money and says, "It doesn't matter. Just buy me ten pairs of women's shoes."

So at two o'clock in the morning, I'm trying to get back to where we're staying, bumming a ride on a horse-drawn milk wagon with this arm full of women's shoes of all different descriptions, no particular size. I know something's terribly wrong, but I'll be darned if I know what it is. When I told Mom about this strange thing, she said, "Well, it sounds to me like that fellow has a fetish." So I wondered what in the world a fetish is. And Mom said, "Well, it's a very deep subject, and when you come home we'll have a heart-to-heart discussion about a lot of things that are hard to explain on the telephone." So the next time I was home, she sat me down and explained that some people just had unusual habits and preferences, and that as long as they didn't try to include me in them, I shouldn't let it bother me.

Smoke Signals

Speaking of the unusual, one of the places we played was Iron Mountain, Michigan and there was an odd local custom there. We'd go down this alley lined with bales of hay waiting to be dumped onto trucks and wagons, to the entrance of a little radio station located there in the back of a building. The place is so small we have to stand our bass player in the next room to get the rest of us in there and keep him from drowning us out. The guy running the radio station has his earphones on and he's tuning up this little 20 or 30-watt station. When he's got it just right, he looks at me and says, "Hey, you." And I say, "Yeah?" He says, "Go out to the alley there and look to your left and tell me what you see." So I go out to look and I say, "I see smoke a ways down the alley there." And he says, "Good, that means we're coming in great." There was a barbershop down the alley listening to the station, and the barber burns a pile of hair out in the alley to signal good reception.

Riding With The Cowboys

Rube's band traveled in two vehicles, a truck and a mammoth old 16-cylinder touring car that had steer horns mounted on the front. The truck went on ahead and played records and made public announcements through a mobile PA system. The big car hauling the musicians would follow the truck, and when we'd come into town, you'd put your hat on. That was the rule, when you enter town, have your hat on, and the music would play and they'd announce where we would be appearing.

And, I was driving. Just a scrawny kid driving this enormous touring car over those rough roads and narrow highways while the other guys slept it off. And we're bouncing all over the map. One night we're in Escanaba, Michigan, the next we're in Centralia, Illinois, and then it's somewhere in Ohio and back to Chicago to do the WLS show. It was craziness.

Taking care of the sound equipment was right down my alley. It was basic, simple stuff, but they needed someone who could keep it running and I was perfect for it. That wasn't included in my deal with Rube, but it just automatically fell to me because I happened to have that talent and knew how to wire things up.

Another reason they liked me was that I was the boy wonder, a hockable product and guaranteed crowd pleaser. And they surely needed an extra driver who could go with very little sleep, and I happened to be that type of person. I didn't realize what a bonus it was for them to have someone to do that type of work above and beyond performing. I was eating it up, and they were glad to let me do it.

Rube was a drinker, and the rest of the band followed suit. There were lots of laughs, but the boozing also caused unpleasantness. One night Booger got into it with Al Mee, the drummer. I didn't realize there was any dissension in the ranks till suddenly I see Booger's fist flying through the air. Al Mee ducks and Booger rams his fist through the dressing room wall, leaving a big hole you could see through.

When we pass back through Waukesha again, it's about time for school to be starting, so I tell Ma, "I'm ready to get off the road because this is a very strange group of people, and anyway, Joe isn't there." So I quit the Texas Cowboys and went back to high school.

The Call from Joe

So I'm back going to school and playing engagements around town when one day Joe Wolverton calls from KMOX in St. Louis where's he landed a job as a staff musician. This is in the early fall of 1932 and it's been over a year since I've seen Joe, so I'm terribly glad to hear from him. He says, "Red, I hear you took my place with Rube." And I said, "Yeah, but I'm back home now, back in school, and I'd much rather be with you." "Well, you can be," he says. "There's some good people running things here and it's a great opportunity. I'm putting an act together to do a morning country music show, and you'll fit right in. The pay's good, and I'd like to have you come down and join me. Can you do it?" I said, "Oh, I'll have to talk to my Mother."

So I'm there with Mother and we're making the beds. She's on one side and I'm on the other, folding the sheets over tight just like the army, and I tell her about Joe's offer. She gets quiet and doesn't say anything right away. She knows if I take Joe's offer it means dropping out of school for good. She had always insisted I finish high school, but Mother was terribly excited about me doing something she wished she could have done, and she's quite certain by now I have a future as an entertainer. Finally, she says, "Well, Lester, it's your life. It's up to you." So it's time to make a decision. I said, "Well, if it's up to me, I don't finish school. Algebra's not going to mean that much to me and who shot Lincoln isn't that important either."

So I dash down to the phone, call St. Louis and say, "Joe, I'll be there."

CHAPTER THREE

St. Louis Blues

As soon as I hang up the phone, Ma and I are in my room packing, and I say, "It's a long ways Ma, how am I going to get there?" And Mom says, "Well, I'll take you down on the Greyhound."

It's 1932, the Depression is hitting hard and jobs are scarce. People are going hungry, and here I am dropping out of school to go off by myself to a strange city. If people wondered how she could turn me loose so far from home in such times, they just didn't know my Mother. She always believed I was going to do something remarkable, that was her faith, and she was willing to put it on the line. I didn't need any pushing, and she didn't worry about me getting into trouble because she believed in me. She supported me in every way, and it sure helped.

So we're on the bus headed south about 400 miles to St. Louis. I've got my suitcase with some clothes and the Red Hot Red outfit she made for me, my harmonica and jug, and my resonator guitar. Mom's got a casserole and some other grub she cooked up for us to eat on the bus. We were both excited about this new adventure and talked about what I was going to do, but I didn't get a lot of preaching from her. She just told me to watch my step and made me promise to call her once a week.

The bus pulls into the Greyhound Depot and Joe is there waiting for us. Mother and Joe are acquainted from my Rube Tronson days, and when she hands me over, she says, "Now Joe, I'm counting on you to take care of Lester." She always called me Lester, never Les or Red. Then she turned around, got back on the bus and went back home without ever leaving the bus station.

This is just a tremendously exciting time for me because this is not a summer thing now, this is for real; my first time to leave home without knowing when I'd be back. I'm with my guitar hero, I'm going to be performing at a big time radio station, and I'm on my own. I could not have been happier.

The Scalawags

From the bus station, Joe took me over to a rooming house on Lindell Boulevard where I met the other guys in the group. Besides Joe, there was bass player Steve Pickel, and Ken Wright, who played the accordion and called himself Sad Sam. So there were four of us in this new group, to be known as The Scalawags.

We all stayed together in one big room, and that first night I quickly realized I was again in with some odd characters. Ken Wright is bald, and he's there with little tweezers, plucking and rubbing each remaining hair like it's the most valuable thing on earth. And me, even at my age, knowing it's a waste of time. If you've only got two hairs, you might as well give up, but not Ken. He's rubbing and patting and wearing a woman's stocking on his head, still hoping his hair will make a comeback. Ken Wright was a sweet, gentle guy who later proved to be very much a friend, but that first night he was looking very strange. Then I see Joe climb into bed with his socks on and learned he never went to bed without wearing them.

There are only three beds, and when it's bedtime, Joe says, "Red, you're going to bunk with Steve Pickel." So here's Steve Pickel, probably 20 years older than me, and when he strips down to go to bed, I can't help but notice he's got a bag tied around his tallywhacker, and I'm thinking it's because he's bashful. I don't know this thing is dripping. I don't know what's going on, or what his problem is.

Things quiet down and everybody is asleep when suddenly there's a loud pounding on the door. Almost instantly, Steve Pickel leaps up out of bed and goes crashing right through the bay window, bag and all. He left his clothes there, he left his bass, and we never saw him again. I never knew for sure what the problem was, but somebody was after him and he was gone for good.

Joining The Union

I've got a job that pays $45 a week, but I can't go to work until I'm in the union and the union is very strict about who gets to join. If they have the least suspicion you have a job waiting, they'll turn you down because you're taking work from somebody who's already a local member. So I'm called into the office and told, "You're going to go over to the musician's union and it's going to

The Scalawags. That's me with the jug and Joe's L-5. Ken Wright is on the accordion , Sunny Joe on the fiddle, and Steve Pickel bowing the bass. Hank Richards is holding the derby hat and the girls were called "Girls of the Golden West."

cost $49 to join. Now, if they know you're here to work for KMOX, they'll bust you, so don't tell 'em anything." And I said, "Don't worry, I'll handle it."

So I take my guitar and harmonica over to the musicians' local on Pine Street, and I wait. Finally, they call my name, Lester Polfuss, and I go into a room where a group of union musicians are sitting around a long table like a jury. They ask me what I want, and I say, "I've come to join the union." They want to know why, and I say, "Well, I moved here and I just feel as though, sooner or later, I'm going to be a musician." They look at each other and then say, "Well, you have to audition so we know you're good enough." I pulled out the $49 cash and put it on the table, but they said, "No, we don't want your money yet. First, we have to hear you play."

So I put the harmonica rack around my neck, and when I open my guitar case, there lays a piece of manuscript paper with "KMOX" written in big letters. It's a list of songs we're going to do Saturday night, and I have to dive on it so they don't see it. Then I get my guitar, look them in the eye, and start singing *The Death of Barbara Allen*, which has about 14 verses. I'm singing and playing guitar in G while playing the harmonica in A, and it sounds like a catfight.

Pretty soon, they say "That's good enough, that's fine," but I just keep on singing like it's the performance of my life. They're ready for me to quit; they're making out my card while I'm still singing. When I finish, they take the money, give me the receipt, and I'm out the door with my union card. I can just imagine the laugh they had over the kid who did the worst audition they'd ever heard, but the laugh was on them.

This happened during the week, and I'm to do my first broadcast on KMOX the following Saturday. So Saturday comes, and during rehearsal one of the union hall guys comes in and sees me with Sad Sam and Sunny Joe, and we're playing like hell. We're good, and he's shaking his head realizing I'd put one over on them at the audition, but I kept my union card. I was in.

Rhubarb Red

I had copied Pie Plant Pete's songs and learned to sound just like him with the guitar and harmonica, and now it was paying off because that's just what the station managers had in mind for me to do. The KMOX guys liked the name Red, but didn't think Red Hot Red had the right flair. So Joe and I were told to come up with a different name for me, keeping Red as part of it. Joe knew how much I admired Pie Plant Pete, so when he suggested Rhubarb Red, I thought, from Pie Plant to Rhubarb, what could be better? So from then on, I was known as Rhubarb Red. I had naturally red hair, but they had me color it each week to shock it up. After those henna treatments, my head looked like it was on fire.

I call Mother and tell her about my strange new friends and joining the union, but the big news is that she's going to hear me introduced as Rhubarb Red on KMOX on Saturday night. When I told her I would get to do just one solo number, she said, "Then pick the longest one you've got." So I told her I'd do *I Wish I Was Single Again*, which can go on for days, and Mom tells me she's going to have everybody in Waukesha County listening.

So I'm all set to sing that song for my Saturday night debut, and the program gets canceled at the last minute. I don't remember why, but we got axed on short notice. Come Monday, I got more mail than anybody at the station, all from Waukesha, all saying how great I was on that Saturday night show. The program director comes in laughing and says, "Red, you're a big draw and you don't even have to be on the air to do it!" My Mom had been on a campaign that wouldn't quit to get support for me from home, and it wasn't hard to figure out what had happened.

The Scalawags were a hit on the morning show, and we were soon playing dates all over the area. The other guys were way ahead as experienced performers, but I caught up quick, learning on my feet with our daily performances. Every bit I saw that got a laugh, every lick I heard, I soaked it up fast and made it mine.

After a couple of days, Joe was fed up with the sound of my National resonator and helped me get the first decent guitar I ever had, a little Gibson L-50 arch top which cost about $45. It was one of Gibson's cheaper models, but better than anything I'd had before. I agreed to sell the Dobro to a cook at Walgreen's Drugstore, but when I went there to get my $25, the cook was gone and so was the guitar. So I never got paid and that was the end of my second guitar.

In this photo Joe is playing my Gibson L-5.

Sunny Joe

Joe Wolverton was a slender, dapper little guy with a wild sense of humor and a way with the ladies. He had more girlfriends than I could count and always had women after him. He had a terrible temper too, and wouldn't back down from anybody. He only weighed 129 pounds, but if somebody tried to cross him, Joe would tear into them like a buzz saw, and he didn't care how big they were. The people at the places where we played soon learned you don't mess with Joe. He could get mad at the drop of a hat, and when he did, it was shoot first and ask questions later, but he was always even-tempered with me. He had promised my Mother he would take care of me, and he did.

Joe was very accomplished on all the instruments he played and, especially, a very fine guitarist who had studied and could read music. He received classical training to be a violin player as a young kid, which gave him an edge over most other guitar players. His slender fingers danced over the neck, and he played with a lot of attack, intensity and precision.

We'd sit together with our guitars and Joe would coach me in what he knew as the correct way to play, which included throwing away my thumb pick and capo. He'd say, "No, no, no, don't hold your wrist that way. You

50

hold your wrist this way and the pick this way." When Joe would go to bed, I'd take my guitar into the bathroom and practice half the night by myself. I couldn't get enough because with Joe there, I was learning something new every day. And I was very fortunate because he was more than a good player, he was a good teacher, spending many hours patiently showing me what he knew. I was blessed to have Joe Wolverton as my mentor at such a formative time in my life. Joe was great to me, and I couldn't have asked for a better teacher or truer friend.

Eddie Lang was the first guitarist I heard do a pull-off, but Joe was the first one I saw do it, and I jumped on it. Eddie and Joe would throw in a one string pull-off once in a while, but I thought if you can do it on one string, why not on all six? So I took it and ran with it, and doing multiple string pull-offs in rapid succession became one of my signature licks.

When I first discovered how to do it, I showed it to Ralph, and he said, "Yeah, so what?" He didn't understand why I was so excited. I said, "Look, I can play all these notes so much faster and cleaner with my left hand if the right hand doesn't have to keep up. See?" But Ralph just shrugged it off, and that's what happens. One person will have an idea and it just sits there, and then someone else will come along and take it and do something remarkable with it. It gets back to the curiosity again, wanting to know what will happen if you do this or do that, and being willing to stay with it until you get something that works.

Joe and I became the best of friends and were both incurable

My brother Ralph and I, early 1930s.

pranksters, so lots of terribly funny things happened in the way of jokes we played on each other. One of the best was the time he got married on the air at KMOX when he and his bride were up on stage in front of a live audience with the broadcast going out across the country. Ken Wright, carrying a shotgun, came pushing a baby buggy up the aisle with me in it, dressed like a baby. I jumped out on stage and yelled, "Stop the wedding! That's my Pa!" The audience thought it was part of the act, but it was a total surprise to everybody but myself and Ken Wright, who was in cahoots with me. It brought the house down and Joe laughed it off, but his new wife, Delores, was pretty steamed.

I was always up to some kind of mischief, and it does enter my mind now that maybe I was trying to keep myself occupied to avoid how lonesome I was. When Sundays came around and there was no show to do, and no rehearsal, all the older guys would take their wives or girlfriends and be gone. I didn't have anything to do or anywhere to go, so I'd just wander down the street and sit on a corner and cry thinking about home and how much I missed it. This was my first time to be alone and away from home, and there were many things happening I didn't fully understand. I got very homesick sometimes, and my off-the-wall antics were how I tried to hide it.

The Scalawags were doing fine, but the Depression was having its effect, and after about six months, KMOX told Joe he would have to let his sidemen go. They kept Joe because he had a following, and I stayed on doing Rhubarb Red as a solo act until the station told me I was to be let go, too. I was headed back to Waukesha when Joe came up with another job for us through our friends in St. Louis.

I was just getting started in my career as an entertainer, and there were talented people at KMOX in the early stages of their management careers who became lifelong friends. There was J.L.Van Volkenberg, the president of KMOX who went on to become an important man for CBS in Chicago and New York; and others like Sid Strotz, Hank Richards, and Holland Engle. It's amazing that these very people all did so well in later years and carried with them our friendship. These same people got Joe and I our job in Springfield, Missouri, then took us on up to Chicago and later helped me immensely in New York. And that was the wonderful thing about those days, that there were people who believed in you and wanted to help you become successful.

On stage at Riverside Park near Chicago. From the beginning, I have always been comfortable in front of a crowd.

CHAPTER FOUR

Springfield Via Kalamazoo

When Joe said he had a job for us in Springfield, Missouri, I hadn't heard of the place. And Joe said, "It's down in the Ozarks. Mr. Foster is opening some new stations down there and he's offering a lot of work if we'll come down and get it going." Ralph Foster was an important man in the early days of radio in Missouri. He had started KGBX in St. Joe, then moved it down to Springfield, and now he was bringing in another station, KWTO.

Joe pointed to St. Louis on the map and said, "Just follow the highway west." I looked, and found Springfield about 200 miles to the southwest. Route 66 ran west out of Chicago all the way to California, and I thought, boy, that's the road for me. So Joe, Delores, and I loaded up Joe's Buick and hit the road to Missouri, but we took the long way getting there.

Kalamazoo

I loved Joe's L-5. Anytime he would lay it down, I'd have it and he'd have to chase me down to get it back. So when we're getting ready to go to Springfield, Joe says, "You like my guitar so much, why don't we go up to Kalamazoo and you can get your own L-5 right where Gibson makes 'em."

So we drove up to Kalamazoo, Michigan and paid a visit to the Gibson factory. Observing what it takes to make a fine guitar and seeing the care they put into their work was an eye-opening education. Some of the wood came from the soundboards of old pianos and everything they used had been carefully selected and aged. The L-5 was the top of the line, and it took three, maybe four months for each one to be seasoned and built to get that great sound. The guy would sit there and tap the top here and tap it there and keep shaving it until it had just the right resonance. If it wasn't good enough, it would be tossed aside to be used on something else because only the very best tops went on the L-5s. Nowadays, a machine does it all and they come out alike and that's it, but not then. Those early L-5s were the result of knowledge and dedication, and it's the imprint of human skill that made them so great.

*Joe's Gibson
L-5, serial
no. 87357.*

The Two L-5s

Joe had called ahead to let Gibson know we were coming, and when we got there, they had five L-5s set up in a testing room for us to choose from. Of these five, four had dot inlays in the neck, and the fifth had block inlays. Out of these five guitars, I picked two; one with dots and the one that had the block inlays. So I came away with two L-5s instead of one.

According to the serial number, Joe's L-5, which had the dot inlays, was made in late 1928 or '29, and I have always believed my L-5 with dots is from the same time. The one with the blocks has a 1930 serial number. Assuming the serial numbers are dated correctly, I can't explain how Joe and I could be there in 1933 and be looking at guitars from 1929 and 1930. Unfortunately, when I could have gotten a reliable answer to this question, I didn't, and now the ones who had the answer are gone.

My guess is that Gibson archived a few guitars each year to be kept in reserve for customers who might want an instrument from a particular time period, or these hadn't sold because of the Depression. Gibson recognized Joe as one of the top guitarists in the country, and when he told them I wanted an

One of my L-5s with block inlays (serial no. 88281) next to Joe's L-5.

L-5 just like his, they made these available to me out of their regard for him. The standard price for an L-5 was $275, but they treated us very well because they needed cows with bells on them. They knew Joe and I could make a lot of headway for them if we both played L-5s, so they sold them to us for $175.

It was just a fantastic thing to walk out of the Gibson factory with two great L-5s and both of them mine. It was something I had wanted for such a long time, and I have since learned the L-5s the best players loved the most came from 1924-25 to around 1934 or so. So I was very fortunate to have gotten two from that time period.

Joe liked my L-5s and I still liked his best, so after I got my own, we would switch back and forth with them. I'd play his and he'd play one of mine for a month or so, then we'd switch back. We did this for as long as we stayed together. Many years later, when he was at the end of his career, I visited Joe at his home in Arizona and gave him one of the first Les Paul solid body

electrics. In return, he gave his L-5 to me. He was playing that guitar the night I met him, so that meant the world to me. So now I have all three of them and they are just precious, like family.

The Ozark Apple Knockers

We left Kalamazoo in great spirits and drove on down to Missouri. On the way, we got our ideas together for our two-man act, to be known as the Ozark Apple Knockers. Sunny Joe would be the lead player and straight man while I would cut up with hillbilly humor as Rhubarb Red. We could be kidding around one second and doing something seriously good on our guitars the next. Joe knew a million songs and I was learning fast, so we had plenty of material. You name it, we could play it.

As soon as we got to Springfield, we went out and found a little bungalow to rent. Joe was ten years older than I was and came from a musical family that had toured since he was a little kid, so when it

came to living on the road, he knew the ropes. He handled everything because I was very naive, just starting, and knew nothing. He was always looking out for me and I was happy to learn from him, so it was a great relationship.

They didn't waste any time putting us to work. We went on the air the day we got to town, and I remember the first song we played was *La Rosita,* and it was on KGBX because KWTO wasn't ready to go yet. KWTO signed on in Springfield on Christmas Day, 1933, located in the same building with KGBX. They were sister stations, both owned by Ralph Foster, so once KWTO got going, they had us playing on both stations. We'd go in at 4 AM and bang on those old carbon mics to activate them and then do the early morning broadcast. After that, we'd be around all day doing various broadcasts, or traveling to various shows we played all over the state.

Ralph Foster owned or was involved with stations all over the map, and we made frequent road trips which he booked for us. We played in Carthage, St. Joseph, Centralia, Joplin, all in Missouri, and we also hit Champaign and Alton, Illinois, East St. Louis, just a bunch of places where he sent us to play. We would go to all these stations and either open them up or play for an event of some kind, then go back to Springfield and resume our local schedule.

We got fan mail from as far away as Australia in response to our broadcasts on KWTO. It was amazing some of the places where people were picking up that 100-watt signal. The station was located down on the low end of the AM dial, which allowed its signal to be heard in several states around Missouri. The exposure put Springfield on the map as a music center and got Joe and me a lot of publicity. We were very well received by the Ozarks people and soon felt right at home there.

Catching Up With Joe

Now that it's just Joe and me, my guitar playing really starts to take off. I had the time to practice and Joe was so good to show me everything he knew. When I first started with him, it might take a few hours or even a couple of days to get the thing he was showing me because I was still finding the technique and everything was new to me. But now I had the technique, so as soon as I saw something, it was mine a minute later, and I was now putting it all together in my own way, no longer just copying. Somebody said I had to have a phonographic memory to be able to learn and retain so quickly. Maybe I did, but it was more than that. It was knowing what was a hockable product. There are lots of things you can do on a guitar that aren't memorable, so they don't mean anything. But other things are like a magnet and you want to hear them again and again. I had a knack for recognizing those and putting them together to create things no one had done before. It came easy to me, and I was no longer waiting to be shown. I was gone.

Joe had a great knowledge of chords and how to use them, and I was eating it up because this was what I needed to be able to play all the great standards I loved and admired so much. He knew them all, so in no time I knew them too. I remember one write-up in the Springfield paper said, "Sunny Joe is without a doubt one of the great guitarists, but that redheaded kid now with

The Ozark Apple Knockers

him is the one to watch." They were saying there was no longer one great guitar player, there were now two, and I felt embarrassed because I knew Joe was reading it. And Joe knew he had a tiger by the tail because no matter what he played, as soon as he played it, I shot it back at him and it was no longer his.

This was the time when I caught up with Joe and then surpassed him because Joe had everything to be the greatest except for one thing. He wasn't blessed with time. When it was my turn to play solo and he played rhythm, it just wasn't there. This is something I think about so often that you have to be given. You have to be given an ear for music, and you sure as hell can't go down and buy a sense of timing. If you're not born with rhythm you just can't do anything about it, no matter how steady your hands are. If that clock isn't working up in your head, then you're neither on nor off; you're just laying there somewhere. Joe knew it, and it was a curse all through his career for as long as he played. He could play fast and clean with the best, but the solid rhythm was missing. It just wasn't in his genes.

Shotgun Send-Off

There's another incident I remember from our time in Springfield. Joe liked to hunt for arrowheads, it was his hobby, and I would tag along with him just to have something to do. On a Sunday afternoon, we'd go down to one of the streams close to town to see what we could find. Now, I had found a girlfriend there in Springfield, a talented little gal who played piano, and we had been fooling around and thought we were in love. On this particular day, Joe and Delores, myself and my gal Lou had driven up to this log cabin where Joe had heard there were artifacts to be bought. So Joe and Dee get out and go up to this country cabin to see about the arrowheads while Lou and I stay in the back seat, and pretty soon we're wrestling.

While this is going on, a man walks past our car and into the cabin and then goes right over to the shotgun hanging on the wall and takes it down and loads it up. He turns to Joe and says, "I'm gonna blow that s-o-b's head off," meaning me. And Joe says, "Holy Christ, what's Red done now?" The man was angry because his giggling kids were peeking out the cabin window right down into our car seeing things they probably shouldn't have seen. So he comes out with the shotgun and puts it right up against the window, right by my head, and convincingly makes his point that we better be leaving his property in a hurry. Joe and Dee are right behind him and jump in the car and we beat it out of there. Joe never stopped kidding me about that one.

Another memory is of one night when I was jamming on the Square there in Springfield. I'm in this crowded little joint with Joe's L-5 strapped around my neck when I hear this sound you don't want to hear. I look down and I've put a big scratch in the top of Joe's guitar. I was standing next to a pinball machine and made contact with the coin slot and gouged the top. This was terribly upsetting to me, and I couldn't bear to tell Joe what had happened. The next day I took it to a furniture store and had the scratch filled in and the finish repaired. Fortunately, the damage was in the darkest part of the top, not in the lighter sunburst, so you really couldn't see it unless you knew where to look. Eventually, I did tell Joe, and I always remember that scratch when I think of Springfield.

I look back on those days and realize they were some of the best times of my life. We were popular, I was making money, I was learning guitar from one of the best, I was romancing my first girlfriend, and Joe and his wife treated me like a member of their family. It was a wonderful carefree time. We were there for several months before we got the offer to go to WBBM in Chicago, and the offer was a dream.

SOUVENIR BOOK-1934

FEDERAL BUILDING

ILLINOIS HOST HOUSE

HALL OF SCIENCE

FOUNTAIN

WORLD'S FAIR CHICAGO

CHAPTER FIVE

Chicago (1934-1938)

While Joe and I were down in Springfield, the guys in St. Louis who helped us get the job moved up to Chicago and word about us got around there. One of the people who heard and took note was S.L. Huntley, the creator of the *Mescal Ike* comic strip. He wasn't a musician, but he somehow knew about Joe and I, and one day a letter from him arrived in Springfield telling us about a job opening at WBBM, including the salary, and audition arrangements. He also wanted us to make transcriptions, and had jobs waiting for us at the World's Fair. He must have been powerfully influential to be able to get us all that work, and we didn't know who he was! Until we met him in Chicago, all we had was that one letter and a telegram after the audition saying the job was ours.

So we said goodbye to Springfield and traveled Highway 66 through St. Louis on up to Chicago, and what a great time it was to land there. The big World's Fair was going strong, the city was loaded with talented musicians jamming all night in more dives than you could count, and we had a good job on one of CBS' top network stations. We continued as the Ozark Apple Knockers doing the daily Sendol show and working as staff musicians on WBBM, broadcasting out of the famous Wrigley Building.

Mr. Huntley used his connections to get us into the Chicago union without the six-month waiting period, so we were able to go to work immediately. And we hardly ever saw the man. He would say be somewhere at 2 o'clock, we'd be there and do our job, he'd pat us on the head and leave. He was an amazing man, and thanks to him, we hit the ground running.

The job at WBBM was a breeze, and we soon started doing shows from the World's Fair for Big Yank Work Shirts and Pabst Beer. Other engagements came along, some of which we did as a duo, and others with added sidemen. And we also did commercials for Peruna, Sendol and the Big Yank work shirt company. So right in the middle of the Depression, we were making money hand over fist, hauling down a thousand dollars a week between us. The money rolling in was just unbelievable, and then something pivotal happened. We've got everything going our way, and out of the blue Joe says, "Red, we've got so much money now, let's go to Australia."

The Split With Joe

Up till then, I'd been happy to follow Joe wherever he wanted to take us, but now we had reached a fork in the road. I said, "What the hell are we going to get in Australia that we don't have here?" And Joe said, "I don't know, I just want to go." This was a problem because I didn't have the slightest interest in going to Australia. I wanted to play jazz and keep working on building recording machinery, which by this time I was very involved in. I wanted to stay in Chicago because, one, I was learning so much from all the great musicians there; and two, breaks were falling my way which were too good to ignore. NBC thought I should become a comedian, using my guitar as a prop the way Jack Benny used the violin, and Sid Strotz was pitching different ideas that had me going on my own as a solo.

This was all happening when Joe said we were going to Australia, and I said "Nah, Joe, I don't think so. I'm going to stay right in Chicago." When he asked why, I said, "Because of Coleman Hawkins, Roy Eldridge, and Earl Hines." I was talking about all the great Chicago talent I was learning from every night. I wanted to expand my musical knowledge through jazz and keep working on my recording problems. I was tired of being labeled a country entertainer, but Joe had no interest in doing anything else. He just wanted to keep doing the hillbilly act, and now he had a wild hair to go to Australia.

So the time had come for Joe and I to split up and go our separate ways after being together constantly for two years. We never had a fight or a serious argument, and I could not have hoped for a truer friend. Joe was like a gypsy; he loved to be on the rove. And eventually, he did go to Australia, and then Japan, where he was very successful. We remained close for the rest of our lives, but that was the end of our road as partners.

The Piano And All That Jazz

So Joe's gone, the World's Fair and WBBM jobs are over, and I'm knocking around as a solo act on WLS and WGN, thinking about what I'm going to do. And I make the most radical decision I ever made in my life. And that is to quit the guitar, quit the whole country thing, to become a piano player and play jazz. I look back on it now and see it was a stupid move, but it was something I had to get out of my system, and there was a reason for it.

There was an anti-Mother seed that had been there since I was born, and that seed was jazz. From the time I could turn the radio on, that's what I was listening for, but Mother only wanted to hear country and hillbilly music because that's what she loved. She had no interest in jazz, but I did, and the only way I was going to hear it was to be where it's played. So I went to this great piano player who played jazz at a little joint close to home, and I told him, "I'm taking piano lessons but I really want to play jazz and I need to hear you play." And he said, "Well, you're not supposed to be in a saloon at your age, but we'll put the bass cover over you so you can lay there and listen." So that's what we did. I slipped in and got behind the piano and he covered me up. And during the evening, a hand would reach down and give me a half a sandwich, and I'd lie there under the bass fiddle cover, eating while I listened. I didn't have a guitar yet and just loved what he was doing on the piano. I was ten, eleven years old and thinking this was what I wanted to do. I wanted to be a piano player, not a guitar player.

So when Joe and I split up, this piano bug was still gnawing on me and the thing I still most wanted to do was play jazz. And every night on the South Side I was hearing all this stuff beyond anything heard before, coming from musicians who were by far the leaders. I'm talking about Art Tatum, Benny Goodman and so many others who were breaking new ground every night, while I was stuck doing mostly hillbilly and country music. I loved that too, but jazz and country are on opposite sides and don't get along too well. So finally, I made the decision to quit playing country music altogether. I dropped the name Rhubarb Red to become Les Paul and play jazz at night. I loved the guitar, but playing jazz was my goal, so I turned the whole thing around and quit the guitar to play piano.

April 1.
Mar 6 1934

A "RED"-APPLEKNOCKER" FROM WAUKESHA OVER WBBM STATION

Lester Polfuss, Waukesha's own "Rhubarb Red", a favorite radio entertainer, now has been signed with WBBM Chicago, and can be heard daily over that station at 3:45 and 6:00 P. M., excepting Sunday.

For the past three months Red has been heard through KGBZ and KWTO, Springfield, Missouri. During his stay there he teamed up with "Sunny Joe" of the South, the pair taking the name of 'The Ozark Apple-Knockers."

The boys arrived in Chicago Monday and were first introduced over WBBM Tuesday.

In the winter of 1933 the team were known as the "Scalawags" over KMOX, Voice of St. Louis, but now Red's many friends and admirers will be glad to know no doubt, that he is now identified by the more dignified title of an "Ozark Apple-Knocker," and possibly also because he has really landed in big time radio with his ever fresh array of songs and tunes.

Les wishes his friends to know that he will spend many of his Sundays at home with his mother, Mrs. Eveyln Polfuss, and brother, Ralph at the Polfuss residence, 320 West St. Paul Avenue.

The first piano job I got was with my trio, backing Jackie Gleason on the North Side at the 5100 Club. Then I played for Joe E. Lewis, the comedian, and suddenly, I was in with these great entertainers, getting to watch them work an audience night after night. You couldn't buy the education I got for any amount of money. And the money was terrible, I was playing for practically nothing, but it was a great privilege. So I would play limited engagements with Gleason or Lewis or whoever, but when they moved on, I'd be back looking for work as a sideman.

Sundodgers Rendezvous

I happened into a job in a little saloon near Lawrence and Broadway called the Sundodgers Rendezvous. The pay was five dollars a week and a place to sleep, and I had to sweep the joint out every night. I started out there putting Eddie Lang records on a floor model crank phonograph and playing my L-5 along with the record. I'd say, "Here's the greatest guitarist in the world, and the next best to play along with him." That was my act. I knew every note Eddie Lang had recorded, so I could play what he could play. Sometimes I would get adventurous and try things, but usually I just played what Eddie was playing on the record. The problem was, when the place would get a few customers in, the crowd noise would all but drown me out, so I wasn't getting anywhere with it.

It was then I went to the owner, Danny Reames, and asked if I could form a little orchestra, and start doing shows. So I built a PA, had a dance floor installed and turned the place into a little nightclub. And it worked, more or less. Danny started making more money, so he was happy, and I was playing piano with the band I put together.

I went from making five dollars playing along with the phonograph to forty-five dollars a week running the show. That was an improvement, but when you compare it to what I was making doing the country act, it was nothing. And it was then I realized—and this is a big thing for me—I realized how difficult it was for a jazz musician to survive. I had friends right there on the same street, people like Anita O' Day, Lord Buckley, Al Lyons, all great talents and all starving. They were beyond me, and I could see how difficult it was for them, and I began to appreciate how much money I had made as a commercial, country player. And just as I was realizing this, another break came my way, and again it was one of my Missouri friends who helped me.

Rhubarb Red Returns

I happened to be walking past the Wrigley Building one day and ran into Holland Engle, who I knew from St. Louis and who was now program director at WBBM. He said, "How you doing, Red?" And I said, "I'm doing all right. I've got more work than I can handle." And he said, "Yeah, I saw your picture outside the Sundodgers Rendezvous. Truth is, you're not doing very well." I admitted I wasn't, and he said, "Well, let's see what we can do." He took an envelope out of his pocket, addressed it to Ralph Atlass, wrote on it, "Hey, listen to this guy," and signed his name. Then he said, "Take this over to WJJD and talk to them. Gene Autry moved to California and they're looking for somebody for their morning show."

The Atlass brothers controlled several important radio stations in the Chicago area. Les Atlass was president of CBS in Chicago and ran WBBM, and Ralph Atlass owned two of the biggest stations in town, WJJD and WIND.

Holland Engle's note got me an audition at WJJD, which specialized in old time country music. I was sitting there waiting to do my thing when I realized the person I idolized so much, Pie Plant Pete, was sitting across the room. He had his harmonica rack and his guitar, I'm sitting there with my harmonica rack and guitar, and it dawns on me we're both auditioning for the same job. Pie Plant Pete was the one who first inspired me to be an entertainer, who let me hold his guitar and showed me the basic chords when my Mother took me to meet him. So I went over to him and said, "Pete, I've admired you all my life. Why are you here?" And he said, "Well, I'm auditioning for a job. Are you auditioning, too?" And I said, "Well, yes, I am." I was at a loss for words, and he just said, "Well, let's see what happens."

They called me in, and the guy said, "Well, let's see if Holly Engle knows anything. What do you do?" And I said, "Well, I tell jokes, I sing, I play the piano, I play the guitar, I play the harmonica, the banjo, the jug. I sweep, I cook, I do anything." Then I did a Rhubarb Red number, and the guy auditioning me was Ben Kantor, the musical director of WJJD.

As soon as I finished, he pressed a button on his desk and said, "Look no further, I've found the guy I want." And that was the beginning of another great relationship because Ben Kantor became like my godfather while I was in Chicago. With that done, I went back out to the lobby, and Pete said, "We've just been told they've found the person they were looking for. I presume you got the job." And I said, "Yes, I

68

did, and I'm so sorry." He said, "Don't feel sorry. That's life." I think Pete needed the job just as much as I did and I didn't know what to do or say. This was the first time something like this happened where I was directly involved, and it made a big mark on me.

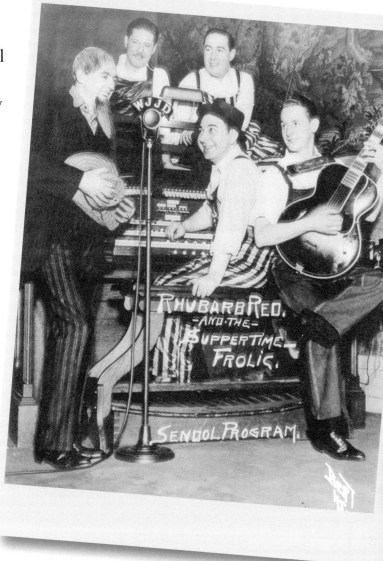

Pete went on to a station in Cleveland that was right next to WJJD on the dial. And it was interesting because I would get his mail. I would get letters from women saying, "I know you changed your name just to get away from me." I even got a cake with a note saying, "Pete, I love you, and will never forget that night." I had copied him so well that many people who heard me thought I was Pete working under a different name.

So I'm back on the air as Rhubarb Red and soon established as a solo act on the early morning show at WJJD. I'd been sleeping on the floor upstairs at the Sundodgers, but now that I was making decent money again, I got myself a little apartment. At night, I was still trying to make my way playing jazz piano, and when I wasn't playing I was out listening to all the great musicians that were everywhere in Chicago.

Art Tatum

There was an interesting situation with the two radio stations owned by Ralph Atlass. WJJD was strictly country, but WIND, the sister station, played all the hip stuff, the jazz and swing. A fellow named Harry Zimmerman was the staff organist, and we used to take turns buying new records for the stations. One week I'd make the rounds and come back with a stack of records, the next week would be his turn. Then various people would audition them and it would be decided which ones went on air. So one day, Harry says, "I've got a record you need to hear." And I say, "Yeah? Who is it?" And Harry says, "Art Tatum."

This was the first I'd heard of Art Tatum. So we sit down and Harry puts the record on and, Holy Christ, I'm shocked. I've heard the great piano play-

69

ers, but never anything like this. He's coming from somewhere else. So the record ends and I say, "Well, to hell with the piano. I'll never be able to play like this guy." Then, when Art comes to town, I go to the Three Deuces to hear him and I'm even more amazed. This guy's hands are enormous, and he can reach a tenth on the keyboard the way most players reach an octave. He's doing things with his left hand nobody ever dreamed of, he's got the right hand going independently, and if it's not perfect, nobody can tell it. I later sat in with him many times with my guitar and we would push each other till the crowd went crazy. This was some of the best playing I ever did because if you're up against Art Tatum, you've got to be good or he's going to flatten you. We became great friends and I was an avid fan of Art Tatum forever, but never again would I consider being a jazz piano player.

Enter Les Paul

So I gave up the piano, but I still had the thing for jazz. So I said, "Well, I'll go back to the guitar. I'll take this inspiration from Art Tatum and all the others I admire and go there with the guitar." And that's what I did. Harry Zimmerman and I started doing a jazz show on WIND with just organ and guitar, and that's when I started using the name Les Paul. I think this was around the end of 1934. And now that I was through with the piano, I was taking my guitar and sitting in at the jazz clubs every night, playing with the greats, and learning from every one of them. This was when I began to get serious about amplifying my sound because with just an acoustic guitar, it was impossible to cut through the horns and drums and noisy, juiced- up crowds who came to dig the music. I wanted to be heard, and I knew the electric guitar was the way to go going all the way back to Beekman's Barbecue Stand. So these were the problems I had been working on all this time. I wanted to be able to record what I was doing so I could hear it and judge it and make it better, and I wanted to be heard without having to beat my guitar to death.

The Django Revolution

Then, maybe six months after I heard Art Tatum, something else happened. I heard Django Reinhardt. When I heard *Clouds* for the first time, I said, "Well, hell, I might as well sell shoes." His music was knocking everybody out, and I was no exception. By this time, Eddie Lang had died and I was hearing few other guitar players, but hearing Django was enough to support the belief that what I was doing was just the beginning, that he was really where the body was buried. I was very intrigued and impressed with the passion and technique of Django's playing, and immediately did what I always do when I hear something I like; I started listening and figuring out what he was doing and making it mine.

I was deeply inspired by Django's playing and also by his group, which included the great violinist Stephane Grapelli. Their sound had a contagious drive, and I caught it. I formed Les Paul and the Melody Kings, and we became a feature on WIND playing all jazz in that style. So now I was like Django, with the guitar and the violin, the whole group, and doing things for NBC.

Doing It All

Now I had everything going at the same time. I was Rhubarb Red on WJJD, Les Paul on WIND, and playing jazz all night in the clubs. This was the beginning of the lifestyle where I worked all day and played all night. I would go on the air at five in the morning doing my country thing, then in the afternoons play the fashion shows or rehearse the trio, and then it was the Melody Kings broadcasts, and playing joints or jobbing dates at night. I never slept like a normal person sleeps. When I got so tired I couldn't go any further, I'd lay down wherever I was and sleep like a dog. Then I'd hear somebody call my name and I'd be up and going again. Many times I would jam all night and then go straight to the station and catch maybe an hour's sleep on the sofa before going on the air. That's the way I grew up. You sleep whenever you get the chance because sleep is not the important thing. The important thing is covering all the fields and making the most of the time you've got. So I was playing country, I was playing jazz, and in between I was working on my electronics and recording ideas. I was doing everything. And the interesting thing is that the people who heard me on WJJD as Rhubarb Red had no idea the Les Paul they were starting to hear about was the same person.

During the time I was in Missouri, I concentrated on acoustic guitar because I was with Joe. It was a question of me making a decision...do I want to experiment electronically or do I want to put my time in and learn to play the instrument? And I chose to just take a rest from my ideas on recording and the electric guitar and study the guitar because I had Joe right there, a great teacher, and I knew there would never be a better opportunity to learn. So that's what I did. After Joe and I split up and I went through my piano phase, I went back to the electronics and began to experiment with amplifying my guitar again.

71

Going Electric - The National Solid Top

There were a few commercially made electric guitars around, but they weren't acceptable. The response was uneven, they buzzed and hummed, I didn't care for the guitars themselves and the available amplification was barbaric. The National String Instrument Company was on the northwest side of Chicago, not far from where I lived, so I decided to take what I had learned from my experiments with the Plaster of Paris and all that, and go see them.

So I went to National and said I wanted a guitar with a half-inch thick solid maple top, and no f-holes in it. They said, "No f-holes? You've got to be kidding." I said, "No f-holes and real thick." They thought I was crazy, but went along with it. This was the first time I had anyone custom build a guitar for me. Paul Barth built it for me, the same size as an L-5, and then I cut a hole in the thick top and put in my homemade pickup near the bridge.

I learned how to wind my own pickups by taking telephone receivers apart, seeing how the coils in the little microphone units were put together, and then applying my own windings to accommodate six guitar strings. I experimented constantly with different windings, different cores, where to place them, how far from the strings, how close to the bridge, doing everything I could think of to locate a better, stronger sound. My pickups were heavy and crude, but they had more tonal power than anything I could go out and buy.

After I got the National put together, I took it out and jammed with it in a few spots around Chicago and nobody really flipped over it. People like George Barnes and Everett Hull regarded it as a curiosity. The worst thing about it was being so cumbersome and heavy. With the thick top and my heavy homemade pickup, this thing carried serious weight. The reason an acoustic guitar has a big body is to resonate and amplify the sound, and I realized for what I was doing, the size of the sound box didn't mean anything. So I learned something useful from it. What I liked about it, and the thing that showed me I was going in the right direction, was that it had remarkable sustain compared to any other guitar I had played. It was a struggle because I knew there was something there, but I didn't know the things that were obstructing it. The National wasn't satisfactory, but it was a big step and an improvement. I was experimenting with my pickups too, very much so, and the amplification, and it hadn't all come together yet.

I didn't hang on to the National very long. Some guy expressed an interest in it one night and I practically gave it away after removing my pickup.

The Toaster

While the National people were building the solid top guitar for me, I was thinking about how I was going to amplify it. By this time, 16mm movies with

In 2004 a gal named Ellen Miller was walking down Broadway on a Monday night, and just happened to pass the Iridium, where I was playing. She came in for the show, and afterwards she came up to get my autograph, and she told me she plays guitar. When I asked her what kind of guitar she played, she said, "It's very peculiar". She had found it in Key West, Florida, and it had no f-holes. She showed it to several experts and no one could shed any light on it. So I asked her, "Is it a blonde National?" She said "Yes!" Then, "Does it have a pickup?", and she said "yes" again. Then I asked "Where was the pickup located?", and she replied "Right down next to the bridge". And that's when I knew that the guitar she had found in Key West was my old National.

sound had arrived, and seeing that type of portable movie set-up gave me an idea. So I went over to Bell and Howell and said to the guys there, "You know the outfit you have for showing 16mm movies? Well, I don't want the projector. I want the speaker box with the amplifier and the long cable, and that's all I want." They said, "What are you going to do with it?" I told them I wanted to try it out as a guitar amplifier. And they said, "Okay, we'll give you one." So they gave me one and I customized it so I could plug my guitar into it, and it worked pretty well. This was the first guitar amplifier I had that wasn't some version of a converted radio, and I liked it because it was portable and easy to carry around. I took it over to the Lyon and Healey music store and they looked at it and listened to it, and then they copied it. And that's how the early

73

Gibson guitar amplifier came into being. All you have to do is put one of those first Gibson amps beside Bell and Howell's 16mm movie speaker from the early thirties, and you'll see they're exactly alike in shape and speaker size.

My amp came to be known as the toaster, and there's a little story behind the name. We were playing a date at the Palmer House there in Chicago, which was located in an area where all the electricity was DC. I plugged in the amp but forgot to plug in the AC converter, and then stepped out of the ballroom. I was out in the lobby when this guy who works for the hotel came up and said, "That toaster of yours, you better go take a look at it." And I said, "You're making fun of the electric guitar? I don't know who you are, but get lost." He said, "Okay, fine, it's not my problem, but there's smoke coming out of it." So I run back into the ballroom and sure enough, smoke is boiling out of my amp. The DC current had burned the transformer up. And from then on, I called my little amp the toaster.

The Larson Brothers

I'd heard about the Larson brothers. They had a reputation for high quality work and were one of the first guitar makers to concentrate on steel string instruments, so I decided to give them a try. They were located in what would be downtown Chicago now, where the Loop verges, but it was still on the outskirts then. When I went to the barn where they worked, there was a sign that said, 'if you want to talk, pull this string.' So I pulled the string and a little bell rang up on the second floor. A guy came to the hayloft door, looked down and said, "What do you want?" And I said, "I want to talk to you about building a guitar." So he pulls on a string from upstairs that lifts the latch downstairs to open the door. I go in and climb the stairs to their workshop area and there's August and Carl, these two brothers, working alone in this barn making great guitars. August sized me up and said, "Just tell me exactly why you're here because I'm a busy man." And I said "Well, that's good, because I'm busy too." These guys were Swedish and I'm German, so we had a way of understanding each other and soon became friends. I made many visits to their workshop while I was in Chicago and August would say the same thing every time he saw me, "Tell me what you want because I'm a busy man."

So I'm there with my idea, and I introduced myself to them as Les Paul. And Carl says, "Well here, you want to try one of our guitars?" So I took one and played something, and he says, "You know, you sound a lot like Rhubarb Red, you're just not as good as he is." And I said, "But I am him, I'm Rhubarb Red." And Carl says, "There's a lot of guys who would like to play like him but you've got a ways to go." I tried to convince them I really was Rhubarb

I no longer have my original Gibson cheapie that I played with Fred Waring,. This ES-250 shown here with my "toaster" amp was a later version of the same thing.

Red and they weren't buying it. But they did buy the idea of making a solid top guitar for me, with no f-holes like the National, only this time I specified making the top much thinner. I ordered a smaller guitar, with a cutaway, 22 frets, and the neck placed so more of them were clear of the body for playing higher up the fingerboard.

So I had them build that guitar for me, and again I sawed a hole in the top and put my pickup in where I thought I wanted it. Then I had to keep making the hole bigger because I didn't like the way the pickup sounded and each time I moved it the hole had to be enlarged. The Larson brothers eventually built three guitars for me, very fine instruments, and I kept sawing them up trying to get the electric sound I knew was there.

The Gibson Cheapie

Finally, I took my little archtop L-50 out of retirement, cut a chunk out of the top, and installed my homemade pickup. This little guitar had lived a rough life and was so banged up the top was caving in. I mounted the pickup in a larger piece of metal to cover the hole I cut. Having it that way, the whole works all together, made the outfit heavier, but also easier to take out and put back in, which I did often because I was always tinkering with it. I had John D'Angelico mount a solid wood section of resonant wood inside the sound box to strengthen it and give it better sustain, and it worked. It was an absolute wreck to look at, but it represented my best ideas up to that time and sounded great.

The cheapie was the first guitar I put two pickups on, and that was later in 1938 when I was with Fred Waring. One of the Gibson guys saw it and said, "Why do you want two pickups on there, isn't one loud enough?" They had no idea what I was doing or what I was after. I loved that little guitar for the way it played and for its electric sound, and it became my favorite. It didn't have the binding on it, and the frets went right over the end, and it just sustained better than the others. It was one of Gibson's good cheap ones. I performed and jammed everywhere with it, and it drove Gibson crazy because they wanted me to play something flashy and expensive.

That little $45 guitar was a very valuable thing to me, and I had a big problem because the top was caving in. All the sawing and banging and the weight of the pickup plate had weakened it, so I would put a sound post inside it, like you would a violin, to support the weakened top. And that was difficult because I had to tie two pieces of string to the wooden post and then try to snake it into place inside the guitar. I'd be laying on the floor all night long wrestling with that thing trying to get it just right, so it was a headache, but well worth it to me.

And Gibson kept saying, "Gee, Red, we'll give you any guitar you want, but you gotta stop playing that beat-up cheapie." And they would keep giving me 400s because that was their new high-dollar guitar. Hell, by the time I left Chicago, I had six Super 400s. They were beautiful to look at but I never liked them because they were big and cumbersome and didn't fit what I was doing. My cheapie wasn't pretty, but it was me. It was the beginning of my sound and I wasn't about to give it up.

First Network Broadcast Bombs

Playing electric guitar with the Melody Kings on WIND established Les Paul as an up and coming name in Chicago radio. My friend from KMOX in

Gibson kept sending me new L-5s and Super 400s to play. They were fine acoustic instruments but I continued to play the cheapie because it was electric, and that's the direction I knew I wanted to go.

St. Louis, Sid Strotz, got wind of it and called me up. He said, "Les, I've got a great job for you and your quartet. We're going to broadcast a show from the Bismarck Hotel every Friday night, and it'll be coast-to-coast on NBC. It's perfect for you."

So I get my quartet together and we go down to the Bismarck to do this show, and it's the first time I'm going to use my electric guitar on the national network. This is 1934, maybe early '35, and being featured on a national network show was a big thing, the thing you hope for, so we were jazzed about it. We go over to the hotel and set up and everything is perfect. I have my amplifier set so it's aimed in toward the mic, and the other guys, rhythm guitar, fiddle and bass, gather around close because we're all playing to one microphone.

The violin player was a fellow named Adolph Simovitz, known professionally as Harry Sims. He was a great violin player, but I remember him best as a guy who was just naturally funny. We were always laughing at Harry because he did funny things without meaning to. When he unconsciously did something wrong or stupid and then realized how funny it was, he always laughed harder than we did. He was a sweetheart.

The night of my first national broadcast with an electric guitar, I had the pickup and the wiring all mounted in a piece of metal, and the whole thing was bolted into the cheapie as a single unit with the shielded cable coming out of it and going to my amp. The show starts and everything is going fine. When it's time for us to play, the announcer gives us a nice introduction and then says, "So here they are, Les Paul and the Melody Kings!" I move quickly toward the microphone and all hell breaks loose. Harry was standing on my guitar cord, and when I stepped forward, the whole works was ripped out of my guitar and hit the floor with a terrible racket. The pick-up works was attached to the bridge and tailpiece, a contraption external of the guitar, so now we're dead because I've got no electric guitar, I've got no acoustic guitar, there's nothing to do but play around it. I tried to sing because I couldn't play my leads, but we were flustered and there was no hiding it. So my first NBC network radio show playing electric guitar was a total disaster. Poor old Harry never stopped blaming himself for it. I'd love to contact him again just so we could laugh about it, but I can't find him.

Forming The Trio

Now that I had the toaster and an electric guitar with good volume and tone, jamming with all the jazz players became much more satisfying, and my playing began to get more notice. I also started playing electric on WIND and was getting a good response there, too. And it's along about now, early 1935,

When the new model Super 400 came out, Gibson always made sure they sent me one. They were beautiful guitars, great for playing rhythm, but the 18" wide body was too big for my taste.

when I'm back doing country to make a living that I come to another decision. Now that I've been through the piano thing, now that I've heard Django and gotten fired up about doing jazz on the guitar, now that I've got a handle on amplifying my guitar, I realize what I want to do next is go to New York.

And to go to New York, I want to form a group that's really good, a real knockout. So I'm thinking about what sort of group to have, when one night I'm backstage at the National Barn Dance and a fellow comes up and introduces himself. It's Jimmy Atkins, and I know him from hearing him sing on WLS as Tommy Tanner. Jimmy was a great singer, a crooner like Bing, and it

79

turns out he's a fan of both Rhubarb Red and Les Paul, and he's been wanting to meet me. Everybody knows now that Jimmy was Chet Atkins' older half-brother, but Chet was still just a kid down in the sticks at this time and hadn't been heard from yet. So we started talking and discovered we had a lot in common. We were both making a living playing hillbilly music and both wanted to get away from it and do the modern stuff. Jimmy was an excellent rhythm guitarist and a gifted vocalist, and when he said Ernie Newton, another WLS staff musician and a bass player, was looking to do the same thing, the first Les Paul Trio was born.

The chemistry between the three of us was great from the start, and we started spending all the time we could rehearsing. The key was we were going to play a million songs, but out of all of them, there would be two gold nuggets, two especially good arrangements we'd have ready to close the deal when the opportunity came. The two songs we picked were *Out of Nowhere* and *After You've Gone*. We rehearsed many many songs, but we kept coming back to those two and concentrating on them, playing them in every style and key until we found arrangements that really grabbed us. We rehearsed those two songs for nearly two years to get ourselves ready.

Three afternoons a week, we'd get together in my little one-room apartment and set up and play. My recording machinery was behind a folding bed, so to record, we'd fold the bed down and crowd around it. I'd sit on the edge of the bed where I could reach the recording controls, and there was just enough room left for Ernie and his bass, Jimmy and his guitar, and my dog. Using the homemade recording machine I'd built, a disk cutter, we would record our songs and then play them back. And this was terribly helpful to us because we could hear what was working and what was just lying there. I was also recording the Melody Kings broadcasts off WIND and using them in the same way. This was when recording became an important part of my whole approach to music. It was terribly interesting because the quality was so poor by today's standards, but to us it was such an advantage to be able to hear what we were sounding like. It was the beginning.

Jimmy and Ernie were both sincere people, and what I liked about the three of us was just how thoughtful and respectful we were toward each other. Our talents fit together in a unique way, which made working together a very positive thing, and we took care not to step on each others' toes. Every Friday, we'd have a meeting to discuss any problems anyone was having, and from those talks ground rules were established which we all followed. For example, there was a rule amongst us that you didn't just go over and pick up another person's instrument without permission. I didn't care who picked up my guitar, but the next guy might feel differently. We respected each other, and it helped us get along great together.

Jim Atkins had an excellent musical ear and was just an outstanding vocalist. When he started singing, people would stop what they were doing to listen, that's the kind of voice he had. He could sell a song, and he was a very solid rhythm guitarist who could play fat chords all over the neck to give us a fuller, more interesting sound. Ernie was a hard-driving bass player and a good showman. He wore a top hat when he played, and had a playing technique that added to our percussion. He had a piece of sandpaper glued to the front of his bass and would hold a drum brush in his right hand while he played. He'd pluck a string and then slide the brush across the sandpaper to create a rhythmic swoosh in time with the music. He was really very accomplished at doing this and it was an important part of our sound. He also mounted a little squeeze bulb at the top of his bass neck, which we would fill with talcum powder. When we'd do *Casey Jones*, he'd squeeze the bulb and the talcum powder would blow up in the air to simulate smoke from the train. That bit always got a laugh and a round of applause. So with Jim's voice, Ernie's showmanship and my little electric guitar through the toaster, we made a unique impression.

Multi-Track Breakthrough

The disk-cutting machine I'd built was really barbaric, but it was good enough to get us on a disk so we could hear ourselves and improve what we were doing. One particular day, rehearsal was over, and I thought, "Oh, geez. I wanted to do *Limehouse Blues* and Jimmy and Ernie are gone. Oh, well, I'll just put the rhythm down and play along with it." And as I started to do that the idea struck me, "Why don't I just record two of these things out and play Ernie's part and then play Jim's part and then play my part?" So I thought about it, and I dug out another playback arm and added it because I've got to cut the record twice on the outside groove to get the rhythm track. So, on the first pass, I recorded the rhythm guitar, and then, on the next set of grooves, I laid down the bass line using the low string on my rhythm guitar.

To do this, I had to have two pickups to play these things back on and be able to start them at the same time. And, of course, that was the toughest thing in the world to do, to take two pick up arms and put them down at the same time and start them off together. But I kept at it and in a few days I had the thing so I could play back a rhythm section in sync and play my part over it. So now, if Ernie and Jim don't happen to be there, I don't have to wait. I can go ahead and do it without them. That was my first attempt at trying to do multi-tracking with the guitar. It was very crude, but it proved a point and it lit the light.

81

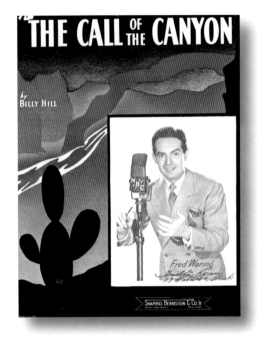

Discovering Delay

Something I discovered in that learning process was the delay effect and the way it could enhance sustain and the fullness of the tone. Very few people know I was the one who discovered that effect which is so common now. Delay was a problem I worked on for years to figure out, and it was so simple. Most all of it is simple, really, once you see it. It's just a matter of chasing it until you realize it's been right in front of you the whole time, but for some reason, you can't see it. You know it's there because the facts are pointing the way, trying to tell you. You can feel it, and you know it can be done, so you just have to stay with it until you figure out how to shine the light on it. Once you do, when it comes clear to you, then you're saying, "Well, hell, that's easy...nothing to it," but getting there will keep you awake all night. It always comes back to the desire to find something out, and being stubborn enough not to quit until you get where you want to go. And this applies to any undertaking in life.

My popularity as a country fixture on WJJD, and the success I had doing shows and county fairs up in Wisconsin, Michigan and elsewhere led to my first professional recordings. In 1936, at the age of 21, I cut my first commercial records as Rhubarb Red, recording four songs for the Montgomery Ward record label, including *Just Because* and *Deep Elm Blues.* I also did some of my first session work then, playing on about 20 sides with the great old blues singer, Georgia White. These were all done with my L-5 during the time I was developing my first electric guitars, and it was getting near the end for Rhubarb Red.

After we got the trio together, we would talk about going to New York, and other times California, when we got good enough.

And I'd say, "Don't worry about the money. I have the transportation and the money to get us there. We've just got to get so good they can't turn us down." My first choice was New York because it was the center of the musical universe, the big time, but I was also drawn to California because Eddie Lang had died and I figured I should be Bing Crosby's next guitar player.

Just before we left Chicago, Art Satherly recorded us at Columbia and gave us the record, as a favor. It was *Casey Jones,* and I still have it. Art knew we were planning to leave Chicago, and after he gave the record to us, he said, "My advice to you is don't give up what you've got in Chicago because you guys aren't ready to go anywhere." Jimmy and Ernie looked at me and I said, "Don't pay any attention to him, we're good. We're damn good, so let's go do it."

We still hadn't decided where to go, we just knew we were going, but there were some differences. Ernie was the type who said, "I'll go no matter what. You say it, Les, and we'll go." But Jimmy was married and a very stable kind of guy, so he was a little more cautious. He said, "Les, are you sure? We've all got good jobs here and we're all settled." And I said, "Listen. I've got so many friends in New York it's unbelievable." And, of course, I didn't know anybody in New York, but I said, "We'll go see my buddy Paul Whiteman, he and I are like this." I had never met Paul Whiteman, and he sure as hell didn't know who I was, but I dropped his name because we had all listened to his national broadcast on NBC called Grand Central Station. So Paul Whiteman became my thing. I think it was that absolute belief I had that we were going to make it no matter where we went that made them able to go along with me. I believed it so much they believed it too. So we made up our minds to go.

Leaving Chicago

It was a beautiful sunny afternoon in June of 1938 when we packed my car at 3900 Sheridan Road. Red Foley was there, the Hoosier Hotshots and many of our Chicago friends, all there to help us pack up and see us off. So we load the car with Ernie's bass, Jimmy's acoustic and my electric guitar and amp, one of my L-5s, our personal stuff, everything we really need jammed into every available space. Everything I had left over, my piano, my guitars, my recording machine, clothes, I just left it there. Some of it I sold, some of it I gave away, but I just left it all because I didn't want to deal with it later. I got rid of my six Super 400s and even gave away one of my L-5s along with a pair of Florsheim shoes. The L-5 came back to me years later and I'm so glad it did, but that day I didn't want it anymore.

When the car was all packed, I took a coin and said, "Heads we're going to New York, tails we're going to L.A," and flipped it and it came down heads. So I said, "It's New York. Everybody agreed?" Jimmy and Ernie said yes, so that was it. Jimmy kissed his wife, we said our goodbyes and were New York bound. Through connections Jim and Ernie had, we were able to hire on at the last minute with a WLS road show headed for New York state on a tour, so we caught up with them and worked our way east playing our last gigs as country entertainers.

For Your Summer Vacation
WORLD'S FAIR
New York
Admission 50¢

"I think there are moments where you can see the world turning from what it is into what it will be. For me, the New York World's Fair is such a moment. It is a compass rose pointing in all directions, toward imaginary future and real past, false future and immutable present, a world of tomorrow contained in the lost American yesterday."

—John Crowly, from the film *The World of Tomorrow*

CHAPTER SIX

New York, New York (1938-1941)

We sailed out of Chicago in my overloaded Buick, finally doing what we'd been working toward since the trio was formed. We were on our way to New York, and couldn't have been more excited about getting on with it.

We tagged along with Lula Belle and Scotty and the Cumberland Ridge Runners as part of the National Barn Dance hillbilly road show, working our way east. This was to our benefit because we were getting paid, and it gave the trio a chance to work with live audiences, which we hadn't done before.

When the WLS tour turned roundabout and started working west back to Chicago, we drove on to New York City, arriving in the summer of 1938. We found our way to the Chesterfield Hotel, a hot spot we'd heard about, and took a room together for $12 a week. It was located on Broadway, not far from Times Square, and a popular hangout for musicians because it was cheap. It was crowded, and Jimmy, Ernie and I had to share the bathtub down the hall with about 20 other guys.

Finding work was tough, but we got lucky and landed a job at the Onyx Club. We began to get offers and were even approached by Major Bowes, but it wasn't what we were looking for. After a couple of weeks, the boys were getting restless. Jimmy was missing his wife; Ernie still had his old job waiting at WLS; and Chicago was starting to look like home sweet home.

The Miracle On Broadway

As the days passed, the guys kept bringing up Paul Whiteman. Jimmy finally collared me one day and said, "Now look Red, are you going to call your buddy or not? We've got to have a job." And I said, "Okay, let's do it."

We go down to the lobby pay phone, and Jimmy and Ernie are standing there when I get Whiteman's secretary on the line. I tell her I'm Les Paul, an old friend of Paul Whiteman, with this great trio he really needs to hear. But she's not buying it, and when I pause for a second, she says, "Sorry, we're not looking for anybody," and hangs up. The guys want to know what's up, and I say,

"They said to come right over!" I figure I've faked it this long, and there's no reason to quit now.

We take our instruments and walk three blocks to the 53rd Street Theatre, where Whiteman's office is located. We're up on one of the upper floors and I'm giving my line to the secretary again, when I see Whiteman through an open door further back in the office. So I wave and say "Hey, Paul!" like he's my old friend. Whiteman gets annoyed with the secretary for letting us in, and we're swiftly shown the door, which slams shut behind us.

So now we're standing there in the hallway, three lost guys toting a bass, two guitars and a suitcase amplifier, and I don't know what to say because now I'm really busted. And just then, a fellow steps out of a nearby restroom, and it's Fred Waring. And I say, "Are you Fred Waring?" And he says, "Yeah, but I'm not looking for any musicians." He goes to the elevator and pushes the button, and I say, "Well, can we play till the elevator gets here?" He says, "Well, there's no law against it, I guess you can."

Quick as a cat, I plug my amp into an outlet there in the hallway, and we jump into *After You've Gone*. We're all watching the floor indicator, and the closer it gets to our floor, the faster Jimmy sings and the faster we play. We're dashing madly to the finish just as the elevator doors open, and now Fred is amused. He says, "Okay, okay, come on and get in." So we crowd into the elevator and go down to the next floor, where the rehearsal studio and headquarters for the Fred Waring show are located. He just happened to be using the restroom on Whiteman's floor because his own was being re-painted, and we just happened to be standing there when he walked out. It'd never happen in a million years, but it was our time and it happened for us.

He leads us out of the elevator and into this enormous room where all the Pennsylvanians and office help are rehearsing and working. Fred gets their attention, and says, "Something just happened. These three hoodlums nailed me in the hallway upstairs, and if you like them as much as I do, I'm going to hire them." So we play *After You've Gone* again, and all the Pennsylvanians applaud like mad because they know the decision has already been made. Fred's going to hire us, and they're going along with it for his benefit.

So we got the job, and it was truly a miracle. In less than fifteen minutes, we went from being down and out with no job and no prospects to joining one of the biggest names in the country and making good money. And this is one of the terribly interesting things about show business. You can have all the talent in the world, you can work hard and steady and be blessed in many ways, but to be successful, you also have to have tremendous good fortune. Meeting Fred Waring by chance and winding up on his national NBC radio show couldn't be made to happen if you prayed for it all your life. Luck is terribly

The Les Paul Trio warming up for the Fred Waring Show: That's me, Jimmy Atkins, and Ernie Newton.

This photo was taken in 1939 during the first television broadcast from Rockefeller Center. Donna Dae is the vocalist, Fred Waring is conducting, and Jimmy and I are on the first row playing acoustic guitars. Notice that the entire orchestra and glee club are playing into one microphone.

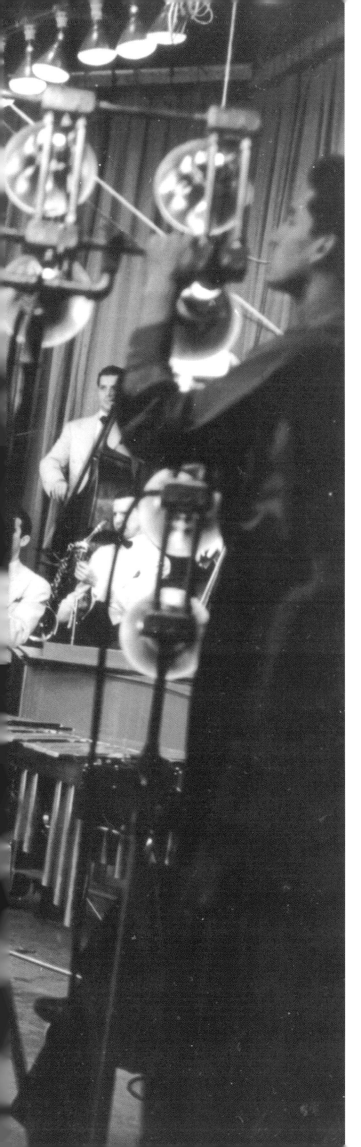

important, and I've had my share going both ways.

Fred put us on retainer for thirty bucks a week while we waited for clearance from the New York union. During the waiting period, Jimmy and I went back to Chicago to get our girls. It was great to be able to tell our friends we were joining Fred Waring and the Pennsylvanians, and would be featured coast-to-coast on his radio show.

In Chicago, I'd been living with Virginia Webb, a happy-go-lucky gal I met while working on the North Side. When we left for New York, I said I would come back for her, and when I did, we went to a Justice of the Peace and got hitched, with Jimmy and Wilma as our witnesses. Then it was the four of us driving back to New York, ready to start a new life.

Electra Court

Getting union cards jumped our pay to $150 a week and allowed us to take furnished apartments at Electra Court, a big apartment building in the Jackson Heights neighborhood of Queens. We heard about Electra Court through the Pennsylvanians, and just about everybody there was a musician or somehow involved in show business. The guys we met there played for people like Bob Crosby, Benny Goodman, Tommy Dorsey and Artie Shaw. Many of them were married, so our wives found new friends too, which helped keep the peace.

The union waiting period ended in November, 1938 and we immediately

89

THE GREATEST IN PERSON SHOW BROADWAY HAS EVER SEEN!

IN PERSON!

FRED WARING AND HIS PENNSYLVANIANS

IN PERSON!
FRED WARING
AND HIS PENNSYLVANIANS
WITH THE WARING GLEE CLUB
AND ALL THE RADIO GANG

POLEY McCLINTOCK
STUART CHURCHILL
SCOTTY BATES
DONNA DAE
RAY SAX
FERNE
TWO BEES AND A HONEY
LES PAUL TRIO
JIMMY ATKINS
GORDON GOODMAN

POLEY McCLINTOCK
STUART CHURCHILL
SCOTTY BATES
DONNA DAE
RAY SAX
FERNE
TWO BEES AND A HONEY
LES PAUL TRIO
JIMMY ATKINS
GORDON GOODMAN

made our network debut playing *Please Come Out of Your Dreams* on Fred's weekly half-hour show sponsored by Bromo Quinine. We became a fixture on the program, playing in the orchestra full time and doing a featured trio number each week. This continued until the summer of '39, when Fred moved to NBC with a new sponsor and a new show called *Chesterfield Pleasure Time.*

The Vanderbilt Theater on 48th Street became the New York home for two live broadcasts each night, five nights a week. Doing the broadcasts in a theatre provided seating for a large studio audience, and we did each show for about a thousand people. *Chesterfield Pleasure Time* was a fifteen-minute live broadcast on the network, followed by a 45-minute performance for the live audience. Then the theatre would be emptied and a new audience seated for the second show.

When I turned the volume up on the electric guitar, it would pick up WEAF in New York, and you could hear "bong, bong, bong," the NBC chimes, coming out of the toaster. When Fred heard it, he said, "Turn it up and we'll use it." So, at the top of the hour, at the right moment, I'd turn up the volume, we'd hear the chimes through the piano mic, and Fred would hit it with the band. The chimes were our sure-fire network cue, which was helpful because nobody wore earphones.

Fred Waring was probably the most demanding guy to work for I ever came across in the music business. Besides doing nine hour-long live shows a week, the big group rehearsed several hours each day, plus there were required rehearsals for the trio. We did two shows on weeknights and the sponsors insisted all shows be aired live, so everything had to be rehearsed very precisely and timed out down to the second.

We traveled by train, and kept the same live broadcast schedule wherever we toured. There were very strict rules about dress code, punctuality and other things, so somebody was always getting fired or docked. Fred was a perfectionist and considered hard to get along with, but gave me slack when I needed it. We became friends, and I learned a lot seeing how he got things done.

The trio became one of the show's most popular features, and the interesting thing is that our country-oriented experience helped us accomplish it. Fred loved the *Casey Jones* talcum powder bit, with Ernie hooting the train whistle sound, and kept it in the act as a guaranteed showstopper during the after-broadcast show for the studio audience. So we were succeeding with the very thing we all wanted to get away from when we formed the trio, only now we were wearing dinner jackets instead of overalls, and playing a lot of jazzy stuff too.

Electric In The Spotlight

Being part of a daily national broadcast brought many things our way, including the thrill of performing for President Roosevelt. And it was particularly satisfying to be the first to really put the electric guitar in the spotlight on national radio. Most people hadn't heard an electric guitar until they heard us, and many guitarists have since told me it was hearing those Fred Waring shows that took them to it. Guys like Johnny Smith, Tony Mottola, and my late dear friend, Chet Atkins, who was tuning us in somewhere down South to hear his brother Jimmy and became fascinated with what he was hearing.

There's an interesting guitar story that ties in with Jimmy and Chet. Once we joined Fred Waring, Chet was listening to our broadcasts and asking Jimmy questions about how we did certain things. I remember Jimmy sending transcriptions of some of our stuff down to wherever Chet was at the time. One day Jimmy came to me and said, "I need to get Chester a better guitar because that old bow-wow he's got is holding him back. He listens to us all the time, and I know he would love to have one of yours. What've you got I can buy cheap?"

Well, I had just the thing, a pretty, customized L-10. Gibson had extended the fingerboard by six frets under the B and E strings so I could play up to the higher F octave. Now that I was playing electric all the time, I didn't need it anymore, so I sold it to Jimmy for $25 and he gave it to Chet. I didn't find out until years later that some of Chet's great early recordings were done with my old L-10. It's a part of Chet's display in the Country Music Hall of Fame now, just a few showcases away from my original Log.

The Trio's Instruments

I kept tearing up guitars experimenting with my electric sound, but I always used my Gibson cheapie when I played electric with Waring, and it drove the Gibson guys nuts. They tried everything to get me to change, but my little guitar had the sound that became my identity on the radio, and I stayed with it until my family of klunkers came along. Until Charlie Christian joined Benny Goodman, I was the only guy on the air going coast-to-coast with an electric, and I wasn't going to alter my sound just to have a prettier guitar.

Jimmy always played acoustic guitar, and used the same instrument, an L-7, the whole time we were together. I think he played that same guitar his whole life. He was a solid rhythm player, always rock steady, with an excellent knowledge of chords and great musical intuition.

Ernie's bass was what you call a teardrop bass. If you look at a picture of it, you'll see it has no hook on the side, no violin curl, the side just slurps down like a teardrop. We were the first in New York to tune a bass with a C on top, and that

The trio, again with Donna Dae and Fred Waring. Putting my stool on a short riser brought the sound box of my guitar up to the vocalist's level.

was because of radio. A bass fiddle strung the normal way produced notes lower than home radios could reproduce. Most radios didn't go down to 42 Hertz, so why have that big string on the bottom hitting notes nobody can hear? So we put higher strings on his bass, and it helped our broadcast sound tremendously. He used the drum brush on the sandpaper with his picking hand to get the boom-shick, boom-shick, and Jimmy always knew right where he needed to be with the acoustic guitar. You listen to those old recordings of ours, and sometimes you'd swear there's somebody in there with a snare drum. It was a two-man rhythm section and it worked great.

A big part of the trio's success, and you'd have to say it was another of the trio's instruments, was Jimmy Atkins' voice. He was a handsome guy, and God gave him a great voice often compared to Bing's. Jimmy loved that because he worshipped Bing and patterned his style after him. He was in that league as a singer; he had the voice and the musical ear, but lacked the gift for putting all the pieces together to achieve the greatness of a Crosby or Sinatra. Mary was the same way. She had a great talent, but she lacked direction. She needed somebody else to steer the ship.

Stage Fright

Mary and Jimmy had something else in common: they both suffered from stage fright. Once at the Strand Theatre, Fred was announcing the trio to the audience when Jimmy turned to me in a panic and said, "What the hell are the lyrics?" And I said, "After you've gone…" And Jimmy said, "Yeah, yeah, that's the first number, but what are the lyrics?" His mind had gone blank just as Fred Waring was joking with the audience, saying, "And now, it's time for the Mozart String Trio." And Jimmy said, "Les, don't fuck with me now, what are the Goddam lyrics!" And I'm yelling back at Fred, saying, "No, it's the Ozark String Trio!"

So Fred is introducing us, Jimmy's in a panic, and it's all happening at the same time. Then Fred says, "So here they are…the Les Paul Trio with Jimmy Atkins!" And as we're hustling out on stage, I turn to Jimmy and real quick sing, "After you've gone, and left me crying…" We do our thing, Jimmy does a great job with the vocal, and nobody has any idea that just seconds before, his brain had locked up due to stage fright. It's an affliction Mary and Jimmy both had to fight for as long as they performed.

94

I am playing my modified Gibson "cheapie." You will notice in early photos of the cheapie, the pickups were different. I was continually experimenting with the pickups to find my signature sound.

The Electric Debate

The trio started out with me playing electric guitar on both Waring shows each night, and right away the comments were flying within the orchestra and the glee club. Using an electric guitar was a new thing, a break with tradition, and controversy sprang up within the Waring group even before letters from across the country started pouring in.

The other musicians had strong opinions going both ways, and it led to confusion. We had decided back in Chicago we wanted to go electric, but there were problems with the way the overall sound of the orchestra was amplified. Effective technology for doing that sort of thing hadn't been developed, and the inherent limitations influenced how the other musicians felt about my electric sound. The violinist, a gal, would say, "Well, I like the acoustic. It's more like I think the guitar should sound with this orchestral music." She's playing an acoustic stringed instrument, and her opinion is that I should play one too. But the sax player was just the opposite. He said, "Boy, now you've got that guitar sounding like a horn and your sound will stand up against any other instrument in the band." Various members of the Waring organization were involved in the debate, which was sometimes intense.

I played an electric when we first auditioned for Fred, so he knew what he was getting when he hired us. But now, due to the controversy, he had the choice of a very fine acoustic guitar, or my electric sound. And, surprisingly, it didn't matter to him which guitar I played. As long as it was entertaining and sounded good, Fred didn't care, so I decided to experiment with alternating between acoustic and electric guitars.

This was happening in 1939, when guitarists were mostly concentrated in the East. For that reason, I used my cheapie and the toaster on the first show, which started at 7 PM on NBC stations east of the Mississippi. For the 11 PM show, which aired in the west, I made arrangements with the engineer to use my L-5 and play to the mic along with the singer. I would sometimes switch the shows around, but usually, the eastern audience heard the electric and the west got the acoustic.

So I'm alternating guitars doing two shows a night on coast-to-coast network radio, and within two weeks, most of the mail coming in for the Fred Waring show is addressed to the Les Paul Trio. When Fred became aware of this, he came to me and said, "It's bothering me and I need to ask you, what is all this mail you're getting about?" And I said, "Well, it's mostly about the guitars. Some people want me to stick with the acoustic guitar, and the rest are saying they like the new electric guitar sound better." I'd been playing acoustic half the time because of resistance to change in the orchestra, but as they heard the differences themselves during the two live shows we played every night,

Rehearsing for the television broadcast during the 1939 New York World's Fair. Jimmy always kept an Epiphone in his pocket for emergencies.

the other musicians began to recognize the superiority of the electric as a lead instrument. When I played acoustic into a microphone, the limitations of the studio monitor system made it almost impossible to hear in association with the other instruments. The only way I could monitor the acoustic was by feeling the vibrations of the sound box against my chest, which made it difficult to play with the expression I was now accustomed to getting with my electric.

For my cheapie, I had a long cord that ran from up front all the way back to the piano, where my amp was picked up by the piano mic. My pickups were low impedance, so I could be 30 feet from the toaster without any line drop. The monitor system was inferior because the speakers weren't capable of reproducing the full sound, or properly matched with the PA amplifier. This was a handicap for some in the orchestra, but for me it was great. From where I sat, I heard my guitar from the amp itself, and also from speakers all over the studio. The combined sound floated through the air like angels flying around the room, big as a house. Everybody heard it, and a growing number of people in both the orchestra and the radio audience began to favor the electric sound. This was the beginning of bringing the guitar out of the rhythm section and into the spotlight as an amplified solo instrument.

Fred and I kidding around.

Going Electric Full Time

Ernie, Jim and I were leaving the studio one night when Fred asked where we were going. And I said, "We're going over to your office to listen to the recordings of tonight's shows." Fred asked, "Is it okay if I go along with you?" And we said, "Sure, come on." So the four of us went over to his office and went into the room where a recording lathe was set up to record his broadcasts. All his shows were live, and he recorded every one of them for his personal archive and collection.

The four of us listened to the trio's performances, one with acoustic guitar, the other with electric, and decided to take a vote on which guitar sound was best. And it was unanimous in favor of the electric, which was a very important turn of events.

Out of curiosity, I asked Fred why he voted for the electric. And he said, "One, it projects better; two, nobody will drown you out because you've got control of the volume; and three, you can make sounds never before heard." Fred didn't like the attention I was getting, but he knew my unique electric sound gave his show an advantage. So after our agreement that night, there was no more half and half. It was electric guitar full time.

Building The Log

Something terribly important developed in 1941 as I continued my efforts to create an electrically amplified guitar whose acoustical properties didn't cause feedback. I was looking for volume, tone and sustain that could be controlled, still chasing the idea that started with stretching a guitar string over a section of railroad rail. The thing that grabbed me about that early experiment was how the string vibrated and sustained almost indefinitely when anchored to the solidity of the steel rail, with no feedback whatsoever. The facts were pointing the way and I was realizing more and more that for electric guitar, the solidity of the neck and body and the way the strings attach were the critical factors I needed to pursue. Other than for looks and ease of holding it, the body of the guitar didn't matter. When I stripped the problem down to that simple under-

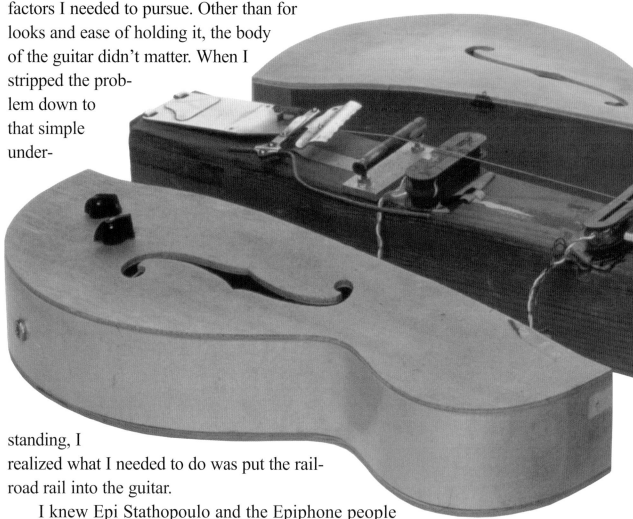

standing, I realized what I needed to do was put the railroad rail into the guitar.

I knew Epi Stathopoulo and the Epiphone people very well, and loved their instruments. I was always a Gibson player, but I admired their instruments and had a good friendship with the Epiphone people. They had a factory on 14th Street, and knowing them as I did, it was no problem to get permission to use their machinery and equipment on Sundays, when the place was shut down. The watchman took a personal interest in showing me how to operate the machinery, and Epiphone was happy to let me in because they were hoping I might convert to their instruments.

Working on Sundays, I took a length of 4x4 pine, put an Epiphone neck on it, wound a couple of homemade pickups and mounted them on the wood. Then I added a bridge and a Vibrola tailpiece, strung it up, and I had the Log. It was crude, but when I plugged it into an amp, it worked. And I decided to take this 4x4 piece of wood with strings and a neck on it into a club, play it, and see what happened.

I took it to Gladys' Bar, a little club in Sunnyside, where I played "The Sheik of Araby" with the same trio I often jammed with, and nobody gave much notice to it. I was getting a very cool, unusual sound with this electric Log, and there was no reaction or curiosity about it, other than it just looked odd. And it did look strange because I didn't have the wings on it yet. It was just a 4x4 stick of wood plugged into an amp, which should've drawn attention. A piece of lumber being played as an electric guitar was something nobody had ever seen before, or even thought of, but it didn't seem to make a big impression.

So I went back to the Epiphone factory, took the sound box of an old Epiphone archtop, and sawed it in half right down the middle. Then I braced up the halves so they could be attached to the sides, and two Sundays later, the Log had its wings and looked more like a normal guitar.

With wings attached, I took the Log back to the same club, and jammed again with the same trio. And to my surprise, there was a great reaction. Everyone started talking about the unusual sound and

The original Log now resides in the Country Music Hall of Fame in Nashville. This replica I built shows the basic construction with the 4x4 running the length of the body.

asking questions about the guitar and my amplifier. There was a positive reaction to the sound I got that night, which was the same sound the same people had heard before. So I came to the conclusion that people hear with their eyes.

When Epiphone asked what I was doing all those Sundays in their factory, I showed them the Log, but they weren't impressed. They were focused on competing with Gibson, concentrating on trying to close the gap, and the Log was too radical for them to consider. What I was trying to prove or where I might be going with it was of no interest to them.

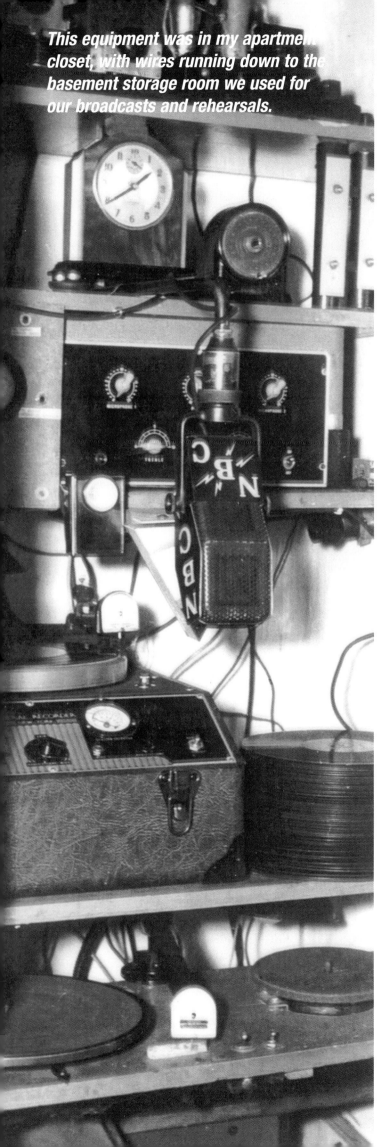

This equipment was in my apartment closet, with wires running down to the basement storage room we used for our broadcasts and rehearsals.

The Booger Brothers Broadcasting System

The little apartments at Electra Court didn't allow for rehearsal room, but there was an empty storage area in the basement, with a rug on the floor and an old piano. The manager let us turn it into our rehearsal studio, and it became a gathering place for the many musicians who lived or visited in the building. Word got around about our open jam sessions, and bang, we had our own after hours club, jamming with all the musicians who were always looking for a good session; greats like Eddie Miller, Joe Sullivan, Bobby Hackett, Lester Young, and Roy Eldridge. It was a tremendously exciting, creative time for everyone involved.

In 1939, Philco introduced a combination radio/record player with a built in oscillator that allowed the phonograph to send a weak broadcast signal to a radio in

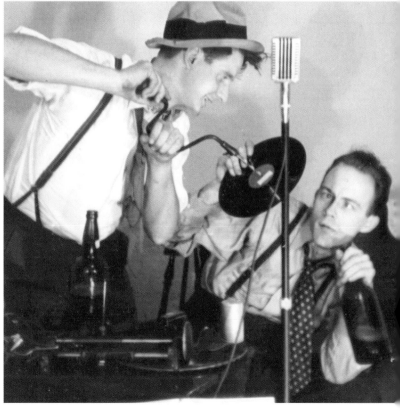

104

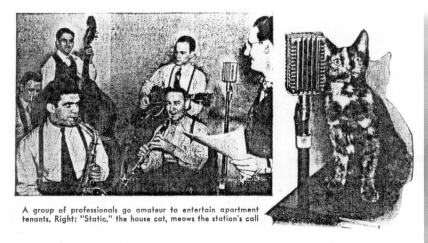

A group of professionals go amateur to entertain apartment tenants. Right: "Static," the house cat, meows the station's call

Tenants Run Apartment Network

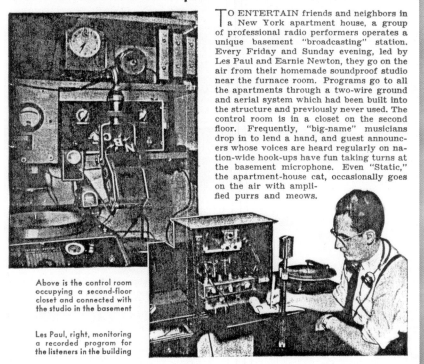

Above is the control room occupying a second-floor closet and connected with the studio in the basement

Les Paul, right, monitoring a recorded program for the listeners in the building

TO ENTERTAIN friends and neighbors in a New York apartment house, a group of professional radio performers operates a unique basement "broadcasting" station. Every Friday and Sunday evening, led by Les Paul and Earnie Newton, they go on the air from their homemade soundproof studio near the furnace room. Programs go to all the apartments through a two-wire ground and aerial system which had been built into the structure and previously never used. The control room is in a closet on the second floor. Frequently, "big-name" musicians drop in to lend a hand, and guest announcers whose voices are heard regularly on nation-wide hook-ups have fun taking turns at the basement microphone. Even "Static," the apartment-house cat, occasionally goes on the air with amplified purrs and meows.

110 *POPULAR SCIENCE*

another room. Jimmy Atkins got one of these things, and when I saw how it worked, it gave me an idea. First, I had a guy build a transmitter that kicked out a signal all the radios in Electra Court could pick up. Then we did a little research and discovered the records we were playing in my apartment could be picked up on car radios up to four miles away. In no time, we turned our basement room into a broadcast studio, and the Booger Brothers Broadcasting System was born.

The one night we didn't do two Waring shows was Wednesday, when we only did the early show. As soon as we wrapped it up, we'd go back to Electra Court and fire up the transmitter. At 9 PM, I'd turn on the mic and say, "The Booger Brothers Broadcasting System is on the air!" Then we'd start jamming and go non-stop until 8:30 Thursday morning, with people all over Queens tuning us in. Some of the all-night joints around our neighborhood would send over food and drinks in exchange for on-the-air plugs, and famous people would drop by and jam under phony names because they were under contract. There were no rules, no set format. We were just winging it, and it took off.

The first to hear us and seek out our broadcast location were guys from the Bob Crosby Band. And they were saying, "Jesus Christ, have you heard this station? They use the foulest language, but they jam their asses off. The station's pounding." And when some guy asked where it was on the dial, they said, "It's all over the dial. It's everywhere."

105

That's me on the left and Ernie on the right. The guy reading into the mic was a parking lot attendant who just walked in and got involved.

And it was true. I hadn't learned how to use a wave trap to filter out the harmonics, so we were showing up at two or three places on the dial, which is against FCC regulations. Hell, the whole damn thing was illegal, and it went on until America got directly involved in the war and the FCC had to shut us down to prevent radio interference at LaGuardia Airport. The Booger Brothers was just a name we made up to go along with all the crazy things we did, and the greatest musicians in the world played some of the best jazz ever heard right there in that basement.

Bob Wills And Charlie Christian

In 1939, Ernie and I had some time off and went back to Chicago to jam and hang out with all our friends there. When we went up to visit my Mother, she said, "Well, it's too bad you don't get a job with somebody like Bob Wills." And we said, "Who?" And she said, "Well, Bob Wills has a show that comes in from Tulsa on Saturday night, and I just love his music." So Saturday night, Mom dials in Tulsa, and we hear, "Take it away, Leon," with multiple fiddles and all this great intricate stuff going on. Mother really loves her country music, and she says, "You should leave that high-hat Fred Waring and go play some real music."

Ernie and I look at each other and say, "Let's get in the car and drive out to Tulsa, just for the hell of it." So we go back down to Chicago, and come the end of the week, we're driving to Tulsa to catch the next Bob Wills show. We get there and find the place and the next thing you know we're on stage with Bob Wills having a wonderful time meeting and jamming with all his cowboy guys. We finished the set, and just as I step down off the stage, there's a skinny black guy standing there, and he says, "Mr. Paul, my name is Charlie Christian. I play the guitar." I say, "Are you any good?" He says, "Yes, sir, I think so." So Ernie hands him a guitar, he plays a couple of really inventive things, and we say, "Geez, you *are* good."

So we invite him up on stage for the next set and he's jamming with us, this one modest black guy amongst all these cowboys, but everything goes fine. This is the first time I ever heard Charlie play or even knew he existed, and we had a wonderful time trading riffs. I told him to get in touch with me when he came east.

Some time later, the phone rings and it's Charlie. He's gotten the job with Benny Goodman, the job that put him on the map, and he needs a guitar. And I said, "Let me talk to Gibson. I'm getting ready to have them build a guitar for me, so I'll just have them make two exactly alike and you can have the other one. We'll have ourselves a couple of blondes."

Gibson built the two guitars using the solid bar pickups I'd been making and using for years. As Charlie became famous, they were identified with him and his unique sound, and became known as Charlie Christian pickups. And the guitars were monsters. They were solid box guitars, with no f-holes, and had a great sound, but the weight of them was absolutely frightening. The matching amps were made of one-inch maple with a 16-tube chassis, plus the weight of the transformer and speaker, so they weighed a ton. And the combined weight was too much, just impractical for guys on the go all the time. So I sent them back to Gibson with that explanation.

Those guitars were a continuation of the early electric experiments I'd tried with National and the Larson brothers. I wish now I'd hung on to them but at the time they were just too much weight to lug around. I was chasing the design for a true electric instrument, not just an acoustic guitar with something added on. I was still a couple of years away from achieving it, but I knew it was there.

107

Ernie with his teardrop bass, on the air with the Booger Brothers.

Jamming In New York

We were very glad to be a part of the Fred Waring show, but certain restrictions came with it. Fred didn't want any of his people getting too much individual attention because every time he made someone famous, he'd lose them. He thought the emphasis should be on the whole show, and on him, and his rules were designed to keep it that way. He didn't want the trio playing dates other than with his show, or making any records independent of him.

So what we did to keep ourselves happy was hit the clubs and after-hours dives to jam with our buddies and all the great musicians who were everywhere. We had our guitars and our bass, just our bare-naked trio, and when we weren't jamming in the basement of Electra Court, we were out finding the greatest places to play. Like down in the Village, and Harlem, where the jamming started after the regular clubs closed and went on till dawn. There was an after-hours place in the back of an undertaking parlor, and you'd have to walk by the drain board with some stiff lying there to get to the scene. And it would be a jam session with Art Tatum and Coleman Hawkins, or Lester Young and Roy Eldridge, the greatest players in the world, and all in their prime. These were the days when very few guitar players were doing anything more than strumming chords in the rhythm section, and it was hard to find anyone to battle with and learn from, like Leonard Ware who played a four-string guitar. Hardly anyone's ever heard of him, but he was very good and I loved jamming with him because he always showed me something different. But the guy I enjoyed most during those days was Charlie Christian.

We used to go up to Harlem to a place called Minton's Playhouse to jam with Charlie and the other black musicians who congregated there. Playing fast came easy for me, and when I jammed with horn players or keyboard guys, we'd have a great time trying to outgun each other. But with Charlie being another guitar player, it was different. I put the heat on him the first few times we got on the bandstand together, but he didn't go for it. Instead, he'd come back with a different idea in the phrasing, with a different line. I saw how it worked, and picked up on it. Charlie influenced my style by showing me the value of laying out to say more with fewer notes. I think I influenced him too, so it was a fair trade. We had a special friendship.

First Records and The Wire Recorder

In October 1939, we cut our first commercial records, doing four sides for Columbia: *Out of Nowhere, Swanee River, Where Is Love,* and *Goodbye, My Lover, Goodbye.* It was against the rules, but Fred knew we'd be snapped up by someone else if he fired us. He didn't want to see that happen, so he let us get by with it.

When we first joined the Pennsylvanians, Fred's *Ford Show* was broadcast out of Rockefeller Center. RCA had a display of glass cases in the hallways there that were part of the World's Fair tours people took to see the history of electronics, RCA and Edison, that sort of thing. Television was just on the verge, and RCA was predicting its future in 1939. In fact, it was just a year later we did the first television show from right there in Rockefeller Center.

One of the encased objects in the hallway was a wire recorder, and Fred arranged for us to have it on loan. He just handed it over one day, and said, "Play with it and see what you get." This was the first serious wire recorder, a prototype invented by Valdemar Poulsen, on loan to RCA. And it's a yard long and a foot-and-a-half high, with a big glass cover. So the Les Paul Trio now has a wire recorder the size of a washing machine.

I had a Wilcox-Gay disk recorder in my apartment, which we were using for recording our rehearsals at Electra Court and also our performances on the Waring show. So we already had a way to record ourselves, but we were interested in the wire machine just to see what it was and be up on what was happening. And what we found is that when the wire is running from the supply spool to the take-up, it rotates. So when you send a signal into the wire, it may be on the front of the wire, the side of the wire, or the back of the wire because the wire is twisting.

The variance in audio quality due to the twisting wire made it unacceptable for professional use, so they passed it on to us to rehearse with at Rockefeller Center. If our number on the show was going to be *Out of Nowhere*, we'd record it during trio rehearsal and listen back to improve the arrangement. Then we'd erase it because there was no practical way to save anything on this barbaric wire machine. So there were problems with the wire recorder, and the Reich was busy over in Germany figuring out what to do about it. And all they or anybody had to do was flatten out the wire so it wouldn't twist; flatten it and make it out of something you don't have to tie a knot in to splice.

Electrocution At Electra Court

Something else happened in '41 that changed my life, and almost ended it. It was summer and we were jamming and fooling around down in the basement studio at Electra Court. There was no air conditioning, it was hot and humid as hell, and I thoughtlessly stuck my sweaty hand inside the transmitter rack. I wanted to change frequency coils, and when I reached into the transmitter to pull out the coil in use, I didn't remember I had my electric guitar in the other hand. My guitar was plugged into an amp, and when my fingers touched the coil, a surge of high amperage electricity was instantly using my body as a conductor between the coil and the guitar. The current caused the muscles in my hands to clamp down like a vise, so I couldn't let go on either end.

It was the stupidest thing I ever did. If anybody knew you should never ever reach inside a hot transmitter while holding an electric guitar, it would be me, but that's exactly what I did, and the current hit me like a bolt of lightning. Ernie happened to be standing in the area outside the broadcast studio and could see me through the window we'd put in the wall. I started shaking and fell to the floor, pulling the rack and everything attached to it down with me. So me, the guitar, the transmitter rack are all hitting the floor, and I'm convulsing and frying. For just a second, Ernie thought it was another one of my jokes, but then very quickly realized it wasn't.

Fortunately, everything in that place was powered by one switch, which was on the wall just inside the door. And Ernie saved my life, no question about it, because he dashed through that door so fast to hit the switch and turn everything off before I was electrocuted. The guys soaked me in cold water till the ambulance arrived. When they examined me at the hospital, the doctors found the current had ripped up the muscles and ligaments in my chest and arms. Both my hands were burned and I was laid up for weeks in a dazed, painful state. In time, the muscle damage healed, but my hands were still numb.

As to when this happened, it had to be right after what turned out to be our final performance on the Waring show, which was May 27, 1941. Jimmy and Ernie continued to do the shows, but our trio never came back.

I went right away to Bellevue Hospital, and the doctors there said what I'd experienced was very similar to being struck by lightning, the results of which, if not fatal, can leave you with handicaps you don't recover from. One doctor was of the opinion that the numbness might never go away completely, so I didn't know to what degree I'd be able to regain my playing ability.

When someone gets electrocuted with such a jolt, it's as though every muscle is ripped from the bone, like your whole body has been stretched out of shape and now has to try and find its way back to normal. I never really believed I wouldn't recover, but the future was very uncertain and the course of my life was changed forever. What I did was very stupid, and now, you will never see me use both hands with anything electronic. It was a good lesson learned the hard way.

Leaving Fred Waring

While I was laid up, for the first time in my life, I had to take it easy. I couldn't jam, perform or do anything I was used to doing because my hands were dead and my energy level was kaput. The down time gave me the opportunity to think about everything I'd done, and what I still wanted to do. I was 26 years old and confident of regaining my abilities, and one day I just woke up and it was clear to me. I appreciated what working for Fred had meant to us, to our careers, but I didn't want to go back to it. I had my sights set on something else. The love for Bing had been building up and building up within me and had finally reached the point where it was time to leave Fred Waring and go to California to find him.

So I met privately with Fred and said, "I'm leaving you. I'm on my way to the West Coast." And Fred said, "Why...did you get another job?" And I said, "Well, I'm going to be with Bing Crosby." Fred said, "I just knew something like that was going to happen, that somebody was going to grab you." He assumed I already knew Bing and wanted to know how I had connected with him. And I said, "Bing hasn't heard of me just like you hadn't heard of me, but he will, and that's where I'm going."

In the early '40s, there was no better place to be than California, and Bing was going to hear of me because I'd made up my mind that's where I wanted to go. I always had the belief that if I made up my mind to do something, to achieve something, it would happen. And it did.

The Trio Break-Up

After I gave my notice to Fred, I told Jim and Ernie about my decision. And I said, "We can do this as the trio, and I'm positive we'll become famous. Are you willing to go West with me?" It was another gamble, just like we'd taken when we left Chicago. Ernie immediately said he would go wherever I wanted to go, but Jimmy was uncertain. He was a family man with a wonderful wife and children and a steady, good-paying job as Waring's featured vocalist, so he was much less likely to make a risky decision. Jimmy was concerned about my plan to get with Bing because they sang so much alike. He felt it might work against him out west; whereas, it was a big strength in New York. And I told Jimmy, "You'll never get anywhere beyond where you are now if you stay with Fred because he won't let you get any bigger." My goal was to go as high as you can get, and Bing was the top. Whatever I had to do to get there, that's where I was going to land eventually.

The three of us talked it over, and Jimmy finally determined the job he had with Waring was just too good to leave for the unknown thing I was proposing to do. So Jimmy decided to stay in New York, Ernie was going to California with me, and that was it, the trio was disbanded. Everybody understood what the other guy was doing, and why. There were no hard feelings, but there was sadness for all of us in breaking up because we'd grown very close, like brothers. Through so many adventures, we had achieved our dream of success in New York and it was not easy to see it come to an end. We had a wonderful career together.

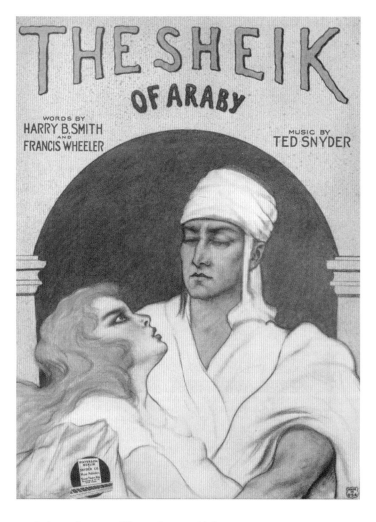

Fate Intervenes Again

We got ourselves ready to go to California, and just as we were walking out of Electra Court for the last time, at the very last minute on the day we're leaving New York, Pat the doorman says, "Les, you're wanted on the phone." And it's Ralph Atlass calling from Chicago, saying, "I've got an opening here for a musical director for WJJD and WIND, and you'd be perfect for it. Would you be interested in the job?" And I said, "Well, it's odd you should call at this particular moment. The wife and kid are in the car, the engine is running, we're all packed and we're leaving for the West Coast. We're headed your way."

I told Ralph about my health concerns, and my intentions with Bing Crosby. And he said, "This job will be easy for you, and it'll be good for you. I'll put your name on the door, you keep an eye on things for me, and pick up a check. You don't have to do anything more than that. When you don't want it anymore, fine, you go on to the coast."

Recovering from the electric shock was going to take time, and when Ralph Atlass offered more than I'd been making with Waring, I couldn't turn it down. So the decision was made to take the job, and Virginia, our month-old son Rusty, Ernie and I left New York and drove back to Chicago.

CHAPTER SEVEN

Back In Chicago (1941-1942)

So I'm back in Chicago working as music director of WJJD and WIND, auditioning and hiring musicians and looking after the musical programming for both stations. When I asked Ralph Atlass what else he wanted done, he said, "Go out and find me some country talent for WJJD." So Ernie and I got in the car and started driving toward Cincinnati. We were listening to WLW, and that's when I heard Merle Travis for the first time. His sound had an identity to it, a ton of personality, and he sounded great. I'd never heard him before, but I knew the name from Jimmy describing Chet's playing. Back in New York, when Jimmy told me his kid brother was good, I asked what he sounded like. And Jimmy said, "He sounds like you and Django and Merle Travis put together." So now it's 1941, and this great finger picking I'm hearing reminds me of what Jimmy said. And when I heard Chet on the radio for the first time, I realized he was right.

The job I had with WJJD and WIND was good because it gave me something I could do while waiting for my hands to come back. And I needed something because not being able to play was frustrating. Working on my guitar experiments helped get some flexibility back, and I started trying to play again as the numbness in my hands began to subside. Then Ralph Atlass called and said "Les, my brother's got Ben Bernie five times a week coast to coast on CBS over at WBBM. You can go over there and make some extra bucks working with Ben Bernie." The numbness in my hands was getting better, and it was a national show, so I joined up with Ben Bernie with the understanding that I was only going to stay until I felt good enough to go on to California.

Ben Bernie called himself the 'Ol Maestro and had been a top radio star and orchestra leader since the early '30s, and now had the new coast-to-coast Wrigley Gum show, Monday through Friday at 5PM on WBBM. He gave me the job of putting together the personnel for his band, the Ben Bernie Orchestra, and knowing everybody in Chicago and New York as I did, I was able to bring guys in quite easily. I got piano player Joe Rann, who I had known back in New York, and the supreme accordion player, Art Van Damme. I also got Wally Kamin, my future brother-in-law and the number one guy in my life, a job playing bass. At the time my parents were getting a divorce back in Waukesha, I was put in Shorewood School in Milwaukee, and met Wally there. We were the same age, and became lifelong friends.

They Used to Call Him 'Rhubarb Red'

Chicago — But that was a long time ago, and now the Milwaukee git-man, Les Paul, is one of the finest jazz box men in the game. Les, whose fretting was a feature of the Fred Waring show until recently, is now on the staff of WBBM-NBC in Chi. That's the perennial ol' maestro, Bernie, catching some of Les' licks. Paul is featured on Ben's Wrigley show five days a week. After Les received a bad shock from his amateur radio transmitter, it was feared he couldn't play, but he's okay now. Les' hands would turn numb as he played. It's half in your mind, the meds told him, so he forgot it.

So that's what I did. I assembled Ben Bernie's Orchestra at WBBM and went to work as a featured member of the studio orchestra, becoming close friends with Ben in the process. I think playing was probably good for my hands and nervous system because everything started getting better.

Ernie Goes South

When Georgie Gobel started hitting it big over at WLS and announced he was going to move to Nashville, Ernie came to me and said, "What do you think you're going to do?" He knew I'd taken the job with WBBM and Ben Bernie and he was wondering what his future was with me. And I said, "I'm going to stay with WBBM until my hands get better and then I'm going to the coast to head for Bing. I'll holler for you if I need you." So Ernie decided to go to Nashville with George Gobel and become his right hand man. We parted with the agreement that if something came up in California that would be good for Ernie, I'd let him know and he'd come on out if he wanted to. In the meantime, he'd have a good job and a chance to go places on his own, so it was a perfect arrangement for everybody.

Gibson Rejects The Log

Not long after I got back to Chicago, still in '41, I went to the Gibson people with the Log. They thought it was a joke and I was laughed at, not scoring too well with the idea of a solid body guitar. They called me the character with the broomstick with pickups on it. It was another ten years before they saw the light.

I continued to experiment with the Log, and during the time I was unable to play, turned my attention to my amplifier, looking for a different electric sound. John Kutilek was an amp builder who took an interest in what I was doing. We worked nights in his workshop experimenting with distortion and overload to fatten up the sound. John was knowledgeable and very helpful in altering my amplifier's capabilities in the direction I wanted to go.

Les The Prankster

I was always a prankster. It was just something about me all my life, and I'm still that way. And one time at WBBM, I decided I wanted to play a trick on everybody in the control room. So I caught a common house fly, went to one of the main microphones they used on the air, opened up the housing, put the fly

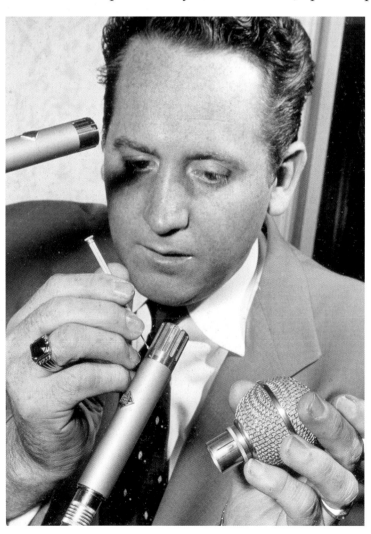

inside, and closed it back up. Then I just sat back and watched them go crazy trying to figure out where the buzzing was coming from. The fly would buzz around inside the mic and then rest for a couple of seconds, and the engineers were going nuts trying to find the cause. Watching them trying to identify the problem just struck me as very funny, and they never did figure it out until I finally told them. And even after I'd been known as Les Paul for many years, those guys never stopped calling me Rhubarb.

116

The Klunkers

The world of klunkers started in 1941. Ahead of that, leading up to the Log, there were all kinds of guitar experiments, but the klunker started in '41, and it's an interesting story. The Log had an Epiphone neck and wings made from an Epiphone guitar, I'd just come away from being involved with Epiphone in New York, and another Epiphone guitar entered my life shortly after I got back to Chicago.

I had moved to WBBM when this guy calls me up who had gotten his hand mangled in a bread-wrapping machine. He's got an Epiphone guitar and amp, and he wants me to have them because he can't play anymore. He said, "I've been listening to you on the radio and love the way you play, and I want to give them to you." And I said, "Well, I can't let you do that, but bring them over and we'll talk about it."

So he brought the guitar and amp to the studio where I was working on my sound equipment and I gave him something for them. He didn't come looking for money, but I insisted on paying him because what had happened to his hand was tragic and I felt bad for him as a fellow guitar player. And I was very glad to get this Epiphone guitar because it had a trap door built into the back, from the factory, which meant I could easily reach inside and fool around with the electronics without having to remove the whole works. This was a great thing because I was taking the pickups and pots out and putting them back every time I had an idea, which was every day, and constantly had to loosen all the strings and pull everything out of the top of the guitar in order to make internal changes and adjustments. I was jazzed to have this trap door guitar because I knew it was going to save a tremendous amount of time, and that Epiphone became klunker number one.

What's In A Name

I name everything. If a guy's got a hooknose, I call him a parrot, and if he's got one eye, he's a pirate. A big car is a Sherman tank, and Wolf, the fellow taking the pictures for this book, is German so I call him Hans. I put names on everything, and the name I came up with for my hotrod Epiphone was klunker. A klunker is a great big beast. It's just a dog, but it's great so it had to be my favorite dog. A family of modified, experimental guitars developed after that first one, and I called them all klunkers. The name just stuck.

I loved this particular model Epiphone because it came from the factory with this "trap door" in the back, so it was easy to get inside there and change the pickups.

Klunker Number One

I took this Epiphone, which was actually a very nice guitar, and started doing my thing with it. I cut a section out of the top and put in my homemade pickups, put heavy strings on it, and a wig-wag, and started seriously experimenting with it. And I was just delighted with it because, with that door in the back, it meant no more fishing the pickup wiring out through the f-hole or loosening strings to take out a pickup. Now I could easily move my pickup placement and make other adjustments, and I took full advantage of it. I changed my mind two million times about the best position for the pickups to get what I was looking for. Putting this customized guitar through the amp I was developing was a big step toward the sound that would eventually be my breakthrough.

Klunker number one became the model for the ones that followed, and I used it extensively while I was in Chicago, and later in California. It was the

My first klunker, Epiphone serial no. 6867. I switched pickups on this guitar so many times, looking for my sound, that I finally had to put a steel plate in the middle of the top to hold it together.

guitar I used on the recording of *It's Been A Long, Long Time* with Bing and other recordings from that time period, and in most of my radio and recording work with the armed forces during the war.

Klunker Number Two

Klunker number two also came to me while I was in Chicago. I found it on the Loop, and it was an odd thing because the store belonged to the future chairman of the board of the company that owned Gibson, and he was a Martin dealer. I'd been looking for a second one ever since I got the first one and realized how useful the trap door design was for what I was doing.

So I walked into this music store with Martin guitars everywhere and there's a trap door Epiphone hanging on the wall for $100. So I took it down and told the guy I'd take it. I was very glad to find it because I had arrived at a place with klunker number one where I wanted to keep the sound I had with it. I still wanted to keep experimenting, and I needed a second one to work on so I could leave number one alone. And that's what I did. I immediately turned the second Epiphone into klunker number two and continued with my experiments.

Klunker Number Three

Within a year, we packed the car and left Chicago, taking my two klunkers on to California. Not long after we got there, I found klunker number three at the Fife and Nichols Music Store on Hollywood Boulevard. I went in one day and there's another trap door Epiphone, so I bought klunker number three from them. And it was very helpful to have three of them because I could establish a standard,

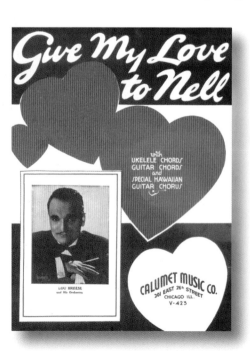

a reference, with one of them and then make changes in the others and be able to hear the difference by comparison. When I got one to the point where it sounded good, I'd leave it alone and turn to another one. That way, I had a reference, a fixed example of what a certain combination of ideas produced. If you just keep changing the one instrument, you can't go back to check out specific differences because you've lost your standard of comparison.

The three klunkers were all exactly the same Epiphone guitar, but each one was different. The ones used with Bing Crosby, on the Sullivan Show, for recording, were each unique. The pickup placement is altered by an inch, the pickup is wound differently, different tail piece, different knobs, and the holes are drilled in a dif-

120

Klunkers Two and Three were the same model Epiphone. They all had certain characteristics in common but the pickups were wired differently. I was using these guitars to look for my signature sound.

serial no. 4108

serial no. 7133

ferent place, just slight variations that were a part of the ongoing experiment to arrive at the best possible sound. By 1946, at the time Django and Johnny Smith jammed in my dressing room at the Paramount, I had built all three and they played two of them. It started in 1941 when the guy with the mangled hand wanted to give me his Epiphone guitar and amp, and each succeeding klunker represented the continuing evolution of ideas. I've still got all three, and the Eppy amp too.

The Klunkers In Rotation

Once I had all three of them going, I switched the klunkers back and forth all the time. I might play number one on a show with Bing, then switch to number two to do a show with somebody else, and go out to the clubs and jam with number three, all in the same day. When I was doing dates on the road, I always traveled with at least two of them. That way, I always had a back-up ready if I broke a string or had a technical problem. The whole idea was that I didn't want to change the guitar as an instrument, I just wanted to evolve the way the electronics were applied to better understand which setup worked best, and why. This was one of the biggest steps toward finding my sound.

I continued performing with my klunkers until I signed with Gibson in 1952. Mary and I made most of our hits with them, and I continued to record with them even after Gibson launched the Les Paul solid body. After the solid body came out, all my public appearances were with a Gibson guitar in one form or another.

California Calling

My hands improved steadily when I started playing again, and once I got on board at WBBM, I played all the time because of feuding between the musicians union and the record companies. The union brass were concerned that the rise of recorded music was going to put a huge numbers of musicians out of work. For a period of time in the early '40s, the national union ordered musicians not to do any recording, forcing radio stations to rely on live music for their broadcasts. I was a versatile player with the ability to back up anybody who came along, so I was kept very busy as an accompanist the last few months I was in Chicago.

WBBM was a high profile station in the CBS network and one of the most successful in the country. As a result of working there, and at WJJD and WIND, I met a lot of big names who either lived and worked in Chicago or passed through on their tours. People like the Andrews Sisters, Judy Canova, Fran Allison, Gene Autry and many others. Many of these friendships continued after I made the move to California because lots of entertainers were gravitating in that direction because of Hollywood and the war.

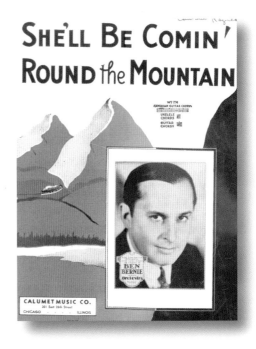

Another important thing for me during this time in Chicago was getting to know Ben Bernie and being a part of his network show. He loved my music and gave me a featured role in his broadcasts, so once again I was appearing regularly on a daily, coast-to-coast show, which again helped establish my unique electric guitar sound with a national audience. Ben had been around for a long time and was a very polished and confident showman, a master at working an audience with his wonderfully smooth speaking voice. I observed how he managed things and took what I learned to heart. He made what he did look easy, but he did it by being well prepared and ready to deliver when the opportunity presented itself. He took an interest in me, believed in me, and we became close friends.

Ben was a hard drinker and you never saw him without a cigar in his mouth. He hadn't taken care of himself over the years, and now poor health was catching up with him. When keeping up his act finally got to be too much for him, he decided to take the advice of his doctors and retire to California. He said if I'd move out to there, I could take over the leadership of his orchestra.

I was ready to go, but my main goal of meeting and working with Bing Crosby hadn't changed, nor was it a new thing. All the while I was coming up through the ranks and paying my dues as a guitar player and entertainer, Bing was the biggest thing going. I was exposed to his music, his records and radio shows, from the late '20s on, and along with him, Eddie Lang. I've already stated how important Eddie Lang was in showing the way to jazz guitar, and in my mind, Bing Crosby and Eddic Lang went together. When Eddie passed away suddenly, I had the immediate thought that I would one day take his place with Bing. Then Bing moved to southern California, started making movies and became the biggest star in the world. So going west to connect with Bing was my long-term goal long before we ever went to New York.

When my hands were basically healed and I was confident of regaining my full capabilities, I gave my notice and my thanks to the Atlass brothers and made the move to California after working out the final commitments in my

contract with WBBM. Ralph and Les Atlass were two of the best friends I ever had. They were nice people and very good to me, and I remember them with great appreciation and very fondly.

The Gig With Gene Autry

Gene Autry and I had known each other from working radio in Chicago during my Rhubarb Red days. In fact, when he left WLS to go to California in the mid-'30s, I took his place. And coincidentally, when I was getting ready to leave Chicago for the coast, Caesar Petrillo, the music director at WBBM, told me my last job for them would be a remote broadcast on the way to California. They asked me to make a stop at Chanute Field and make an appearance with Gene Autry on his radio show which was doing a broadcast from there.

So leaving Chicago, we went to Chanute Field and found Gene. I got up onstage to play without benefit of any rehearsal and made the mistake of playing a C6 to start a song. It was a fatal mistake because when I played the sixth chord, Gene couldn't hear his note. He was used to hearing a plain C, and when I hit the C6, he just froze in front of the mic. I'm standing there looking at him, and he's looking at me, and I thought, "Holy Christ, what's wrong?" Then I realized what I'd done, hit a plain C chord, and it was "Back in the saddle again..." I learned right then, if the guy you're playing with calls for a C, you hit a C, not a C6. Don't go putting butter on it unless you know it's gonna work.

CHAPTER EIGHT

California Bound (1943)

I said goodbye to my many Chicago friends and headed west in the spring of 1943. It was me, my piano player friend Joe Rann, and whatever we could jam into my Buick. Virginia and Rusty, our young son, stayed in Chicago. The plan was to see what the situation was going to be, find a place to live, and then go back for them. It was terribly exciting to finally be headed west, and

Big Cut on U. S. Highway 66 at Hooker, between Lebanon and Rolla, Missouri, in the Beautiful Ozarks

after stopping off for the date with Gene Autry, it was Route 66 all the way to California.

Joe Rann was Joe Rannozizzi, sometimes called Fox-Hole Joe because he had a bad eye that kept him out of the service. Joe was a military reject and I hadn't been inducted yet, so we drove to California together and shared expenses on the trip.

Arrival In Hollywood

We arrived in Hollywood at night and found our way to Graumann's Chinese Theatre. And while we were checking out the cement slabs with all the footprints and handprints of famous movie stars, I noticed the Cinegrill, a show lounge in the Roosevelt Hotel across the street. And the Cinegrill sign said, "Bud Glen and His Trio."

Well, Bud Glen just happened to be a bass player I'd worked with in Chicago. So we go into the Cinegrill, and within 15 minutes I'm up on the stage jamming with Bud and his guys. And a fellow sitting right down front starts making requests. He wants to hear *Avalon, Limehouse Blues,* and *The Sheik of Araby.* After I play them, he then tells me he's from the musicians union, and I'm to be fined for performing on CBS without union authorization. I had barged in and started jamming without realizing Bud Glen's group was doing a live remote broadcast on CBS. When the union man gave me his card, he said, "You're good. I'll see you Friday." So my first night in Hollywood, my introduction to California was being busted by the union.

Reasoning With The Union

I went to the union office as ordered, and was told I had the right to offer an explanation as to why I had broken union regulations before they levied my fine. Spike Wallace was the union president, so I asked him, "Mr. President, if

your wife asked to go dancing on Saturday night, would you take her to the Palladium, or would you stay home and dance in the kitchen?" "Well," he said, "I'm sure she'd be offended if I expected her to be happy with dancing at home." And I said, "Well, I play guitar the same way, and it sounds much better at the Cinegrill than it does at home." We both started laughing, so I didn't get fined, but I didn't get a union card either. The rule was you could play individual dates, but until the six-month probationary period passed, you couldn't take steady work as a musician.

Spike and I both enjoyed our little confrontation, and a personal friendship was established which later proved to be very important in helping me survive. And from that day on, everybody associated with the Los Angeles union treated me like a friend.

Finding A Place To Live

A few days later, I was back in Hollywood walking down the street where CBS and NBC were located and saw Gene Autry. And Gene said, "Red, what in the world are you doing here?" And I said, "Well, I came out here to see what Hollywood's all about." And out of the blue, he said, "Do you have a place to live?" And I said, "No, I don't. I've been staying with Bud Glen and I'm looking for a place." And he said, "You're in luck." This was during the war, and there was a housing shortage in L.A. because of all the military activity. Gene said, "My band leader has been inducted and he's leaving today. There's nobody in his place, and it's just around the corner."

We were standing at the intersection of Sunset and Vine, and Gene said, "Just walk a couple of blocks to Gordon Street, and it's the second house on the left. Don't say anything to anybody, just go on in and start living there. Pay the rent at the end of the month and the landlord won't know the difference, nor will he care." So Gene's accordion player shipped out, and I moved into his house the day he left.

Talk about luck! Due to the war, it was hard as hell to find anything to rent, and here I find this sweet little house for forty dollars a month, completely furnished including dishes and silverware, and it's located exactly where I want to be, right in the middle of the entertainment and radio center of Hollywood.

NBC, CBS, and the Palladium were right at the end of the block, almost on the doorstep of this great little house. So now I had a place for my family, and a perfect location for doing my thing to try and get with Bing. And we stayed there until we moved to the place on North Curson Avenue.

It wasn't long after that I got my induction notice and got involved with the Armed Forces Radio Service. The AFRS headquarters were located right down the hill at Gordon Street and Santa Monica Boulevard. So I could get in my car in front of the house, release the brake, and let it roll downhill to the army base where I worked without ever starting it. I would roll to a stop without the motor running, and the guys at the base would laugh and say, "Here's Les in his electric Cadillac."

The New Trio

One of the first things I did was contact Ben Bernie, and the news wasn't good. Ben was deathly ill and being cared for at Ida Lupino's Hollywood mansion. She and Howard Duff were his friends, and were looking after him. When I went to see him, he was lying on a stretcher by the pool, too sick to be concerned with his act any more. So any opportunity I might have had through him was out the window. He passed away soon after my visit, and two or three days after that, I formed a new trio and started forming my plans for getting into NBC and connecting with Bing.

Joe Rann was an excellent piano player, so I hooked up with him and we started playing together, hitting the clubs to jam and looking for a bass player. I learned that Bob Meyer, who had played bass for me in the Melody Kings back in Chicago, was working the area with his own jazz group, so Joe and I went to one of his club dates. Bob was a good bass player who shared my appreciation of Django's music, and with a little convincing, he disbanded his quartet and joined us to complete the trio.

My little house was too small for rehearsing, so we set up a rehearsal space in a spare bedroom at Bob's place, re-tuned his bass like Ernie's, brought in an old piano and started getting our act together. Radio was booming and there were opportunities everywhere. In no time, we were playing club dates and making transcriptions for a company that shipped them all over the country for broadcast, but I wanted more.

During my whole career up to this point, I was constantly exposed to Bing Crosby. He was big on the radio, big in the movies, and sold more records than anybody. Bing was huge, and my number one priority was to connect with him. And to do that, I needed to find a way to get into NBC.

129

Invading NBC

NBC was just a couple of blocks from my house, and one of the first things I did after we got settled was locate the studio where Bing did his weekly *Kraft Music Hall* show. Joe Rann and I went over to NBC and sat there watching to see what we could learn. And we saw Bing arrive and park his car, and took note of which door he went in.

Now we knew where the broadcast was done, and the next step was to figure out how we were going to get past the security guards and get inside. It never entered my mind to go to Bing's office and approach him that way because everybody in the world was already there. I had a different idea in mind entirely, and as we continued to observe the situation, a plan began to take shape. Every Thursday about noon, the cast and crew on Bing's show would arrive to rehearse for the evening's broadcasts on the NBC network. We knew from observing that Bing went in through the artists' entrance, and we knew the cast and crew took a break at five o'clock to go out and eat or have a drink before coming back to do the broadcast.

D-Day

So finally, I tell the guys I've got a plan. When there's the big commotion of everybody going on break at five o'clock, we're gonna back into the place. So here we go. Bob Meyer is lugging his bass, I've got a guitar in one hand and my amp in the other, Joe Rann is with us, and we slip into the parking lot acting like we belong there. As the cast and crew start coming out, we blend in with them and then start causing a commotion at the stage door. I yell out, "Did you bring the music?" And Bob says, "I thought you had it." And I say, "No, no, I left it on the music stand. You were supposed to get it." And Bob says, "Well, I forgot it." So I say, "Okay, then we've got to go get it." So in the confusion of all the people piling out the door, with the guard standing right there, we enter the stage door pretending to go after our music, and we get away with it.

Once we're inside, we go down this long hallway lined with broadcast studios of various sizes with signs on the doors saying Studio A, Studio B, and so on. Most of these studios have musical instruments and scripts laying around, so we know they're in use, but Studio E is empty. We go in and turn on the lights and there's the piano we need, so I plug in my guitar and we start to play. Pretty soon, a jolly little guy with wire glasses and a straw hat walks into the room carrying a clipboard. He's checking his schedule, and he says, "I don't see anything booked for Studio E. Who are you guys?" And I say, "The Les Paul Trio." He checks his clipboard again and says, "Well, it's not written into the schedule here." We talk and find out he's Bill Gilcher, the musical contractor for NBC. And I say,

"Well, I've got to level with you, Bill. We're not on your list because we backed in here, we crashed the joint. I wanted to get in here and be heard because I've got a damn good trio. Let us play something for you, and you be the judge."

Another Miracle

Before he can protest, we start playing. He listens for a short time and then says, "Stay right here, don't leave." So he goes out and comes back with Tom Pelouso, the music director. Tom listens for a bit, and says, "Jesus Christ, you guys *are* good...you're *real* good...and boy, could we use you. Just stay right here, I'll be right back."

So he runs out and comes back with this big tall guy, and who is it but my buddy from St. Louis and Chicago, Sid Strotz. And I say, "Sid!" And he says, "Red! How the hell are you?" I had no idea Sid had moved up the ladder to become vice-president of NBC, or that he was even there. He asks me what I'm doing there and I tell him how I've just arrived in California and how we'd just backed in through the stage door to invade NBC. He laughs and says, "Well, you guys have a job starting right now." And I say, "Great, but what about the union?" So Sid picks up the phone, calls Spike Wallace, they have a laugh about this crazy guy, me, and my union problems are over. The six-month waiting period is waived, and just like that we've got our cards and making union scale working for NBC.

A Star On The Rise

So they signed us up and we were immediately on the job playing sustainers, filling unscheduled air-time with commercial-free 15-minute shows as "Les Paul and His Trio" with an added vocalist or whatever. Word got around that we were versatile, and we would often be called upon to back a vocalist who was guesting on NBC without their usual accompaniment. All the while, I was on the lookout for Bing. When we were working, we would see him walking in the hallways or talking with network brass, but had no good way of approaching him.

Being a staff musician at NBC immediately plugged you into everything that was going on with many important people. We were doing nine network sustainers a week, and were also allowed to make appearances on other radio shows, even on the other networks. Things started happening terribly fast because once we started playing on NBC, then *everybody* got to hear us. When they were taking a break from rehearsing, Amos and Andy would come in and listen to us play our sustainers, and they weren't alone. Lots of people were taking note of us. We became very popular, and I had the freedom to go anywhere I wanted, so getting hired at NBC was a tremendous break.

This is one version of Les Paul and his Trio, with Paul Smith on piano, Cal Gooden, Jr. on acoustic rhythm guitar, and Bob Meyer on bass. Throughout this period you can see different photos of my klunkers and you'll notice that in every picture the pickups are different. I was constantly searching for the perfect combination to match the sound I could hear in my head.

133

On The Big Screen

Jack Benny's orchestra leader heard some of our sustainer shows and was impressed. This fellow was also involved in directing musical scores for various movies, and after one of our performances; he approached me and said he had something for us. The next thing you know, I was on a movie set with my group at Universal Studios, doing a number for the film called *Sensations of 1945*.

Then I got a bit part in a Paramount film. In the scene I'm remembering, I was a milkman and I clanked the bottles together. Ginger Rogers heard the musical sound and started to sing from her upstairs window. When she leaned out and started singing, I grabbed my guitar out of the milk truck and played for her. This movie either never came out, or if it did, it may be that my part was edited out in the final version.

There was another movie, this one featuring jazz, called *Sarge Goes to College* in which I was in quite a band. There was Abe Lyman on drums, Joe Venuti on violin, Jess Stacy on piano, Jerry Wald on clarinet, and Wingy Manone, the one-armed trumpet player. There was also a fellow named Don Ripps who played the bass harmonica like nobody I ever heard. The line up of musicians was the best thing about that movie. It was done at Monogram, which was famous for being low budget. The movie was released and did nothing. It was a bomb, and after that, I decided to stick to what I knew best, which was playing guitar and working on my recordings.

In 1947 I appeared with several other well-known musicians in a Monogram Studios movie Sarge Goes to College. *Jack McVea was the orchestra leader, with Abe Lyman, Joe Venuti, Jess Stacy, Jerry Wald, Wingy Manone (holding trumpet), Don Ripps, Candy Candido, and Russ Morgan. The actors were Alan Hale, Jr. (who played the role of "Sarge"), Noel Neill (who later played Lois Lane in the Superman serials), June Preisser, Warren Mills, and Freddie Stewart (wearing glasses). Right after the end of World War II, millions of GIs went to college, where jazz music was the new thing.*

135

CHAPTER NINE

Armed Forces Radio

I received my induction papers in the fall of '43 and was headed into the service. Shortly after receiving my draft notice, I'm walking past CBS when Bobby Sommers, a guitar player I know, stops me and says, "My mother just died and I need a favor. Would you grab my guitar and fill in for me on *Suspense*?" This was a popular radio drama for which the group he was with provided music. And I said sure, I would be glad to do it.

So I go into CBS and sit in with his group while the show is being produced, and during a break, some of us start jamming. These guys are all accomplished musicians, and in no time, we're pushing and challenging each other and having a blast. When Gordon Jenkins, the orchestra leader, hears what we're doing, he flips for it.

Meredith Willson

The next thing I know, a guy taps me on the shoulder and says, "My name is Meredith Willson, what's yours?" I tell him, and he says, "Well Les, if you're ever inducted into the service, I'd like to have you in my orchestra. I'm Captain Meredith Willson, and I'm in charge of the Armed Forces Radio Service."

I knew who Meredith Willson was because he was also the musical director for NBC. And I said, "Well, I've already been inducted, but I've got a problem. I've just made arrangements to go with Glenn Miller." And it was true. I was all

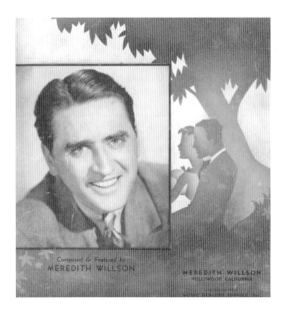

set to go with Glenn Miller's band as soon as I got processed in. He said, "If I can arrange to have your orders changed and have you with us in Hollywood, would you agree to it?" And I said, "I'd be happy to, I'd prefer it." Glenn Miller was going to be traveling all over the world, and with Meredith, I could stay in Hollywood and still do my bit.

So within a week of going into the army, I'm back living in my own home. I'm officially stationed on the same street where I live, and now a member of the Armed Forces Radio Service, the AFRS. It's amazing, the damndest story in the whole world, but that's exactly what happened.

On Duty

I made the AFRS aware of my interest in electronics and recording and got assigned to the department producing programs for the Armed Forces radio network. Also, with Meredith Willson, I had two other jobs to perform. One was with my trio, and we were busier than hell doing shows with Kate Smith, Dinah Shore, anybody you could think of who would want to do intimate dates for the Armed Forces network. We'd do 15 minutes, a half hour, whatever the show called for, doing medleys of songs, talking to the soldiers and tying everything together. The second job was to play in Meredith Willson's AFRS orchestra accompanying the dramas, doing all the fills and segues, again doing whatever the program called for.

So I had three jobs to juggle while in the service: helping produce variety shows for the troops, playing electric guitar with my trio, and acoustic guitar with the orchestra. I had obtained a blonde L-5, which I played exclusively when an acoustic guitar was called for. It was a beautiful instrument with an excellent tone, but I didn't keep it. Cal Gooden admired it and usually played rhythm on it with the trio, so I gave it to him after I got discharged from the service. Cal died young, and that guitar never resurfaced. I've always wondered what became of it. It was my army guitar.

Jazz At The Philharmonic

In the summer of 1944, Nat Cole and Norman Grantz came to see me. Norman was promoting the first *Jazz at the Philharmonic* show. This would be the first time anything other than classical music had been presented at the Philharmonic Concert Hall, and would also feature black and white musicians playing together on the same program, which was not commonly done in those days. And Nat says, "Les, we need a guitar player. Oscar Moore's locked himself up in an attic with some chick and he's not available. What about you?" I said, "Well, I'm still in uniform, I'll have to ask my boss." So I talk to Meredith Willson about it, and he says, "Well, if you just get rid of all your identification, then you can go do it and I won't see."

This had all happened very quickly, and there was no thought of a rehearsal. The musicians gathered, we made up a tune list, and started playing. And as we played, the music progressed and the energy created by the group started building and just kept going on up. It just so happens that Nat and I are from the same school of thought, with the same way of doing most things in music. And on that day, on that stage, we were a perfect marriage. Immediately, as soon as he'd play something, I'd play it back to him, and vice versa, and we both kept upping the ante.

The audience was almost entirely black, a very savvy jazz audience, and they immediately picked up that something special was happening. Very rarely do you witness an explosion such as this was. It was an uncanny, sensational performance. Nat knew it, I knew it, and the audience knew it. I remember looking out at the audience when we finished, and they were throwing their hats in the air. Every man and boy wore a hat then, and there were hundreds of hats filling the air. They were cheering for what had just happened because they knew it was pure. As a performing musician, this was one of the great rewarding moments of my life.

We didn't know the performance was being recorded by AFRS, but later learned that a fellow who loved jazz had brought in a disk recorder and recorded the whole thing on one microphone. Nat and I both had restrictions about using our real names in association with the recording, so when copies were pressed, I was listed as Paul Leslie and Nat as Shorty Nadine.

As a younger musician, back when I was jamming in the clubs in Chicago and New York, I had that gunslinger mentality, always trying to outplay everybody. But I came to the realization that you'll never be the best because there is no such thing. What I did do was always try to do the best I could on all levels. If you don't do that, then you let down when everybody in the audience is hoping there's going to be a knock-down, drag-out fight between the two greats. So I tried to never let down to the point of disappointing the audience. If they came to hear you, they should get their money's worth. They're rooting for you because they believe in you, and sometimes, something great happens. It's happened many times in my lifetime, and what happened with Nat and I at the Philharmonic was one of the best.

Acoustic Electric

While I was in the AFRS, Navy scientists came to Meredith Willson looking for help with a subterfuge box they were working on, a simulator to plunk in the water and fool the enemy into chasing it instead of a ship or a

submarine. They needed someone with a keen ear who also understood the physics of sound to contribute what could be heard and relate to it electronically, and I got the assignment.

What they needed to do was determine what was missing between the sound of the device and the sound of an actual machine, a real ship. So they put me underwater in a diving bell, and I listened while they sent out different signals. What they wanted me to do was identify the different distortions in the sound, the inner modulations creating the unwanted frequencies interfering with the sounds they wanted to produce. So I did that for them, and once the Navy got the bugs out of it, the device worked and was used in the war.

They were dealing with quartz crystals and barium titinate, the piezo, and I immediately saw its potential for musical instruments. After the war was over, I kept working with barium titinate with the thought of using it to make an amplified acoustic guitar. I was intent on the idea for the acoustic-electric and devoted much of my time to it, trying one experiment after another, even after we moved to New Jersey. This involved making the pickup, and also where to put it. Do you place it under the bridge? Do you place it under the string itself? Do you place it on the back of the instrument? It was an interesting problem because it was a very high impedance device, and anybody knowledgeable in electronics knows this poses a more difficult problem because high impedance is more sensitive to outside interference.

I was very interested in all the different applications barium titinate could be used for, from checking vibrations in a car to deep-sea fishing to amplified sound. There are other types of material being used now, coming from normal crystals dug out of the ground, natural phenomena from Earth that have the ability to function as a transducer under pressure of the string. The piezos are used in many, many of the acoustic guitars you hear today which are plugged directly into an amplifier, with wonderful results.

After working on it for ten years, I had done all I could do with it. By then, Mary and I were hitting it big and I had to make a decision. Either I'm going to play the Paramount, the Sullivan show, the Listerine show, or I'm going to hibernate in a room like a mad professor, working with quartz crystals and barium titinate and not making any money. And the worst part was, when I got it perfected and took it to Gibson, they turned it down. They weren't interested in it at all and rejected it without a thought.

I didn't have sense enough to protect my ideas, and years later, I think Barcus-Berry came along and patented it. At the time, I didn't have much interest in patenting anything. I just had this hang-up where the acoustic-electric guitar was something I craved to hear, but not with the thought in mind that I was going to patent it and license it and make money on it. I was making my money by playing and doing other things, so money wasn't the goal. The goal was to make the thing work. I worked my ass off for ten years to build it, and then moved on to something else.

Natural Energy

Something I've often been asked about is how I've been able to maintain such an intense pace over such a long period of time in trying to perfect all my ideas, and it came up while I was in the armed forces. They conducted a test to find out what kind of person lasts the longest, using a variety of methods on different soldiers. The idea was to determine how long a person could go without sleep and still function properly.

As I recall it, there were two testing groups. In one, the person was free to do whatever he wished to do without restriction. If he wanted to play basketball all day, he could; if he wanted to read, he could; if he wanted to listen to the radio, he could. He could do anything he wished to do to stay awake. In the other group, everything was restricted and regimented, with specific routines that had to be followed. An hour of this, ten minutes of that, exercise so many times a day, do your laundry or whatever. Every minute of the day and night was scheduled and accounted for. And the point of the test for both groups was to find out who could stay awake the longest.

When I was selected to participate in this test, I said, "Sure, I'll do it, and I'll tell you right now, I'm going to walk over every guy in the army with this thing." I don't know why, but I've always been able to go with very little rest. So they put me in the group who could do whatever they wanted to do, and I went for eleven days with no sleep. Nobody else even came close to this record, and they were suddenly terribly curious about me, asking, "How'd you do it? What is it? Does it run in your family?"

I couldn't answer it for them then, and I still can't. As far as I know, it's not a family trait. I don't drink coffee or do any drugs, and never have. It's a natural energy somehow connected to the curiosity factor, the desire to know something and to keep digging until you find it, like a drive that's just built-in. Sometimes I don't like it because I would like to lay down and throw the switch and get some sleep. I would say I suffered from something, but I haven't found anybody who can tell me just exactly what it is. And it's still with me. It's nothing at all for me to go two or three days with little or no sleep, even at my age.

Sound Recording In The War Effort

The programs we were producing at Armed Forces Radio headquarters in Hollywood were going out worldwide to entertain the troops and keep up public morale. Our job was to take pre-recorded entertainment from various sources and edit it into variety shows, which were then transcribed for distribution on the Armed Forces network. We produced 72 hours of programming every week using a series of disk recording machines. Maintaining this schedule week after week was tedious and exhausting, but I learned many things about disk editing that proved useful when I later built my own studio.

Besides being involved in the technical side of producing AFRS programs, I also participated constantly as a musician and had the privilege of playing to a far wider audience than would otherwise have been possible. The purpose of everything we did was to keep our soldiers in touch with home, and it was also aimed at the enemy. So the whole world was being saturated with the entertainment we were constantly producing and serving to the Allied Armed Forces.

Thinking back to when Jimmy, Ernie and I were trying to make use of that wire recorder at NBC in New York, we were then seeing what the problems were. And little did we know that this was going to play an important part in World War II. We were rehearsing with this device, saying, "Well, the recording wire twists and turns around, and the twisting screws up the sound, so this is not the answer." But instead of sitting down and figuring out the obvious, that you should flatten out the wire and change it to some kind of flexible material that would wrap around a recording head, we just tossed it aside and said, "Well, wire isn't the answer." But the Germans didn't do that. They stayed with the problem, and they solved it.

Here's where the problem we didn't solve came in. What do you record on? Other than the wire recorder, the only thing the Armed Forces or any of us could do was to try and scribe onto a disk. So we would take the glass or aluminum disks and gouge a groove in the acetate coating to record our performances. Then vinyl pressings would be made and sent out to all the various places for broadcast. And as the war progressed and the propaganda got more complex, we found we had a very serious problem. The Nazis were much faster than we were, and the audio quality of their broadcasts was much better.

Superior German Recording Technology

We would have discussions about this, and say, "No one can move faster than we can. They can jump through a tire, they can fire a gun, they can build airplanes and boats, but we can do the same things faster and better. So how come they can record and edit faster than we can, and their quality is better than ours?"

They were getting their finished product faster and better than we were, and we were baffled as to how they were doing it. I would stand there and watch our fellows do their job and they'd have three transcription turntables going. They had the same speech by Hitler on machine one, two and three. There are two guys with earphones and keys to cue the disks up for the purpose of altering Hitler's speech. Maybe you want to make him cough, or you don't want something he said to stay in the speech, so you have to delete it to take it out. We would have to do this by going from one turntable to the second turntable to the third. The script with the first disk goes to the point where you want to make the change, and at that point you kill it. Then the next machine starts after the part you want taken out, and you put it all together on the third disk, press it, and send it on out. The problem was that the succeeding generations of recordings caused a step down in audio quality that was very noticeable, and it was a lengthy process. Hitler would be all around the world with his speech while we were still there trying to get our stuff together.

They were just light-years ahead of us with how efficiently they were producing audio, and it wasn't until we took back France and got into Luxembourg that the German tape machines were discovered and we figured out how they'd done it. With magnetic tape, they had no loss of quality between the beginning and the end of a program or speech, where our disk went all to hell as it went inside. Just picture a phonograph record. As the needle moves toward the center, the quality deteriorates because of the tracking error and becomes more evident the further in you go.

So they had that advantage until the end of the war when we got hold of the equipment they'd invented, including the magnetic tape itself. It was a revelation to us, and little did I know at the time it was going to be so important in my life.

I don't usually wear a tux when practicing in the garage! I must have been on my way to a performance somewhere. I later gave this blonde Gibson L-5 to Cal Gooden, my rhythm player.

In this picture Cal Gooden and I are playing with Tommy Todd on the piano and Clint Nordquist on bass. I believe this photo was made at Paramount Studios.

CHAPTER TEN

Swinging On A Star (Connecting with Bing)

In 1944, after about a year in uniform, I was discharged from active duty with an agreement to continue producing programs for the war effort. Working at Macgregor Recorders cutting transcriptions for the Armed Forces network gave me the opportunity to record many outstanding musicians while gaining further knowledge of the techniques and accepted standards of professional recording. With so many musicians caught up in the war, jukeboxes and phonograph records were more and more replacing live music in the clubs and on the air. The handwriting was on the wall, and I was now very serious in learning all I could about audio recording. The Macgregor engineers were very helpful in showing me what worked, and where the unsolved problems were.

I went back to doing sustainers for NBC as the Les Paul Trio, sometimes adding a piano to make it Les Paul and His Trio. My personnel was unstable because of the war, but the guys I worked most consistently with were Cal Gooden, Jr. on rhythm guitar and either Clint Nordquist or my old buddy Bob Meyer on bass. On piano, after Joe Rann, there was Buddy Cole, Hal Dean, Bob Armstrong, Paul Smith, Tommy Todd and the great Milt Raskin.

Milt Raskin had the uncanny ability to know just when I wasn't going to play and his hand would be right there, adding just the right thing in the space I left open. Or if I was going to play, he was out of the way and playing around me, giving me room. None of the other piano players I played with could do this, or even realized it needed to be done. The difference between good and great is the ability to take the right note and put it in the right place. To be able to do this without effort is genius, and Milt had it. He had some personal problems, but as a piano player, Milt Raskin was the best, hands down.

My group was often called upon because we had the ability to take any type song and make whoever was performing it sound good. Word of our versatility got around, and we began appearing on programs like the *Elgin Watch Show*, *What's New*, Jo Stafford, Paul Weston, George Burns and Gracie Allen, Fibber McGee and Molly, and numerous other radio shows. But not with Bing. He had the top radio show in the nation and had won an Oscar for best actor. He was bigger than ever, and we hadn't yet succeeded in getting his attention. My time in the service had put it on hold, but my number one goal was still to connect with Bing.

The Emergency Room

As a wartime precaution, NBC had constructed a tiny, windowless studio called the emergency room. It had concrete walls and was outfitted with equipment that could operate on batteries or generators, so the network could keep broadcasting in case of an enemy attack or power failure. It was like a little bunker, and nobody ever used it. It was just there in case it was ever needed.

After maybe a month being back with NBC, I noticed a pattern in Bing's Thursday routine. Just before his show, he would go into the emergency room, stay a little while, and then come back out. The reason for this wasn't hard to figure. He wanted to be left alone for a little while before the show, and that little studio was where he liked to go. It was quiet and private, he could go over his lines, he could take a drink and think about what he was going to do. He carried a little medicine bottle and would take a couple of slugs. So every Thursday, just before airtime, this is what he would do to get ready for the weekly coast-to-coast broadcast. The little emergency studio was his hideaway, and that was the opening I'd been looking for.

The next week, I went to the secretary who assigned the rehearsal rooms and said we wanted to rehearse in the emergency room. And she said, "No one ever goes in there, it's just for an emergency. Why would you want to be cramped into that little room?" And I said, "Oh, we love the sound in there because everything is so close and we can hear ourselves so well. It's a special great-sounding room for us, and we'd just love to have it." And she said, "Okay then, you got it."

148

Meeting Bing

I hadn't said anything to my guys about Bing's habit of going into the emergency studio, or that I had a plan for meeting him. I just told them if we're in there rehearsing and someone walks in, don't stop, keep right on playing.

So Thursday evening rolls around and we're crowded into this tiny room rehearsing. We're playing like mad, the cement walls are creating a slapback, and it sounds amazing. Then the door opens, and sure enough, it's Bing. When the guys see who it is, they stop dead, and Bing says, "Oh, excuse me fellas, I didn't know anybody was in the room." He starts to retreat, and as the sound proof door is closing, Clint Nordquist blurts out, "Geez, that's Bing Crosby!" And I say, "Keep playing!" So we start up again, and the door reopens. Bing sticks his head in, and says, "Do you mind if I listen?" And I say, "No, not at all." So Bing stands in the door, and we're tearing into *Back Home Again In Indiana.* When we finish, he says, "What do you guys call this little outfit?" I say, "The Les Paul Trio." He says, "So you're Les Paul, huh?" I said, "Yeah, we're on staff here at NBC." And Bing says, "Well, not anymore. Now you're working for me. I'll see you next Thursday." And just like that, Bing hired us and we're just falling over, happier than hell.

Bing leaves because he's got his show to do, so I go out the door after him. He's walking away and down the road a bit, and I say, "Hey, Bing?" And he stops and says, "Yes?" I say, "How much?" He says, "One thou," and starts walking again. And I say, "Hey, Bing?" Bing turns again, "Yeah, now what do you want?" I say, "How much for the other guys?" He says, "Don't worry about it, I'll put them in the band." So he put Clint and Joe in the band for the *Kraft Music Hall* show, and I took the featured place that had once belonged to Eddie Lang, just as I had dreamed I would.

The following week Joe Rann decided to go back to New York. He had work there and he just liked New York better, so he went back to Brooklyn. To replace him, I hired Buddy Cole, one of the finest piano players in Hollywood. So my trio guys were in the band every week, and I would just noodle behind Bing as a featured part of the show.

It's Been A Long, Long Time

Being associated with Bing was a major step up. Bing was very aware of his influence, and he tried to be helpful in other ways, too. A good example of this came when we recorded *It's Been a Long, Long Time*, the first recording we did together after I'd been with his radio show for a while.

It was just Bing, myself, Cal Gooden and Clint Nordquist on the session. Bing always recorded first thing in the morning, and it was still early when we finished. He knew I'd been up all night before the session, so he asked," You

149

When we recorded It's Been a Long, Long Time *with Bing in 1945, it was just Bing and me, with Cal on rhythm and Clint on bass. Bing liked to keep it simple.*

hungry?" And I said, "Yeah, sure." So we went next door to this little restaurant to get something, and Bing said, "I noticed you weren't too enthused about what we did in there. What could we have done better?" And I said, "Well, most of it is technical stuff." I told him I thought the sound wasn't being equalized properly, and that reverb should be added in certain areas, and they should have him much closer to the microphone. In those days, you put one mic in the room and everybody played to it. Bing would be standing a foot away from the microphone when he recorded his vocals. Today there are multiple microphones on everything, and everybody sings close to the mic. Times have changed for the better, and this was the beginning of it.

Bing liked my ideas, and the recording of *Long, Long Time* was a tremendous number one hit for him in '45, an absolute monster, and being featured on it gained a lot of notoriety for me. Millions of people became aware of my electric guitar sound because of that record. It was a huge boost for my career.

150

Bing's Offer

Shortly after recording *Long, Long Time*, Bing called and said, "Let's go for a ride. I've got an idea for you." So he came and got me and we were in his car driving up Sunset Boulevard, when Bing said, "What I've got in mind is the Les Paul House of Sound. I think you should have your own studio, and run it your way, and teach music and recording. It'll be like the Fred Astaire dancing school thing, only it'll be the Les Paul House of Sound, and we'll put it all over the world."

Bing was willing to do this for me, and I'm sure anybody else would've leaped at the opportunity, but I said, "Well, I don't know..." We kept driving around the neighborhood, going up and down the streets looking at places, and finally I said, "Bing, I love the ride, but I don't think I'm interested in taking this tangent because if I got involved in something like that, it would take me away from playing, and playing is what I love." And he just said, "Okay," and was very gracious about it. He dropped me off back at North Curson Avenue and headed for the golf course. I had turned him down, but Bing's proposal led to a new idea which turned out to be terribly important.

151

CHAPTER ELEVEN

The Garage Studio

When Bing dropped me off at home, my two buddies, Lloyd Rich and Vern Carson, were waiting to hear about the ride. I said, "Oh, it went fine. We

My little bungalow at 1514 North Curson Avenue in Hollywood.

The driveway at left led back to the garage. I can't believe we couldn't find a picture of it, or the patio.

ended up going up and down Sunset Boulevard and all around, looking for a place to build a studio." I tell them about Bing's idea for going worldwide with the Les Paul House of Sound, and then I tell them I turned it down. And they both say, "Are you nuts? Why?" They found it hard to understand how I could turn down such an offer from the biggest star in the world.

These two guys were special friends, to me, but they were so different they could hardly talk to each other. One was a guitar player, and the other was an army buddy I'd worked with in the AFRS. They were close friends but couldn't have been more different. Lloyd, the guitar player, was way out there in his thinking. For him, there was no end to the universe. It just went on and on and he went right along with it, always going further and further out. Vern looked down into the electronics, that's what he knew and understood, and that was his world. He didn't want to go any further.

Building The Studio

So we're talking about Bing's idea of me having my own studio, and Lloyd says, "I'm good at building, and if you'll park the car outside, we can bring the piano out from the house, board up the garage doors, and build your studio right here." So that's what we did. We closed and sealed the garage door, threw some rugs on the floor, paneled it with Transite, and used the little side window for an entrance.

Transite was an acoustic tile made of asbestos and full of holes like peg-board, only thicker. For years, in every city, it was used in all the recording and broadcast studios to get that resonant sound. It had a spank at about 6K that was just great for a man's voice, anybody's voice. It had that ambient snap to it, and you could only get it with that material, so I considered it a necessity. Counting the Transite, nails, rugs, paint and everything else, the amount of money I spent getting the garage ready to be a studio was about $600. To set this thing up electronically, using the stuff I already had and adding what we needed to get started, was another four or five hundred dollars. So it came to somewhere around $1000 to build and outfit the studio. And after we got it built, for three months I didn't charge anybody anything to record in the studio. If a player was good enough to make a record, I would record it for nothing. And in doing that, I would learn how something should be recorded. I was *serious* about recording now. I was determined to solve the problems of the AFRS, Decca, Columbia, Victor, and the other recording studios that all did things I wouldn't do or that I wished to do differently.

153

Lansing Speakers

This was well before we started using magnetic tape, before Ampex. I again had to build a disk-cutting machine, and in this one, we perfected the things I'd learned from the ones built previously. Eventually, we built a second disk cutter, but all we thought of at first was getting the studio built, the acoustic quality of the studio sound, and the mixer. Many people became involved in helping accomplish what we were trying to do. There was Vern, Lloyd, myself, a fellow named Art Partridge, and a long list of people who were somehow important in getting it up and running. Many people took a contributing interest.

For instance, we had to determine the best speaker for our purposes because we can't judge the quality of anything unless we are getting a reliable reference on the reproduced sound. In the Midwest and on the East Coast, I had friends in places like Bell Labs, but the West Coast was foreign to me. I hadn't been there long enough to know where to look for the right people. Then Vern said, "Jim Lansing. He builds a darn good speaker out of a little place over on Vine Street. Why don't we go over and talk to him?" So that's what we did, and lo and behold, that's where our studio monitor came from. When Capitol and Decca heard the sound we were getting in the garage, they were converted. Most of the world followed suit on the same speakers because they were so good. Jim Lansing set the standard.

After I installed Lansing speakers in the garage, I was so impressed I put them in my guitar amps. In 1951, when Mary and I played at the Grand Ole Opry, Chet Atkins was on the show as a sideman in the band. Chet and I had become friends by then, and as soon as he heard my amp he was down on the floor with a flashlight trying to see what kind of a speaker I was using. I said, "Wait a minute, after the show I'll take the back off so you can look at it and see what it is." Chet had a tremendously good ear for sound, and he knew something different was being used. He was going to find out what I had in there if it was the last thing on earth.

I was using a 15-inch speaker, and it was a boat anchor, so my amp weighed a ton. The sound guys in Nashville were just stunned by the sound of this speaker because no one had heard of Jim Lansing or had any idea what he was doing. He was building what is called a coaxial speaker, and because of my connection with him, I was the first to get them and put them to use for recording and performing. The Lansing coaxial speaker was unheard of then, but for the sound I was after, it was perfect. And, of course, the whole garage studio thing, Lansing speakers and all, would never have happened if it wasn't for Bing asking why I wasn't pleased with a record we were making, and then driving me up and down Sunset Boulevard pitching the idea of the Les Paul House of Sound.

I made records for people without charging a fee in order to discover what I needed to learn. If a concertmaster wants to bring in a legitimate quartet from MGM to record classical music, it has to be done in a certain way to effectively capture that particular sound. The next guy who comes in might say, "I want you to record my group like it's in a smoky joint, and I want it to sound just like you're sitting in this joint listening to it. It's got to be raunchy."

The idea was to capture the feeling of a live performance in a studio setting. So when we built the garage studio, I was thinking, "How do you record a French horn in an orchestra? How do you mic it, how do you capture that instrument's particular sound and the sound of the whole orchestra? How many people can you put in a room and still get a good sound?" I once had seventeen people in the one room studio, and they couldn't breathe, so I learned how many was too many. And the rug, does it stay down or come out? Do we paint here or do something else? Do we slant the window this way or that way, or should it stay straight? We were asking all these questions, and we had to answer them for the French horn, accordion and bass player; for the piano player, the guitar player and everybody else. Those first few months in operation, we were constantly experimenting, to get the desired sound in our recordings.

This was a tremendously exciting and creative time because both sides were coming at me at once. One side was the engineers with their interest in the electronics angle and what they could learn and also contribute, and the other side was all the singers and musicians who wanted to be involved in what we were doing for their own reasons. We were learning something new every day, and the commercial studios were going crazy trying to figure out what we were doing, and how we were doing it. And the truth is, we weren't doing anything they couldn't have done, if they'd had the freedom and drive to do it. We were trying anything and everything we could think of, and when something worked or it didn't work, either way it would lead to something else.

The Fraternity of Sound

There's something about the camaraderie of engineers that's very similar to musicians, especially guitar players. Guitar players are like a clan. We love each other no matter how we play the guitar. There's just some unspoken thing, which all guitar players have in common. We'll hang out together even when we're not playing, and we have a feeling for each other, like a brotherhood. I don't think one saxophone player ever talks to another sax player away from the gig, but guitar players are a very close bunch, and I found it to be the same with engineers. So in the garage, we had musicians creating, we had engineers creating,

and everything married because we were all in it together. And you couldn't have planned it because trying to plan it would've killed the creative chemistry. It was a very special thing that happened there, because it had to happen.

And this was a situation where for the first time, the engineer was also the musician. I was after a better way to capture and reproduce sound, but you couldn't identify the qualities that made it better until you heard it. It was vague when you were searching for it, yet definite because you heard it in your head. So we just kept chasing after it, trying to find ways to turn thoughts into sound waves.

Hum Hiss Paul

I was extremely picky, a perfectionist, about every detail of every recording, so much so that I used to get ribbed about it. I knew this old fellow named Harry Merns, one of the head engineers at RCA, and when he saw me coming he'd say, "Here comes Hum Hiss Paul." I would hear something in a recording, a buzz or hum or some other sound that didn't belong, and the engineers would say, "Nobody will ever notice that. It's nothing, it won't show up. It's a great record, leave it alone." And I'd say, "Well, I hear it and I don't want to hear it." So we'd keep doing it until I was satisfied we had it right.

Harry Merns was a great character. A religious, stiff kind of guy, but a very gifted sound engineer. After we moved to New Jersey, he built a lot of what I needed, including the control console for the eight track, which required an incredibly complex wiring job. When I say he was a character, I mean he was like most of my other friends, just a different kind of cat, and a unique individual. All my friends were that way, and they didn't always understand each other, but I could communicate with each one of them one hundred percent. I had 40 great friends in California who were very important in my life, and I couldn't have done what I did without them.

More Than Just The Sound

We had an audio engineer's club called the Sapphire Club, and we'd meet once a month to seriously thrash out how we could make a better mousetrap. This was what the meetings were all about, and the garage studio got a lot of interest from some very gifted guys. It was at one of these meeting when a fellow got up and said, "Listen. We've got a stomach pump here and we're going to put it on Les. We want him to cough up on a lot of this stuff because, by God, it is driving us crazy!"

A similar interest came from Columbia. I had no idea I was bugging them so much until the president of the company approached me in Atlantic City.

Columbia had a convention there at the same time I was appearing at the Steel Pier. And the Columbia guy says, "We've figured out what you're doing. We built one and we know what it is now—it's a limiter." I was glad to let them think they had the answer, but they couldn't have been more wrong. There were no limiters, and they still had no idea what we were doing to get the audio quality that was keeping them all awake at night.

Another label issued a letter of warning to their R&D people, saying to find out where the demo came from if you're considering signing someone. And if it was made in Les Paul's garage, put it aside because it's probably the sound you're listening to, not the artist.

But it wasn't just the sound. Judgment also played an important part, and I'm convinced this is a gift. You don't get it out of a book or achieve it by practicing. It's like going down to the store to buy rhythm or perfect pitch. You can't do it. These things are God's gifts. So it's not only the studio, or the artist. The producer and the audio engineering are equally important. This was the beginning of the era that has become common today, where one person can write, produce, arrange and perform. I was doing everything myself, right down to delivering the masters to the label.

What The Big Labels Couldn't Do

The problem with all the major companies was, when someone wanted to do something, no matter what it was, the response would always be, "Well, we've got to get an okay from New York." If NBC in Hollywood wanted to change a microphone or throw a switch to change impedance, they'd have to get confirmation from New York. Days would go by to accomplish this simple thing. But in my world, if I want to throw the switch, I just do it and that's it. We wound our own heads and did almost everything ourselves, so we were much quicker, and we had the freedom to do anything we wished to do. If you had an idea, no matter how radical, you could try it. The big company guy couldn't do that. He'd say, "Well, I can't do that unless they have a meeting and the boss okays it."

Bing Takes An Interest

Bing didn't lose interest in me because I turned down his studio idea, and continued to visit the garage regularly. One night he called and said, "What are you up to?" I said, "Oh, we're busy recording something." And at this particular time we were recording in the living room of the house, not back in the garage. Maybe a half hour later, the doorbell rings, and it's Bing with a caravan of six limos parked out in front of my little house. So in comes Bing with Howard Hawks, Frank Capra, Andy Devine, John Scott Trotter and several others. There must have been a dozen important people in the living room of our tiny little house, and Bing had brought them over just so they could hear a recording we'd made and experience the sound we were getting. Introducing me to all these people with his endorsement was important in getting the word out about what we were doing, and another way he supported what I was doing.

Because of his contract with Decca, Bing never recorded in the garage, but he liked to drop by and listen to whatever I was working on. One night, he came over and said, "What have you got that I can hear? I just want to hear something you're recording." So I played my recording of Kay Starr singing *I Can't Get Started* And he kept saying, "Play it again." He listened to it over and over and just marveled at the sound because he'd been involved with recording for a long time and could hear the difference. He stood there with a drink in his hand, and said, "Les, I've been all over the world and I've never heard sound like this in my life." And this was all being done on acetate using the disk cutters we had built ourselves.

The Garage Sound Couldn't Be Duplicated

The sound we were able to get in our homemade studio we were never able to recreate anywhere else. And we tried. Sherman Fairchild flew out to California with his top people to try and duplicate the garage to the last letter. They took a tape measure and measured everything down to the inch, drew out detailed plans, and then reproduced the whole thing in Long Island City, New York. Precisely the same dimensions were used with identical materials, Transite, the whole bit, but it didn't work. The sound wasn't the same, or as good.

Now, you could say the California garage was just somehow special, be glad it happened and let it go at that. But actually, I was wanting to reproduce that sound elsewhere because people like Tex Beneke, who had taken over the Glenn Miller Orchestra, and other top performers were wanting me to go into RCA or Radio Recorders, whatever studio they were associated with, to produce for them the sound I got in the garage. We tried, but never succeeded in matching it completely.

I think the reason for this was many variables contributing together. And by changing one thing, however slightly, other things were changed, too. Guitars are like that. Some will stay in tune, and some won't, no matter what you do. So, in the garage, everything was complementary. We designed it, built it, over a period of time as we experimented along, so it was in layers from the ground up. When you take the finished thing and try to rebuild it all at once, even though you think you're doing everything the same, you're not. There was something different, something lost in trying to recreate it.

Who Was There

It would not be possible to remember all the people, famous and otherwise, who passed through the garage, who came to record or who came because they'd heard about it and just wanted to see and hear what was being done. There was Bing all the time, the Andrews Sisters. Art Tatum, Tex Williams, Pee Wee Hunt, Pat O'Brien, Gene Autry, Judy Canova, and on and on. I met W.C. Fields on a movie set, and he recorded the only audio disk he ever made there in the garage. Another time, Bing's wife, Dixie, brought the four Crosby kids over and we recorded *When the Blue of the Night Meets the Gold of the Day,* which was his theme song. It was a Father's Day surprise for Bing, and that's always been one of my favorite records.

Andy Williams and his brother Dick practically lived at our house for a time there. Andy was one of my favorite test subjects for new recording ideas because his beautiful tenor voice was very consistent, which helped me learn things I needed to know. He came in once and did 21 takes on *Who Broke the Lock.* Then he listened to all 21 of them, and said, "Well, I think 12 was the best one." I agreed, but had switched the numbers on him. What Andy thought was number 12 was really number one. It was the first take. I tried this again with someone else, and the same thing happened. So I learned, if the guy doesn't blow it, the first or second take will usually be way up front. As the number of takes increases, he gets better and perfects it, but the quality of the performance gets worse. So technical perfection is not the answer. It's the spontaneity, the freedom you have before you get boxed in by becoming repetitious, that puts something into the recording people want to hear again and again.

Cutting A Door

When we started building the studio, we put the piano inside the garage before we sealed up the doors. After that, we had to come and go by crawling in and out the window. Along comes a guy who wants a nine-foot grand piano and we can't get it in there. So we have to tear the whole damn garage door down and plow through the workshop to get this gigantic piano in there just for this one guy to do his date. But he's going to make 50 sides and he's a great piano player, so we did it. And again, this would never happen anywhere else.

The piano player was Calvin Jackson, an excellent piano player, but he had a quirk. We had to hire a girl to just sit there in the studio while he played.

161

Playing with Cal and Clint, plus a couple of unknown musicians. My little Eppy amp is in this photo.

He said it inspired him, and he didn't want to do anything but look at her and play the piano. So we not only had to tear a wall down to get the grand piano into the studio, we had to find a pretty girl to sit there while he played, just so he could look at her. When he was done, when all the sides were cut, he went home, the gal went home, we took his piano out, and that was the end of it. When we were putting the garage back in shape after those sessions, we took the opportunity to cut and install a regular door. Calvin died some time ago, but I've still got those 50 sides, and they're great.

Fender and Bigsby

All the sound guys were showing up. Leo Fender, Paul Bigsby, they practically lived in my back yard, and it wasn't because they liked the shape of my nose. They were chasing some of the same problems and knew something important was going down, and they didn't want to miss it. There were country artists, too, guys like Spade Cooley and Tex Williams. And where are they? Out in my backyard. And what are they playing? Electric guitars. They were more interested in the electric guitar sound than the recording stuff, and if they're going to be playing through a speaker, Fender wants to be there to find out what's right and what's wrong. Everybody wants to know what we're discovering so they can add it to what they're doing, and we were doing the same thing.

This was the wonderful part of what I had there, the fact that you'd step out of the garage where all this great stuff was happening, and there's a big, open patio with a fireplace and a couple of orange trees and some chairs. It was our meeting place, and Leo and Bigsby and I, everybody, we would sit there for hours just goofing off, talking and jamming with our ideas about guitars and amplifiers and speakers. It was like an open forum for electronics and guitar ideas, whatever anybody had on their mind. We would joke and argue and compare our notions, and those conversations, those brain sessions, changed the world.

163

CHAPTER TWELVE

Along Came Mary

I was already doing nine sustainer shows a week playing jazz and pop music when Harry Brubeck, NBC's program director, told me he needed to fill nine more shows. When he asked if I knew anyone who did a different kind of music and could handle it, I said, "You know, I used to do a country thing back in Missouri and it was very successful. Why don't you do nine country shows?" And Harry said, "That would be great, but I don't know a thing about country. I wouldn't know where to start." So I told him about the Ozark Apple Knockers, the Scalawags, Rhubarb Red and the whole thing from back in St. Louis and Chicago, and then said, "I've got the whole act right here in my head. If you want me to do it for you, I'll do it, no problem." Harry said go for it, and I agreed to work up the nine shows for NBC, based on my old act.

And I practically had the act together already because my guitar player also played violin and could do the hoedowns, and my keyboard guy also played the accordion. Doing Rhubarb Red again would be easy and fun for me, so all I needed to complete the package was a girl singer, someone to feature during each show to provide some variety.

So I'm walking down Sunset Boulevard with this new thing on my mind, and there's Eddie Dean coming out of CBS, where he's rehearsing Gene Autry's radio show. Gene was with him, and I tell them I'm looking for a cowgirl singer to be a part of these country shows I'm going to be doing. And Gene says, "We've got a girl that just might work. Come on in." So we go in and listen to the Sunshine Girls, a trio featured on their show. The one Gene's recommending is standing in the middle, pretty as a picture, and I'm favorably impressed. After I hear them, I tell Gene, "Well, she looks good, and she sings on key. You're right, she might work out okay." I didn't talk to her then, but Gene gave me her phone number and name, Colleen Summers, and I called her the next day.

And now it's another of those amazing connections that happen when you're not expecting it. The first thing I find out is she's a guitar nut. When she answers the phone, I tell her it's Les Paul calling. And she says, "Not *the* Les Paul?" And I say, "Yeah, *the* Les Paul." She thought it was somebody kidding around, and said, "Well, I don't believe you."

We talk, and she's very knowledgeable about the different guitar players who were known at the time, which was very striking to me. And here's the amazing thing: she had heard me on NBC with Fred Waring, and then with

164

Bing on *Long, Long Time* and on his show, and she was a huge Les Paul fan. We talk about doing the country shows for NBC and she agrees to come for an audition, but she's still not convinced I'm really Les Paul. So I give her the North Curson address, and we agree on a time to meet. Time passes and I'm out front of our little house picking up a year's worth of beer bottles and newspa-

pers, trying to mow knee-high grass with a push mower, when this gal pulls up in her little car. I'm like Johnny Carson doing one of his bits, wearing a checkered shirt, hillbilly hat, baggy army pants, and army boots with no laces. I haven't shaved and look like hell. She looks at the address on the house, and then asks, "Can you tell me where the Les Paul studios are located?" I say, "Well, just follow the driveway back to the garage and you'll find it."

She walks past the house back to the garage, and there's no door, no way to get in. My guys have to lift her in through the window, and they're just starting to run through something with her when I come in from mowing and go into the control room. And they say, "Oh, there's Les now." Her eyebrows go up, and she says, "That's not Les Paul, that's the gardener!" So now her doubts have been confirmed, and she's looking for the exit, ready to get the hell out. I go into the studio, grab a guitar and let go with a couple of fast runs, and she says, "Oh, my God, you *are* Les Paul!" And that did it. Now we're all laughing and having a good time, and that's how Mary and I met for the first time.

The audition went fine, and afterward, the two of us went out to get something to eat. It was then she told me the reason she was reluctant to believe I was really Les Paul. It was because I was her favorite guitarist, who she had defended in argument after argument as being the best, always making my

165

case to those who believed Django or whoever was better. When she first saw me, the way I looked was a shock because it didn't fit her mental image at all. It was a train wreck. It was a funny situation, and every time we thought of it, we'd be laughing again.

We agreed we would do the radio programs with her as the cowgirl singer, but we both knew it wasn't going to end there. We started to plan the shows that very night, and it was like we had known each other all our lives. We got quite intimate in our conversations and the sense of attachment was immediate. That's when I started calling her Mary, rather than Colleen, so we wouldn't tip our hand that we were getting involved.

The shows were billed as Rhubarb Red and the Ozark Apple Knockers, featuring Mary Lou. No last name, just Mary Lou. For each show, I'd do my Rhubarb Red, Mary Lou would sing a song and we'd do some comedy bits. These were pure country shows, which was all Mary knew. She'd never sung a pop song in her life up to that point. So we started kidding around, singing country songs together, and had a blast with it. It worked great because we were nuts about each other.

Rhubarb's Reprise

It was a lot of laughs to be Rhubarb Red again, and I did things during those shows that were absolutely beyond the wall forever. The network had writers who scripted the shows, so we had lines we were supposed to read. At rehearsal, I'd stick to the script so everything timed out just right, but for the actual show, the script goes out the window. Now I'm looking down like I'm reading it, and everybody in the control room is looking at the same page, but what they're seeing isn't what they're hearing. I'm ad-libbing, and I see the producer's papers go up in the air.

Another time, Mary had rehearsed *I Love You So Much It Hurts Me* in the key of A, so on the live show, I start the intro in C. She had the most frightened look on her face because she knew something was terribly wrong. I'm playing the intro in the wrong key, she's thinking I've made a mistake, and then, right at the last moment, I modulate and land it so she's right where she needs to be, and away we go in A with everybody in the band cracking up. Another time, she was doing her number and I set the sheet music she was holding on fire. I did something unexpected every show, so it never ended.

And, of course, the complaints would come in from stations like KOB in Albuquerque, saying, "That show is out of control, it's an insult to the audience, and if you don't take it off, we're going to leave NBC and go with CBS or Mutual." And Harry Brubeck would say, "But it's so funny. I listen to those

transcriptions over and over." It *was* funny, and it was fun. I've got those shows on disk, and they're priceless.

By the time we finished doing those shows, Mary and I were madly in love. Virginia and I were separated by then, and Mary and I became inseparable. I think what impressed her was not just the guitar; it was the sense of humor and the fact that we had so much fun. That's a very important part of any relationship. The laughs. And that's why we liked to travel so much. The road trips gave us time to kibitz and think and just enjoy each other's company. You can't do that when you're under pressure to get something done, with people looking over your shoulder all the time. With Mary, I didn't have to be anything other than who I was, and it was the same for her with me. We knew we had found something terribly rare.

Souvenir Of
HERB WARD   DON FRENCH
Sunset
Off Vine   CLUB ROUNDERS   Across
From N.B.C.
EV Wallace - Your Host

Club Rounders

In the meantime, a couple of guys connected with Las Vegas built a night-club, and one of them was a guitar player. Herb Ward liked my music so much he built this place called the Club Rounders just to give me a place to play. He said, "I want you to play there and be happy with the money, and just make yourself at home. We'll do live broadcasts, and it'll be your thing. You do it however you want to do it."

They put a huge picture of me on a 12-foot square signboard and hung it on the front of the place, and I set up shop with my trio and became the head-line attraction. It was me, Cal Gooden, Bob Meyer and Paul Smith doing live broadcasts from the Rounders damn near every night. Those shows were all

168

transcribed for air check purposes, and I wish now I had saved them because a lot of riotous stuff happened.

The Rounders was located at Sunset and Vine, right across the street from NBC, only a couple of blocks from CBS, and just a half block from Mutual Broadcasting. ABC was also nearby, so the big four were all within a couple of blocks. It was a public place with a private feel, so the stars could rub shoulders and pal around and be themselves. Any time somebody working at one of the networks had time to kill, the Rounders is where they would congregate.

I'd now played on hits with Bing and the Andrews Sisters, so my stock was up, and the Rounders was the "in" place to be. From other guitar players to famous entertainers to those you'd never heard of, everybody who was anybody was in and out of there all the time. On any given night, in the audience would be Bing, Art Tatum, Artie Shaw, Benny Goodman, Barney Kessel, Meredith Willson, Groucho Marx, Joan Davis, Bette Davis, the Andrews Sisters, Bugsy Siegel and on and on. And they kept coming back because we had such a great time.

Our shows featured a lot of ad-libbing back and forth with the audience, but never once did a celebrity come on stage with us. This wasn't a scene where you would put someone on the spot by inviting them up to sing or kid around. The entertainers and musicians in the audience enjoyed having the pressure off and watching us cut loose without a net. It was just me and my trio doing everything from country corn to jazz, and we played it over the top every night. Nobody knew what might happen next, so we had a lot of laughs. Those were great audiences, and it was during this time I became more skilled at live entertaining and improvising with whatever came up to give people a good time.

After the Rhubarb Red thing for NBC, Mary Lou went on an extended tour with Gene Autry and we missed each other terribly. Once she got back, she lived in that club. She would run up a huge tab coming in there four and five nights a week with her sister or a girlfriend just to sit and listen to her favorite guitar player and the great little group I had there. She had sung with me on the country shows, and we were involved personally, but there was no thought of her doing anything with the Les Paul group. She was strictly country, and it never entered either of our minds for her to do anything else.

What brought the Rounders Club to an end was that Herb Ward was flying back from Reno or Vegas and his plane collided with high-tension electric lines. Everybody in the plane was cooked, and all they found of him was his ring. This guy was larger than life, with a shady past. He was the one who created the place and kept it going, and without him, everything changed. It was no longer the same, and then it burned down. So it was over.

169

Highway Getaways

Mary and I were going together while I was still married, and we tried not to flaunt it or do anything to hurt anyone's feelings publicly. We loved to get in the car and drive because then we could get away from the telephone and just enjoy each other's company without feeling watched. Out on the road, it was just the two of us, and that's what we wanted. We developed the practice of driving through the night, then getting a room so we could rest during the day, which was a natural for us because we were both night people.

We loved to drive and listen to the evening radio shows like *Dragnet*, *Suspense* or the *Lux Radio Theater*, whatever we could find on the dial. We both loved country music, so we were listening to that, and then we were listening to great jazz late at night. We had tons and tons of great music to listen to while we traveled, and we loved it all.

On The Way Up

Following the hit with Bing, I recorded *Rumors Are Flying* with the Andrews Sisters, which also did very well. The Andrews girls were preparing to do a national tour just as our record was hitting, and I was invited to join them with my trio. This is 1946, when they were at their peak making hit records and starring in movies with big names like Bing and Bob Hope. We played extended engagements in Cincinnati, Cleveland, New York, Chicago, Philly, Detroit, San Francisco, more towns than I can remember. The tour was coast-to-coast, and we were everywhere.

We got second billing as the opening act and then stayed on stage to back up Maxene, Laverne and Patty while they performed. Starting at noon, we'd do six or seven shows a day wherever we appeared, and nearly every one a sellout. Repeating the routine day after day was exhausting, but we were a good fit musically and it was great to be included in their popularity. They had jazzy, tight arrangements which were a blast to perform, but there was another big plus for me. It was on this tour, while playing the Paramount in New York, I finally met Django.

Meeting Django

I had been listening to Django's music since 1934, but it wasn't until December 1946 that we met. He and Johnny Smith came to the stage door of the Paramount and said they wanted to see me. The doorman yelled up the stairs, "Les, there's someone down here wants to see you. His name is Django Reinhardt." So I hollered back, "Yeah, right. Send up Jesus Christ and a case

170

of beer." I thought someone was pulling my chain, so I wised off.

I'm in a dressing room on the sixth floor, hanging out with my trio between shows. I've got my shirt off and I'm shaving when the elevator door opens and out step Johnny and Django, with an interpreter. He says, "Hello, Les." And I am just stunned because it's really him. There stands Django Reinhardt, the one musician I idolized, admired and respected above all others. There were two klunkers on the bed, and immediately Django picked one up and asked to borrow a pick. Out of the handful I had in my pocket, he selected a tiny one with my name printed on it. Then he took off on *Rose Room* with Johnny playing rhythm on the other klunker, and I was just amazed at the way he handled my guitar.

My high E string was .014-gauge, the low E a .056, and I used a high action. So usually, when somebody picked up one of my guitars, they'd say, "Holy Christ, how can you play this thing?" But Django sat down on a chair and played it like he owned it, like it was part of him. He just beat the hell out of it, and hearing his unique sound coming out of my guitar was a tremendous thrill. My amp was down on stage so he was playing acoustically, and it was a great thing for me, a great moment in my life.

He jammed hot for 15 minutes or so, and then it was time for our next performance. We all went down together, and when I went out to do the show, Django stood in the wings and watched. And you can imagine how I felt during that performance. If there was anybody out there I really looked up to and admired, who I accepted as superior to me, it would be Django. So with him standing there watching me play, you can rest assured I was nervous. But we went out and did our thing and it was fine.

After that, Django and I would see each other every so often. He was on tour with Duke Ellington, I was with the Andrews tour, and we kept hitting the same cities at the same time. We were in Chicago at the same time, in Cincinnati, in Philly, and each time we'd get together. And Django kept telling me how he was tired of it all. He was discouraged and wanted to go back home to his wife and son. "No more. I've had it," he'd say through the interpreter. He was lonely and very unhappy with what he was experiencing in the United States because he wasn't well received at all. He hadn't come with people who understood his rhythms and knew his kind of music. He came over alone assuming it would just fall together like it had back in Paris, but it didn't happen that way. Ellington's band was not prepared to accommodate his style, and it had him upside down.

And we talked about it. Django said, "They don't like me in America, do they?" And I said, "They sure as hell do. You're the greatest in the world. You're just misplaced. When you come back, I will personally see to it and make sure you're directed properly." I didn't mean as a manager or booking agent, but just to see that he had the right situation musically, and that no one would take unfair advantage of him.

I planned to do that for him, and I would have, but he never came back to America. When the Ellington tour ended, he went back home thinking he had failed. And I had a soft spot in my heart for him because he was the leader, he was definitely the leader, but he was terribly confused because of his reception here, and there wasn't anything I could do about it.

The Headless Guitar

It was also during this tour I introduced my headless aluminum guitar. Using sheet aluminum and an old neck, I built an electric guitar with the tuning gears below the bridge instead of up on the headstock. There was no headstock on this guitar, just the nut at the end of the neck where the strings were anchored. The guitar was very light, with a removable back so it was easy to work with, but there was a problem.

Before the show started, I would tune the guitar precisely. We'd go out and do our first number, which was *Caravan*, and by the time we finished that one song, my tuning would be a half tone off. So I'd come off the stage and say, "Damn, I gotta quit drinking because I'm not getting this guitar tuned right. This is bad news." For lack of knowing better, I blamed my tuning problem on the fact that I was drinking beer before the show. So

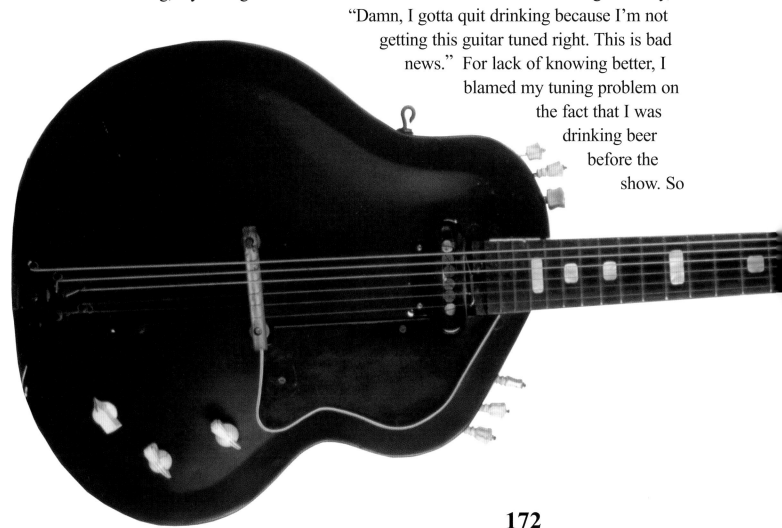

172

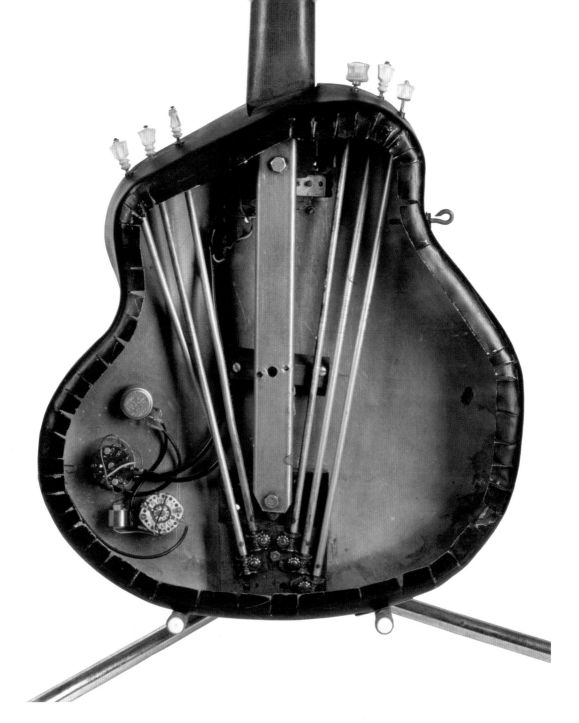

I'd get the guitar back in tune, go out and do the next number, and the same thing would happen again. Finally, I realized the cause was heat from the stage  lights. I was tuning the guitar backstage where it was dim and then going out on stage into the spotlights. The aluminum was so responsive to the hot lights it was knocking the guitar out of tune every time. So that was the end of using the aluminum guitar on stage, and I went back to my klunkers for the rest of the tour. I did use the aluminum guitar occasionally for recording because it had a unique sound, and it's still in my collection.

Buying A Car On Stage

Something else terribly interesting happened while the tour was in New York. One day the girls came into the theatre in a state of excitement with Maxene saying, "We won, we won!" They had won a Buick convertible in a raffle of some kind, and now they had it parked in the hotel garage and didn't know what to do with it. With the tour going on, they really had no use for it, nor did they want the bother of dealing with it. They said, "We need that car like we need a hole in the head." And I thought, "Geez, I could use a new car. That'd be great."

So we're on stage doing the show, and I'm thinking about the car. I pick my moment and say to Maxene, "Hey, you want to sell the car?" And she says, "Three thousand bucks." And I say, "You've got a deal." So I pulled the cash out of my pocket and bought the car right there on stage, while we were performing.

It was a fancy Buick convertible, but it had to be the worst Buick ever made. I had six rear ends put in that thing and it never was right. The gears just couldn't be made to mesh properly. And I remember Mary saying, "It just wouldn't feel right unless we were on a lift." And we had it on a lift many times because there was always something going wrong with that car, like it was jinxed. And that's the car Mary was driving when we had the accident.

Turning Point

While the tour was in Chicago, Ma came down from Waukesha to see the show. And she said, "I heard you on the radio last night, Lester. You sounded great." And I said, "Mom, you didn't hear me. I've been doing seven shows a day with the Andrews Sisters. I haven't had time to be on the radio." And she said, "Well, I thought it was you." I told her it had to be someone else, and then she said, "Well, whoever it was, you should sue them. When you plug that thing into the wall, you all sound alike." When Mother said all electric guitars sounded alike, she had a point. And I said, "Mom, I can't patent it, I can't copyright it, nobody owns this thing called electric sound." And she said, "Well, when your own mother can't tell you from someone else, there's something wrong."

174

I couldn't stop thinking about what she said, and the more I thought about it, the more it bothered me. So I made the decision to quit the tour. Lou Levy was Maxene's husband, and also the Andrews Sisters' manager. When I gave my notice, I told Lou they could keep my trio till the tour was over, but I had to get back to my studio and it couldn't wait. I did my last series of shows with them and then went back to California to find a sound my Mother would know was me. I took a year and did nothing but work on creating a sound that was different. I succeeded, and my Mother was the reason. Once again, she got into the act.

Onstage with the Andrews Sisters, playing my aluminum headless guitar.

CHAPTER THIRTEEN

Back To The Woodshed

Mother's observation that electric guitarists all sounded alike got under my skin. I'm quite sure other guitar players and musicians who were aware could tell a difference between the sound of my playing and the sound of George Barnes or whoever, but it wasn't them I was concerned with. Mother was my tester, my sample audience. If she thought all electric guitars sounded alike, I knew she wasn't alone, and that was my problem.

Starting in early 1947, I holed up in the garage to concentrate on creating a sound that would set me apart and establish an unmistakable identity. This was my goal, and everything was up for grabs. I decided to take all I'd learned about audio recording at AFRS, at NBC and Macgregor and everywhere else, and marry it to my ideas and experiments with the electric guitar. So that's what we did, and it all came together in that little garage, all focused on creating a new sound.

Lester's Mad Lab

We experimented with the guitars, the pickups, the amplifiers and speakers, everything connected to producing the sound, and at the same time, the techniques of recording the sound were constantly refined and improved. It was me and my little circle of engineering buddies, and no idea was too crazy to try. We varied the lathe speeds, tried every microphone placement imaginable, and ran my pickups directly into the mixer and cutting heads of the disk recorders to get a pure electric sound. And it never stopped. When something worked, we added it to our bag of tricks. When it didn't, we made a note of it and kept going to the next thing. We were more or less applying the scientific method of learning by doing, trying anything and everything just to see what could be observed from it, to see where it would lead. And one of the important things I learned was to lay the rhythm parts down first and save the lead parts for last.

I'd been winding and modifying my own pickups since day one, but new ideas had evolved since moving to California and experimenting with the pickups is something we got deeply into. This is where my little family of klunkers with the trap door in the back became terribly important. They were my reference points for judging the results of each modification on the pickups and internal wiring, and after countless variations, I finally got the big, round tone I was craving to hear, the fat, ballsy sound with the big wide highs that became my trade secret.

After months of trial and error, we developed a method of layering multiple tracks onto one disk while suppressing the groove and line noise that increased as each layer was added. We succeeded in doing what the record companies had not yet figured out, achieving an audio quality not heard before. Once again, it was the curiosity factor driving us, and now I was just one important discovery away from the signature sound, which my Mother or anybody else could immediately identify. A sound nobody else could get.

Delay

The remaining important element in achieving my goal was controlled delay. The recording studios created reverb by recording in tiled rooms and empty halls, or by projecting sound from a speaker into a bare concrete room where a microphone recorded the bounce, but the range of these effects was limited and didn't produce what I wanted. I was after a different sound, and I knew it was right there. I just hadn't heard it yet.

One night Lloyd Rich and I were out having a beer and I told him about my problem. I said, "I don't want the empty concert hall reverb because it just lays there and muddies everything up. I want an actual echo I can control." And Lloyd said, "You mean an echo like the same note repeating again as soon as you play it?" When he said that, the light went on and there it was. An extra playback cartridge just next to the recording head was the answer, and I knew it as soon as the idea flashed into my head.

So Lloyd and I went immediately back to the garage and started doing surgery on one of the disk cutters, experimenting with placement of a second arm wired to play back what the cutting stylus had just inscribed. As soon as we started getting a result, as soon as I heard the clear echo enlarging the tone with rich sustain, I knew I'd found my sound. This was a terribly exciting discovery. After a couple of days experimenting with where and how to place the second playback head to be able to vary the desired duration of delay for different recordings, I was on my way to a whole new world.

I still did some recording with other artists, and would go out for the occasional engagement with the Andrews Sisters or with Bing, but I otherwise stayed locked up in the garage. I knew we were onto something big, and it was "Do Not Disturb" for about a year so I could concentrate in private. I had my good buddies Vern and Lloyd, Art Partridge, Wally Jones and others who were coming and going and contributing, but I was otherwise keeping a lid on it. Nobody knew what I was doing in the garage, not even Mary.

Creating the New Sound

A stack of instrumental sides startlingly different from anything ever heard before accumulated during this time of intense experimentation, which began in 1946. *Lover* was the first one I finished, and the way it was recorded is a good example of how multi-layering was done using two disk recorders.

You'd lay your first track down on a disk, then listen back and play something along with it while you used the second machine to record the combined sound on a second disk. You repeated that step as many times as it took, discarding one disk after another, until you got those first two tracks blended just right. Then you'd take that two-layer disk, move it over to the playback machine, and repeat the process adding the third layer, the fourth layer, and so on. Each time you added a track, you were mixing it with everything you'd layered before onto a fresh disk.

Each new layer caused the previous ones to lose fidelity, so the instrumental parts had to be built in reverse order of importance. To get the lead parts out front, they had to be done last, and the same technique had to be followed when we later started layering Mary's vocals. And this is the interesting thing about using the disk machines. As you built a recording, you saved the disks that represented each combination of layers, in case you wanted to compare something or do something over. This was before stereo came along, so everything was in monaural sound.

Lover was the first recording where I attempted to combine all my inventions and effects, the hot pickups, the varied disk speeds and my different playing techniques into a multi-layered recording where I played all the instruments. It was eight layers deep, with the first layer being the percussion. Using a snare drum and cymbals, I put down a simple, solid rhythm track as a basis for the layers to be added, which were various guitars.

I experimented with several different guitars in the process of building *Lover*, and when I wasn't hotwired directly into the mixer or the disk cutter, I used an early Fender amp modified with a Lansing speaker. There were several different versions where I used the aluminum guitar and others in various combinations, but for the final version, the one that became the hit, it's mostly the Log and my favorite klunker you hear, and we went through about 500 disks to get there. Finishing *Lover* completed the creation of my signature sound, which came to be known as the New Sound.

Wally Jones

Wally Jones was a very important person in all this. It was he who built the little mixer that was so important to what we accomplished in the garage, and later when we were living and recording on the road with the tape recorder. Thanks to Wally and the "Wally box," if we wanted to record elsewhere, we could still duplicate the recording effects we previously could get only in the garage. Wally Jones played a big part in our success by helping us cut loose from the garage and be able to do our thing anywhere we went. But here's another very interesting, odd thing. Never could I get Mary to sound good in the garage. I never made a record of Mary in the garage that was worth a darn. This was very unusual. And yet with the road equipment Wally Jones made for me, Mary got a great sound everywhere else. We recorded hits like *Tennessee Waltz* in the living room on North Curson Avenue, but none in the garage.

179

We were invited to many Hollywood parties, and they always wanted us to bring our instruments. Here, Cal and Clint and I are rendering one for Roy Rogers and Sonny Tufts. Must've been a cowboy party!

Soon after I finished *Lover*, Mary and I went to a party and I took the acetate with me. It was at Jim Moran's place and there were a number of musicians and show business people there drinking and enjoying themselves. It was a casual scene with the record player going, so when no one was looking, I slipped my disk on the spindle and then stepped back to see what the reaction would be. And the reaction was great.

It was the usual noisy hubbub when the record started to play, but within a few seconds, it was the only thing you could hear. The room went quiet as everyone caught the sound, and then all hell broke loose. Nobody knew what it was or who was doing it and the questions were flying. But Mary knew immediately, even though she hadn't heard it before. She said, "I know who that is. It's Les!" Then everybody wanted to know what it was and how I did it and what I was going to do with it. That's how *Lover* debuted for the first time outside the garage, and based on the reaction it got, it was time to find a record company.

The Capitol Breakthrough

I knew the people at Decca through Bing and Jack Kapp, so I went to them first, but they weren't interested. They thought what I had was interesting, but it was too radical for them. I was in negotiations with Victor for a time, but a misunderstanding squelched the deal, so I had to keep looking.

Capitol was the new kid on the block and I hadn't given them a thought until I was walking out of NBC one day and saw a guy across the street hanging a canvas sign that said "Capitol Records." So I went over and found they had located their offices upstairs over the Music City record store there on Vine Street. In fact, the brother of the guy who owned the record store was Glenn Wallichs, the president of Capitol Records. He, Buddy deSylva and Johnny Mercer had started the company just a few months earlier. I asked the guy hanging the sign who I should talk to about my records, and he said, "Well, you'll have to make an appointment." So I said, "Okay, I'll go make one," and shot up the stairs.

It was late in the afternoon, the end of the workday, and everybody was clearing out. I saw a door that said "Vice President," so I opened it and walked in and there was Jim Conkling putting his toothbrush and socks into a travel bag. I introduced myself, and he said, "Oh, I've heard of you, but I'm on my way out the door to catch a plane for New York. I'll be back in a few days and we'll make an appointment for you then." And I said, "Well, okay, but I've got to play this record for you." There was a turntable there in his office, and he said, "If you know how to operate that thing, go ahead and put it on and we'll listen while I pack."

So I put *Lover* on, and when he hears it, he's just frozen, listening in amazement. He says, "My God, how many of these recordings have you got?" And I say, "I've got 21 more, and this is probably the worst of the lot." And he said, "Well, it's new, it's different, it's a guaranteed hit."

He grabbed a piece of paper and wrote up an agreement, and we both signed it with the understanding that an official contract covering all the details would be drawn up by the lawyers within the week. Then he was off to catch the plane and I was back out on the street thinking, "Holy Christ, what just happened?"

Jim took my word for it that I had the other recordings, but I didn't really have 22 ready to go. *Lover* was the only one I considered ready to be released. The others were still in the process of being created, all in different stages. It took months to build those recordings the way I was doing it, and now that I had the echo delay, there was much more to do. But Jim Conkling was just knocked out. He said, "I've never heard anything like this in my life. It's the damndest thing I've ever heard and it's going to be a hit. You've got a deal." This was in late 1947, and that's how it happened that I signed with Capitol Records instead of one of the other labels.

There was disappointment when Decca and Victor fell through, but it turned out to be a blessing because it directed me to Capitol. They'd only been going for a year or so when we connected, and they had a more progressive attitude. They had Johnny Mercer and Kay Starr, who was doing very well, and were looking for newer things, so it was a natural fit. They were looking for musical innovators, and I was given more freedom with them than I would've had anywhere else.

Artistic License

Thanks to Jim Conkling, they agreed to let me do my recordings in my own studio and deliver the masters to them for release and distribution. This gave me control over what I was doing technically, and with my music, which was absolutely unheard of. This was a time when everything the artist did was controlled by the label, including which songs were recorded and how they were arranged. It was a terribly important break for me to get on board with a company that had enough foresight to stay out of my way and let me run with what I had. It was exactly what I needed, and it was also to their great benefit. During the next few years, Mary and I sold millions of records and were a major factor in establishing Capitol as one of the powerhouse labels of all time.

A short time later, Jim Conkling, Glenn Wallichs and some of the other Capitol guys came to the garage to see what I was doing. I played the 22 recordings for them, one after the other, and they were stunned. Their heads were spinning because they knew what they were hearing was going to turn the recording world upside down. They wanted to get the first record out right away, and there was considerable debate as to which one it should be. When they asked for my choice, I said we should go with one of the weaker ones first, so we'd have somewhere to go on the next one. *Lover* was finished, so it was decided to go with it first, with *Brazil* on the B-side. So I delivered those masters to Capitol, and then it was just a matter of time waiting for the record to be pressed and released.

182

With the release of Lover, the first of my multi-track "New Sound" recordings, Capitol posed me for this gag shot where I am supposedly playing all these guitars at once.

CHAPTER FOURTEEN

Fateful Journey

Mary and I had been committed to each other for over two years now. I was thinking seriously about a change in my personal life, and it was time for her to meet my family. So after a New Year's Eve date with Bing and squaring everything at Capitol, Mary and I hit the road for Waukesha. It felt great to be going home with the news of my solo record deal and the impending release of *Lover*, but there was a problem. Soon after we left California, I started running a fever and feeling sick.

We stopped in Flagstaff to sleep, and when we got in the room, I said to Mary, "Open the windows, I'm dying in this heat." She said, "But it's not hot in here. There's something wrong with you." We're up in the Arizona high country, with the wind blowing, and I decide to get some beer. So I'm walking to this little beer joint, walking down the highway wearing this little sheepskin jacket with no shirt underneath. It's January, colder than hell, and I'm burning up. And I'm thinking, "This isn't right. I should be freezing to death." Something was wrong, but we'd traveled too far to turn back.

After we're back on the road, I go to a doctor, and I'm told I may have Rocky Mountain spotted fever, or undulant fever, or some kind of brucellosis. They misdiagnose this thing and don't know what the hell it is, but I know I'm sick, and getting worse.

We drive on up to Waukesha and spend some time with Mother, and it goes great. Mother was not always one to approve of the women in my life, but she and Mary got along fine. She was terribly excited to hear about my contract with Capitol, and she could see Mary was right for me, so she accepted it with a good heart even knowing I was still married to Virginia. Mary and Mother quickly became friends, which was very important because they were the two most important people in my life. I also introduced her to my Dad, who had married the nurse and changed his ways. He was critical at first but took a liking to her as soon as they got acquainted. It was wonderful that Mary meeting my family went so well, but I was feeling rotten, and still running a fever.

I saw another doctor in Wisconsin, hoping for a cure, but it didn't go my way. So now we've got to go back to California, and I'm supposed to go see George Barnes when we pass through Chicago. George had called and said, "Come on over to the house. I want to hear about Bing and the Andrews Sisters; I want to hear about California." I had said okay, but now I was running a 103 fever and very ill, and had only one thought: to get back to Hollywood where I could rest and kick this thing.

When we got to Chicago, I didn't call George and I didn't stop. We just kept driving, and now we're back on 66, headed west. I always did the driving, but now the fever and chills had me. By the time we got to St Louis, Mary had to take the wheel so I could lie down. We continued on our way, and somewhere down in Missouri, ran into a winter storm.

The Wreck
January 26, 1948

Now it gets hard for me to remember because I've got a terrible blank from the time of the accident. I've tried many times, but it's very difficult to go back and relate to it. My mind just refuses to go there. I don't remember passing through Springfield, but we had gotten into Oklahoma and the further west we went, the worse the weather got. The guy on the radio was saying, "If you don't have to drive, don't, because this storm is nasty and the roads are treacherous." It was afternoon, with sleet, snow and ice covering the highway. If you grew up in Wisconsin, you knew about winter driving, but Mary wasn't used to snow. In fact, she'd never driven in this kind of weather.

Over The Edge

I was lying in the front seat, half asleep listening to the radio, when I heard Mary scream and felt the car swerve. I rose up quickly to see we were sliding sideways up a bridge ramp. I kicked Mary's foot off the brake, and for a very short time did manage to straighten the car out, but it was too late. I remember saying, "This is it," and I know I put my arm up around her, to protect her face, but that's all there is. From reading news reports about it, I know the car went off the side of a railroad overpass and dropped 20 feet into a ravine. There were no seat belts, and we both went through the roof of the convertible as it went off the bridge, along with my guitars and whatever else was in the back seat. It's probably a good thing because the car landed upside down in the frozen river. If we hadn't been thrown out, we'd have been killed.

The accident happened where the railroad crossed under the highway, between the towns of Davenport and Chandler, Oklahoma. There was no traffic due to the storm, so it was hours before we were found. In going off the bridge, our car had broken telephone and telegraph lines running alongside the railroad tracks. It was the interruption of service that alerted the phone company there was a problem, which led to our being found. Otherwise, who knows

185

how long we'd have laid there in the ice and snow.

The police came, and the ambulance, and they took us to the nearest hospital, which was in Chandler. I believe the convertible was towed to Chandler also, but I never saw the car again. I've been told there were photographs in the newspapers showing how badly mangled it was, but I've never seen those pictures.

Mary was banged up but not seriously injured, which was a miracle, but I was busted all to hell. My back, collarbones, a shoulder and six ribs were bro-

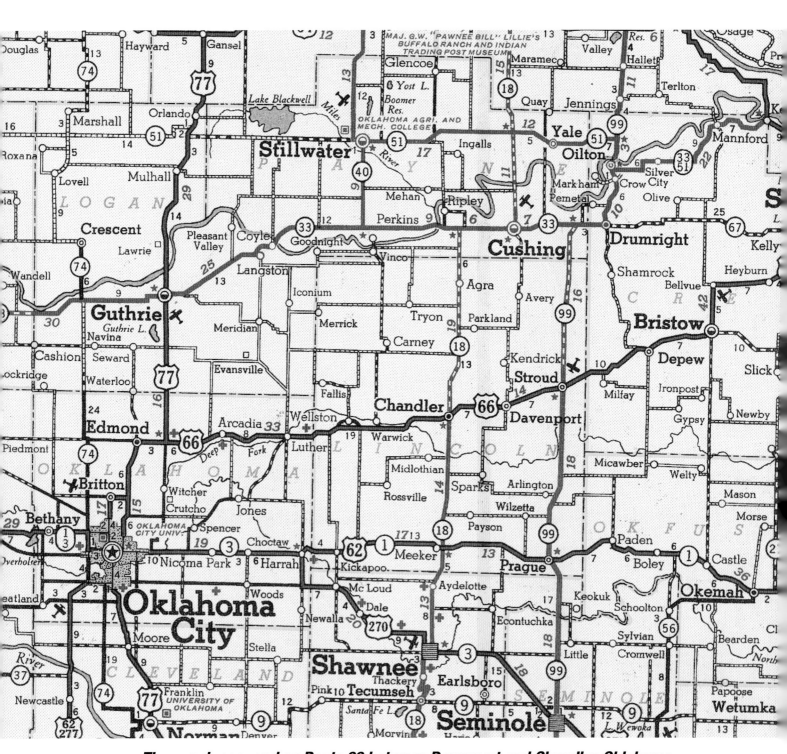

The wreck occurred on Route 66 between Davenport and Chandler, Oklahoma.

ken, I had a fractured pelvis, a punctured spleen, and my nose was smashed. The arm I'd put around Mary, my right arm, was completely shattered and the elbow crushed to a pulp. On top of everything else, I contracted pneumonia lying out there in the snow unconscious for what they said was eight hours before help arrived.

I remember waking up in the hospital and being so relieved to learn Mary was okay. When I heard they were going to transfer me to Oklahoma City, I remembered Ken Wright, my old Scalawags pal, was now living in Oklahoma City. I asked that he be located, and then I was gone again.

So they took me by ambulance to Oklahoma City, and as they were wheeling me into Wesley Hospital, I opened my eyes and there was Ken Wright walking right beside me all the way. And I said, "What happened to you? You look like hell." Ken had the most frightened look on his face, and I was letting him know Rhubarb Red was still alive. I can't tell you why, but seeing him was terribly comforting. He was my friend, and he was there, and it was important. I have always loved him for being there when I needed it. After that, I'm told I passed out and was near death for some time while they worked on me in surgery.

Good Knight

I had something else going for me that night. A surgeon at the hospital, Dr. Robert Knight, just happened to be a longtime fan of my music. We hadn't met, but he knew who I was and was personally involved in saving my life, and my arm. Another doctor there was certain the arm couldn't be saved, and wanted to take it off. And I heard Dr. Knight say, "He's not driving a hay rack, and I'm going to fight to keep it on." A serious difference of opinion was going on out in the hallway, and I could hear what was being said.

When they came back into the room, I said, "Doc Knight, I'm choosing you as the one I'm going to talk to and this other guy has to go." The other doctor was holding a book of some kind, and he slammed it down on the hallway floor when he walked out. I was doped up, and this bit of drama seemed terribly odd. And I told Dr. Knight, "You gotta save my arm."

My elbow was gone and what was left of my arm was in such bad shape that amputation may have been the appropriate medical procedure, but Dr. Knight refused to do it. He said, "Anybody can take it off, but I'm going to try and save it." Then he worked on me for hours in the operating room, tending to my other injuries to stabilize my condition and keep me alive. Later, he did a series of surgeries on the arm, trying to piece it back together enough to save it. And it was the general opinion of everyone involved that if I did survive, I

187

would never play guitar again.

News of the accident and my condition soon spread to the national news, and there were many, including my Dad, who predicted I wasn't going to make it. And I know I nearly died.

There was a point where it was very simple, where dying would've been the easy thing to do. It felt like hanging from a ledge by the tips of your fingers, and it's killing you to hang on. And you think, "Why am I doing this? Let's just let go, and then it will all be over." And I said, "Should I let go?" I saw the light at the end of the tunnel, and I was thinking about going that way, but then I heard the sounds around me coming through, and it was the doctors and nurses working, fighting to save me. And I thought, "If these people are willing to try this hard to keep me alive, then I'll try too." So I decided to fight instead of give up. And Dr. Knight told me later, "We almost lost you. You damn near died." It was rough.

Aftermath

Mary returned home to California and went back to work with Gene Autry, but I wasn't going anywhere. I had pneumonia, and with broken vertebrae and ribs, the coughing was total hell. I was rigged up like a trapeze act in the hospital bed, and it would take me till lunchtime to eat the oatmeal they gave me for breakfast. My mental state was shot. My future as a musician, as an entertainer, as the person I'd always been was one big question mark. Those first weeks in the hospital were a very dark time.

About a month after the accident, *Lover* was released, and just as Jim Conkling had predicted, it shot up the charts. Ken Wright brought a radio so I could hear my record on the air, and not even that cheered me up. I was alive, but my old life was over.

It was while I was in the hospital in Oklahoma that the opportunity to play the Blue Note came up. I was talking to my brother on the phone, and he said, "That record of yours is saturating the Chicago area. It's all I hear." He told me Dave Garroway was playing *Lover* over and over and raving about it on his radio show. Ralph said, "He carries on about it so much, it's embarrassing."

So from the hospital, I called Dave Garroway at WMAQ, where he did a very popular jazz show. And he said, "I'm so enthralled with what you're doing with the electric guitar. I love your sound and what you've done with this recording." Garroway was also the music director for the top jazz club in Chicago. And he said, "I book the acts for the Blue Note, and when you're ready to travel, I want you to come back to Chicago and play an extended engagement." And I said, "I promise you when I'm able and ready to play again, I'll be there."

So playing the Blue Note was something I could look forward to while I was recovering, like having an ace in the hole. It took a year and a half, but we did play there, and the success of that engagement was very important in establishing Mary and I as a successful act.

Time To Think

I passed the time by reading and listening to the radio. Ken Wright would bring me things from the library, and I read one book after another about electronics, audio engineering and human behavior, whatever I could find to take an interest in. After two months in Oklahoma City, the broken bones and other injuries were mending, and I was gradually feeling better. But the right arm was still a mess. Dr. Knight had stayed with me and done as good as he could in saving my arm, but it wasn't working. It wasn't healing and it was getting worse.

It was during this time I got the idea for the synthesizer, when I was day after day laying in that hospital bed thinking about how I could continue if the worst happened and I lost the arm. And that's when it came to me. I had the plans drawn out in detail, but after my arm was saved I didn't pursue it. If I had built it, as far as I know it would have been the first synthesized musical instrument. I still have the original set of detailed plans.

In discussing the situation with my arm, I finally asked Dr. Knight, "Who's your mentor? Who would you turn to with this problem?" And he said, "Dr. Francis McKeaver. He's the best bone specialist in the country, but he's at Good Samaritan Hospital in Los Angeles, and you'd never make it if we try to move you." And I said, "I'll make it. Get me to him."

Back to California

Seats were removed from an airplane to make room, and I was flown back to California on a gurney with a private nurse in attendance. If I remember correctly, this was in late March of 1948, two months after the wreck. When I

189

got to Good Samaritan Hospital, Dr. McKeaver walked in and said, "Well, we can answer one question for you. You've got infectious mononucleosis, that's the cause of your lingering fever." They never did diagnose the fever in Oklahoma, and I had it a year before it finally cleared up.

Once again, the subject of amputation was discussed. The doctors debated whether or not the arm could be stabilized enough to heal, considering the infections and other major problems. Dr. McKeaver and his team decided to take a piece of bone from one of my legs and use it to replace the crushed elbow. A metal plate was to be screwed into place to reconnect my upper arm bone to the forearm, with the grafted piece of leg bone as a living connector in place of the elbow. There would be no more elbow joint. Once it was set and grew into place, the bend in my arm would be permanent. So I told Dr. McKeaver, "Put my forefinger in my bellybutton when you set it. That's how I hold the guitar, and I'll still be able to play." So that's what they did, locking my right arm in the frozen ninety-degree angle I still live with today.

An odd, funny thing happened in the course of that surgery. When they opened up my arm, they were surprised to find Phillips head screws in the bone. Dr. Knight had implanted them in Oklahoma, but Dr. McKeaver wasn't aware of what type they were until they discovered it on the operating table. And he had no Phillips head screwdriver. So someone was sent out to buy a Phillips head screwdriver and bring it back to the operating room. It was sterilized, and the operation continued.

I came out of it in a chest cast that went completely around my body and down to my hips, and also went out my right arm, which was crooked at 90 degrees and held out from my body with a stick between my arm and my hip. They just took a broom handle and sawed it off to fit and built it into the cast. So they plastered me up and I was in that cast for six months. My left arm was free, and I developed improved dexterity with my left hand through constant use.

The surgery was successful, but there was a long way to go. My right hand stuck out of the cast and was terribly weak and swollen, so I started right away to exercise my fingers, doing whatever I could to try and restore feeling and movement. It was similar to the situation after the shock at Electra Court. The doctors said there was potential nerve damage, that I shouldn't count on regaining full use of the hand, but I wasn't buying it. I was determined it was going to come back and that I would play again, even if I had to learn how all over again.

191

CHAPTER FIFTEEN

On The Mend

It was rejuvenating to be back in Hollywood, and to know my arm was finally starting to heal. By now my second son Gene had been born, and Virginia took Rusty and Gene and went back to Chicago, and Mary moved in with me on Curson Avenue. This was a frustrating time of recuperation, and she took care of me like an angel. I don't know what I would've done without her.

Right after I was taken back to California, a union man came to visit me at Good Samaritan, and it was another miracle. This little hunchbacked man came into the room, so hunched over he could only look at the floor. I'm lying there looking at this little man who's looking at the floor, and he says, "Hello Mr. Paul, I'm from the musicians union. We're sorry you're having such a rough time, but you're very lucky because you're insured by the musician's union." But I wasn't insured by the union and never had been. He was there because the union people in L.A. loved me. Spike Wallace and Phil Fisher and all those guys, they just got together and fixed it up so I was covered. They picked up my medical bills in California, and it saved my butt. In my memory, that's one of the kindest things anybody ever did for anybody else, much less for me.

The success of *Lover* and *Brazil* was another terribly positive factor. Both sides went high on the charts and Capitol was selling a ton of records. "Les Paul and the New Sound" was everywhere. And it was a new sound. Nothing like it had ever before been heard.

As soon as I was able to get from the house back to the garage, Jim Conkling came to see me. He said, "You're hot and it's time to release another record. What have you got?" *Lover* was the only recording I'd finished before the accident. *Brazil* had been acceptable as a B-side, but I didn't have anything else ready. And Jim said, "You're going to be in that cast for months. What are we going to do?" And I said, "Well, we'll improvise."

Adapting To The Limitations

I could fret okay with my left hand, but couldn't get my right hand on the strings because of the cast. It was very awkward, and there was no way I could hold a guitar in a playable position. My solution was to take a guitar stand and have it altered to hold my guitars at a height and angle matching the arm cast. The guitar had to be almost vertical and raised considerably in order to get my right

192

hand on the strings. I couldn't grasp a straight pick, so we jammed a thumb pick on my swollen thumb, slapped a guitar into the elevator stand, and I starting putting down parts.

One of the first recordings I finished while wearing the body cast was *Caravan*. I took the disk from before the wreck and used the aluminum guitar to add the lead track. And then I got an idea. Lloyd and Vern were there, and I said, "I want you to go out and find a pump organ." So my buddies found one and brought it into the studio. While I pumped with my feet and chorded with my left hand, the guys swiveled the volume pot on the mixer off and on, off and on, in time with the music, and another side was finished. So the odd sound you hear in *Caravan* is that pump organ, and that's how I got my first wah-wah effect.

It was while working on *What Is This Thing Called Love* I first played my own bass part, using the lower strings on one of my klunkers. The sound transferred to disk better than an actual bass, producing a fuller sounding lower end. I used the Log to lay down the lead and sent it on to Capitol with an instrumental called

Hip-Billy Boogie for the B-side, again using the Log. The record was released in April of '48, and was another immediate hit. *What Is This Thing Called Love* went to the Top Ten and kept Capitol off my back for a while. And that's how it went. I finished a number of recordings during the spring and summer of '48, and gave them all to Capitol to be released over a period of time.

It was also during this time we recorded Mary's first vocal for Capitol, a song I wrote called *Until I Hold You Again*. It was recorded in the garage with people rounded up from the neighborhood as a background chorus. I layered drums, banjo, bass and guitar parts together, and then added the vocal chorus

193

A secretary at Capitol Records signs my cast.

and Mary's lead to finish it. When we were getting ready to record the group, I said, "Everybody sing out, but don't try to sound like singers. Just be yourselves." It was unrehearsed, and that's what I wanted. Plain, normal people singing, where some have a good ear and some don't. The record didn't chart, but it made some noise and laid the groundwork for what was to come.

Jim Conkling was concerned with Capitol's momentum, but I had my own reason for needing to sell more records. It was a tremendous blessing when the union stepped in to take care of my medical expenses in California, but the medical bills in Oklahoma amounted to many thousands of dollars, which I had personally paid. From the time they put me in that Oklahoma City hospital, no matter how ill I was, they were there with a pen and checkbook and I had to approve a check for $10,000 every couple of weeks. By the time I returned to California, I was completely wiped out. The royalty checks from *Lover* started coming in just in time to keep us alive financially.

Looking For A Voice

While I was laid up, I did a lot of thinking about where I wanted to go with my career, and where I could go with it after the accident. My experiences had been pointing to it all along, and I realized one of the things I need-

194

ed was a vocalist, a girl singer.

The facts were from different worlds, but they added up. One world was doing the tour with the Andrews Sisters. When my trio and I would come out and play our jazzy stuff, the audience would applaud like, 'That's good. That's very nice.' Then the Andrews girls would start singing, and the crowd would go nuts. They were connecting with the audience by giving them what they wanted to see and hear, and I got the message. Another world was when I did the country radio shows with Mary. When there's a guy and a gal and they're playing off each other to the audience, it's something everybody can relate to. So that was another message, another piece of the puzzle.

I also knew that with the new technique of multi-track recording, I didn't want to limit the rest of my career to playing all the parts on instrumental arrangements. I knew the public would eventually tire of it, no matter what I did to keep topping myself. And here was another big fact: what is bigger than a vocal, especially a ballad vocal? Nothing. You've got to have that if you want to go as far as you can go. In thinking this out, I said to Mary, "Help me find a singer."

So we began looking for a singer, and several were considered. Rosemary Clooney, Kay Starr, Doris Day, and others auditioned, but I couldn't make up my mind. I still had no thought Mary was the one I was looking for, and neither did she.

Club 400

Now we jump ahead to 1949, a year and a half after the accident. Mary and I had gone to Mayo Clinic to have the last cast removed from my arm.

The first time Mary and I performed together was in my home town of Waukesha at the Club 400, which was owned by my dad and my brother. My old friend Warren Downey played bass for us.

And the doctor said, "Well, practice a little bit each day and in six weeks you should be able to go back to work." I said, "What about six days? I've got to play in Waukesha." My Dad and brother were opening a saloon there called the Club 400, and I had agreed to play for their opening night.

We drove on to Waukesha, and during the trip, my arm puffed up terribly. I called Dr. McKeaver and said, "My arm is like a tomato." He laughed and said, "Well, prop it up on some pillows and the swelling will go down. Just take it easy and you'll be okay."

I had called ahead and asked my brother to find a bass player and a guitar player so I could play the job as a trio. But when we get there, I find out my brother hasn't hired anybody. He said, "I thought you beat your foot loud enough on the floor, you didn't need anybody else." So I called my old bass player buddy, Warren Downey, and he said he'd be there, but there was no guitar player to be found. I needed a rhythm guitar to go with the bass to make this thing work, so I looked at Mary and said, "I've got an extra guitar in the car, you're my rhythm guitar player."

Well, she was back-pedaling fast because one, she had a problem with stage fright; two, she didn't want to embarrass herself in front of my family and friends; and three, she didn't know the lyrics and chord changes to my

196

songs. We'd been together nearly four years by this time, so she'd heard my arrangements a thousand times. She was a solid rhythm player and knew the basic chords, but she'd never done any pop stuff, and that was the problem. So I said, "I'll get someone to come in and read off the lyrics to you, I'll call out the chord changes as we go, and we'll be fine." She was reluctant and terribly nervous about it, but finally agreed to do it.

First Date

I was a little nervous too, but we got up in front of the hometown crowd, and we did it. I believe our first song was Mary singing *I Only Want A Buddy, Not A Sweetheart.* We followed with some of her other cowboy songs and some pop things like *Sweet Sue* and *Jealous.* The crowd was calling for *Lover,* but there was no way Mary and I could reproduce the recorded arrangement in that situation. And there was another problem. Due to the condition of my arm, I was having a rough time and couldn't finish the songs. To cover it, I started joking around telling stories. And that was the first time I came out and started kidding around on stage like I do now on Monday nights.

In trying to do the songs Mary didn't know, I would call out the chord changes as we played along. When she missed one, I'd stop the music and say, "Wait a minute, what are you doing there?" And she'd say, "Oh, did I hit another wrong one?" And I'd say, "Yeah, here's what you should play there." She'd play it, the audience would laugh, we'd laugh, and on we'd go. It all happened very naturally and fell into place just like we'd planned it. The crowd adored her singing and we got through the night despite my difficulties. And that's when it dawned on me that Mary and I could perform together and do something unique. That's when I knew I'd found my singer, and that she'd been right there with me the whole time.

But my Dad didn't agree. During the show, he was sitting on the stairs watching us perform and he kept looking at me and shaking his head 'no' because he didn't approve of what he saw happening. Afterwards I said, "Dad, it'll work. She understands what I want her to do, she never misses a note, and she's the one I want to be with in life." But he still shook his head and said, "You're a roughneck and she's too delicate. I wouldn't do it." He thought the world of Mary, and he knew how driven I was with my music and ideas. He didn't want to see her go down that road with me because he saw what was bound to happen.

197

Opening The Stage Door

The next day, Mary and Warren and I set up down in the basement and started finding our way. The first song we rehearsed together with the thought that we were going to carry this thing forward was *Sentimental Journey*, a number one smash for Doris Day. Mary had the gift of solid rhythm, and when I heard her voice wrapped around that song, I knew it was going to work. Now all I had to do was find a spot for us to get the act into shape, a place where we'd have an audience.

So we got in the car and drove down National Avenue in Milwaukee until we saw a little jazz joint. It was a little club called the Stage Door and the marquee said "John Kirby and his Sextet."

It was the middle of the afternoon when I went inside and asked the bartender where to find the owner. He pointed his finger toward the ceiling and nodded toward the stairway. So I went up the stairs and knocked on the door. It's a hot day, and this guy comes to the door stripped to the waist. He says, "Yeah, what do you want?" And I said, "Well, I'm here to talk to you about a job." And he said, "Well, the act I just had in here died, and I lost my ass. I'm shuttin' the place down." And I said, "Will you consider staying open if I'll bring my group in and play for nothing? I've got a different thing going with this group and I think you can make some money." And he said, "What have I got to lose? Okay."

Mary Gets Her Name

Now we've got a place to rehearse with a live audience, and I've got to name the act. So I grabbed a Milwaukee phone book and said to Mary, "We're going to pick a name for you, and it's not going to be Mary Lou." I'd been calling her Mary for four years and loved the name, so that wasn't going to change. It was a last name I was going through the listings looking for, a rich sounding, and short name. There was Rockefeller, Astor, and then I ran across Ford. And I said, "Hey, what about Mary Ford?" And she said, "Whatever you think, Les." So I said, "Yep, that's it. That's your new name. Mary Ford."

So we started working nightly at this little Milwaukee club, practicing hard to get our routine together. Crowds were small at first, but by the time we closed out the engagement a couple of months later, we were the hottest ticket in town. Our last night there, the night we closed, there was a line of people a block long waiting to get in.

When we finished our run at the Stage Door, Mary and I had been away from home for three months and it was time to take a break. We had a few weeks before the Blue Note, and I needed to get back to California to do some recording and have Dr. McKeaver treat my arm.

198

Les Paul At Home

Right after we got back to Hollywood, I made some inquiries and landed a syndicated radio show with NBC. It was another sustainer, at first called "Les Paul at Home." The name of the show came from having my own recording studio, which was now becoming well known, but we soon changed the name to include Mary.

I started out producing the 15-minute shows using the two disk cutters, creating finished programs in the garage that were then delivered to the network for broadcast. NBC aired the show every Friday evening on their west coast feed to all their stations west of the Mississippi River. Each episode followed a pattern, which included Mary's vocals, my playing, and a running gag woven through each episode.

Mary was always referring to my "electronic gadgets" and we had fun writing scripts around the multi-layering, which was a featured element. In one episode, Mary decided to connect her Hoover to my equipment to see if she could vacuum all the rooms in the house at the same time. In another, I invented the gas-powered guitar, which led to laughing gas and a lot of crazy sound effects.

We made recordings of songs in the process of producing the shows, some of which were released as phonograph records by Capitol. *Cryin'* and *Dry My Tears* are examples. They were released as the A and B-sides of a single in 1950. *Dry My Tears*, the B-side, was also used as our radio theme song.

We were paid just $150 per show, so the money wasn't much, but Mary's voice and my new sound got a lot of exposure and it helped establish us as an up and coming act. The downside was that we were obligated to produce a new show every week, and that meant we were stuck in the garage because we couldn't get the effects we needed anywhere else.

CHAPTER SIXTEEN

The Gift From Bing

I didn't see it coming, but when Mary and I went back to California and got the new radio show, I was about to get my first tape recorder. And when I did, it set us free. Magnetic tape was the beginning of a revolution in audio recording, and how it came full circle to me through Bing is a terribly interesting story.

You have to go back to 1945, at the end of the war, when Germany was defeated. The Allies were occupying all the Reich's scientific research facilities, and a couple of Signal Corp officers, Richard Ranger and Jack Mullin, were among those assigned to investigate the communications technology and equipment which had been developed by the German military. In doing their thing, they discovered the magnetophone, a recording machine the Germans had invented, along with magnetic recording tape. The army confiscated these devices for government purposes, but Richard Ranger and Jack Mullin each managed to privately ship a small number back to the States before leaving Germany, along with reels of ferric-coated recording tape. Disassembled and shipped in several packages, two magnetophones landed in Jack Mullin's garage in San Francisco, and two went to Richard Ranger in New Jersey.

A Glimpse of the Future

When Sherman Fairchild came out to California to take measurements at the garage studio, he was impressed with what he saw and heard us doing with disk recording. A short time later, when he was made aware of Dick Ranger's tape machines, he suggested I should be informed about it.

At this time, I was in New York to play a show with Paul Whiteman and Judy Garland. We were rehearsing in the empty theatre when this little guy came walking toward us waving his arms. And I said, "Are you trying to get to me?" He said, "Yes, I need to talk to you. I'm Colonel Richard Ranger, and I have something Sherm Fairchild thought you would like to know about." And I said, "Okay, what have you got?" And he said, "I have a German recording machine that records on coated tape instead of disks or wire. It's called a tape recorder, and I have it over in Jersey if you'd like to see it."

Of course, I did want to see it, and went with Colonel Ranger over to Belleville, New Jersey where his electronics workshop was located. On the way, he explained how the tape machines had been discovered in Germany, and how he managed to acquire a couple of them. And when I saw this magnetophone, I went into shock. I was just stunned because there it was, right in front of me. And that's when I said, "They did it! They figured out how to flatten the wire."

Spreading the Magnetic Word

Bing had been involved in a serious dispute with the sponsor over his desire to pre-record his shows, which NBC wouldn't allow due to the inferior broadcast quality of transcriptions. As a result, he quit NBC and the Kraft Music Hall show and moved over to ABC, who agreed to let him try pre-recording with the understanding he'd have to go back to doing all the shows live if the ratings went down. Philco was his new sponsor, and Bing was in the process of putting his new show together when Colonel Ranger introduced himself to me and demonstrated his tape machine.

I was aware of Bing's problems, so the first thing I did when I got back to California was immediately tell him about the magnetophone. And he said, "A what?" I said, "It's a tape machine, a recording device, and it's an answer to your problem. You can be at home, on the golf course or anywhere you want to be with this piece of machinery, and you can record good, clean audio." I explained the advantages of how it worked, and he said, "Find this guy and get him out here." This was the first step in Bing getting involved with tape, and it would come back to me in a big way.

Colonel Ranger came out to Hollywood and demonstrated his Rangertone recorder, based on the design of the German magnetophone. Bing was very impressed and wanted to immediately place a large order, but Colonel Ranger said he could only make one or two a year. And Bing said, "Well, that's not going to work. I have to find someone who can build a number of them quickly because I need them now." So right there is where Colonel Ranger missed the boat and Ampex entered the picture.

Ampex

When Jack Mullin and his partner, Bill Palmer, demonstrated the magnetophone in San Francisco, it created a huge sensation. One of the people who heard about it and took an interest was Mr. Poniatoff, the guy who created the Ampex Company. When he saw first-hand what the German machine could do, he jumped on it and brought Jack Mullin into Ampex to supervise the engineering of an improved American-made version of it.

Mullin next demonstrated his machine for Bing, and was invited to record

201

a performance of the Philco show for testing purposes. And this is terribly interesting because that same show was also recorded on disk, and when the two recordings were compared, it was no contest. Jack Mullin was then hired to supervise the recording of all Bing's shows, using his two modified and improved magnetophones and an improved version of the tape he brought back from Germany.

Convinced that magnetic tape was the way to go, Bing went personally to Ampex and laid a check for $50,000 on the president's desk. He gave the money to them at no interest, with no obligation at all other than the fact that it was for them to build a group of machines as quickly as they could. So Ampex went to work, and six months later, the first Ampex Model 200 tape recorders were delivered to ABC in Hollywood and put into service, replacing Mullin's magnetophones.

The Tape Breakthrough

It was the off-season in '47 when Jack Mullin was invited to tape record a show, and what they got on tape that night became the first show of the new season a couple of months later. I remember this because I was there. Bing called and said, "Les, I want you there next Thursday." And I said, "Okay. What are we doing?" And Bing said, "We're recording the first Philco show on tape, and I want you to sit in the control room and observe so you can tell me what's not being done properly."

So that's what I did. I sat there while the show was being performed and recorded, taking it all in with the aim of seeing what could be improved. After the show, we were driving down Sunset Boulevard and Bing said, "Well, what did you figure out?" And I said, "How much do you pay the engineer?" He looked at me like I was nuts and said, "Hell, I don't know." And I said, "Well, I'll tell you. You pay your producer $5,000 a show and he sits there on his ass and doesn't do a damned thing. And your engineer, who does everything important to your sound, gets $75 a show and also empties the trash and sweeps the floor. What you need is a $5,000 engineer." And Bing said, "Who should I get?" I said, "The best guy I know, Murdo Mackenzie."

So Murdo was hired as Bing's technical director and began working with Jack Mullin to produce Bing's ABC show on tape.

Using his two upgraded German machines and a pair of scissors, Mullen edited around the best vocals and skits, and there was great improvement in the show. And this is also when the laugh track was created and used for the first time.

After the Model 200 had been out for a year or so, Ampex came out with the greatly improved Model 300, which established a new standard of audio fidelity for recorded sound and led to the first NAB standards, based on Harold Lindsay's design patents.

Turning Point

One day in July 1949, about 18 months after the accident, out of the blue, Bing pulled up at our house on Curson Avenue. Mary was in the backyard hanging clothes on the line, and I was back in the garage working on our new NBC show, laying down parts using my guitar stand contraption. Bing came in and said, "Hey Les, come on outside, I've got something for you."

So we went out to Bing's Cadillac, and when he went to the trunk, I was expecting to see a Philco radio or a set of golf clubs. I had no idea what he was up to until he raised the lid, and Holy Christ, there sat one of the first Ampex Model 300 tape machines. And he said, "This is yours, for what you've done for me."

This unexpected gift was Bing's way of saying thanks for putting him in touch with the whole idea of magnetic tape, and I was very surprised because up until that moment, I didn't know the Model 300 was available, nor could I afford one. Bing didn't own any interest in Ampex, but Crosby Enterprises had become their exclusive sales agent, which proved to be very profitable. So he was returning the favor full circle. It was a gesture of respect and friendship I'll never forget, and it changed my life forever.

I had one good arm, and between the two of us we got this big thing out of Bing's trunk and into the control room. Then Bing said, "Well, I'll leave you with your toys. Have fun." So just like that, I've got my first tape recorder.

203

After Bing left, I immediately went back to working on the radio show because there was a deadline for delivering it to NBC, and I was always getting it to them just in time. It was the fourth show I was working on, and while I was recording it on disk, I kept staring at the tape machine. I hadn't turned it on, hadn't even plugged it in, I just kept looking at it and thinking. And I very quickly began to realize that I could use the tape recorder to do what I was doing with the two disk cutters if I could figure out how to do sound on sound on tape.

And that's when it hit me. I grabbed a piece of paper and wrote down the idea that was suddenly there in my head, and it was like God had done it. The idea just flashed into my mind that the way to do it was to add a fourth head on the machine, and I immediately drew out a rough design for doing it.

Then I went hobbling into the house yelling, "I've got it! I've got it!" Mary came out of the little laundry room next to the kitchen, and said, "What have you got?" And I said, "I've got a new invention, the tape recorder, and I just figured out how to do sound-on-sound with it." And she said, "What in the world are you talking about?"

So I told her about Bing coming over and giving me the tape machine, and showed her my drawing to explain what I had realized could now be done. And Mary said, "What does this mean to us, what's it all about?" And I said, "It means all the stuff we've been confined to doing on two disk recorders, we can now do on one tape machine!"

I was talking about what it took to produce our radio show, multi-layering tracks with the disk recorders like I'd done on *Lover* and *Caravan* and *Nola*. I was talking about the first sound-on-sound on tape, which led to the first true multi-track recordings and the eight-track machine Ampex later built for me. And it's then I told Mary, "Forget the laundry, forget everything because there's something much bigger. We can now do our radio show without the garage. We can do it with the tape recorder and still play the Blue Note in Chicago. Just toss everything aside and start packing."

So Mary immediately began to close up the house and pack while I called Dave Garroway in Chicago to finalize the dates for our engagement at the Blue Note, just as I had promised. Then I went back to the garage to finish the last radio show produced on disk and sort out the equipment we would need to take with us.

At this early stage, nobody knew more about tape recorders than Jack Mullin, so I quickly went to him with questions I had about wiring in the fourth head. With his input, I drew out the design plan for what I wanted to do, which was add a second playback head to my Ampex recorder.

Then I called Ampex and told them I'd blown a head on my 300 and need-

The Ampex 300 could record at 7.5 ips or 15 ips. This photo shows where I added the extra head.

ed to order another one. I did this because I didn't want them to know what I was up to. I wanted to keep the idea under my hat until I could experiment with it and see where it was going to go. I gave instructions for the new head to be sent to the St. Lawrence Hotel in Chicago, where we would be staying during the Blue Note engagement.

All these things happened in a very short period of time, and then we were packing the car. Besides the tape machine, I took the little mixer Wally Jones built for me, my guitars and modified Fender amp, one microphone and a mic stand, a couple of pairs of headphones, cords and connectors, a few tools and a soldering iron, and that was it. Mary packed everything else we needed, our clothes and personal stuff, I shut down the studio and locked up the house, and we took off for Chicago in my 1942 Cadillac.

CHAPTER SEVENTEEN

A New Beginning

Leaving the security of our home and studio behind worried Mary terribly. From the moment we were in the car driving away, she kept saying constantly, all the way to New Mexico, "But what if your invention is not right? What if it doesn't work?" And I would say, "It's right. Don't worry about it. It'll work, I guarantee it." We kept on driving, and she kept repeating, "But you haven't tried it. It's just a drawing on paper. What will we do if it doesn't work?"

So all the way across the desert, across the Great Plains, Mary keeps saying, "Oh no, it'll never work." And I keep saying, "It's gonna work, believe me, it's gonna be great." But with Mary's constant doubting, I began to think maybe I was making a mistake, and the closer we got to Chicago, the less sure I was. I was worried because if it didn't work, there was no way we could do the radio show properly.

I was still in rough shape from the accident. When the big cast came off, I had immediately been hit with extremely painful sciatica, and I had to wear a brace on my back and use a crutch to get around. The medical bills from places other than L.A. were still eating us up, and I knew if I blew the radio show, there would be consequences much more costly than the $150 a week we got paid for it. So we rolled into Chicago excited about playing the Blue Note, but nervous about meeting our contract for the radio show and whether or not my idea for sound-on-sound was going to work.

The Theory Is Proven

When we got to Chicago, the new playback head from Ampex was waiting for me at the St. Lawrence Hotel. So the first thing we did, before we informed the Blue Note or Garroway or anybody else we had arrived, was take the tape machine up to our room and set it up with my mixer and our microphone. We had taken a chance on my idea, and I couldn't wait to find out if it was going to work.

As soon as we got the equipment into our room, I grabbed a phone book and started looking for somebody to drill holes in the 300 so I could mount the fourth head on it. And in the yellow pages, I found a guy with a drill, and his name was Goodspeed. And I said, "That's the man. Goodspeed has got to be the guy."

So Mr. Goodspeed brings his drill up to the room, and says, "Okay, what size do you want these holes to be, and where do you want them?" I'd already marked the spots on the Ampex, so I tell him the screw size, he puts in the bit, and drills the first hole through the metal transport plate. And then it hits me. There's all kinds of wiring and mechanics underneath, and I didn't think to look before he drilled. It's a tremendous relief when we look inside and discover nothing damaged. I could've blown the whole thing right there, but we got lucky.

After Goodspeed drills the second hole, I mount the new head on the machine and wire it in the way Jack Mullin showed me. And it's slow going because I'm walking with a crutch because of the sciatica. Not a cane, a single crutch, and still having problems with my arm, leg and back. So I'm hobbling around and having to use my left hand, but I finally get it done. And now it's time to find out if my idea is going to work.

I started the tape and recorded Mary saying, "One, two, three, four; one, two, three, four." Then I rewound and started recording again while Mary said, "Hello, hello, hello." And when I played it back, we heard, "One, two, three, four, hello, hello, hello." And that was it. We had sound on sound. My idea worked great, just like I thought it would.

And Holy Christ, what a thrill it was. I threw the crutch in the air and Mary and I danced around the room out of pure joy. And I said, "Mary, I'm doing the show without my crutch. Leave the damn thing in the room. The invention works!" And I walked all the way to the elevator without it and didn't feel any pain in my leg or back because it no longer mattered. We were just floating because it was such a great relief. So then we went down and opened the show at the Blue Note, and got fired.

The Blue Note

Opening night at the Blue Note was a Monday in late August, and the place was jammed. Gene Autry was in Chicago at the time, and he was there. Ella Fitzgerald, Billie Holiday, Artie Shaw, critics from all the trades and newspapers, they were all there to hear Les Paul the jazz musician. There was also a sizable group of country fans who remembered my old Chicago days and were there to hear Rhubarb Red. Everybody in the place knew about the accident and my physical problems, and they were waiting to see if I could still play the way they remembered.

This was my first important appearance since the wreck, and the place was completely sold out thanks to Dave Garroway, who had done a tremendous job publicizing us on his radio show. He also booked the engagement and arranged for us to be paid $1,000 a week. He was one of my biggest fans ever.

Opening night, I decided to have a little fun with Dave as a way of saying thanks. He hadn't arrived when we began our first set, so I told the audience, "When Dave Garroway comes in, when I say the word 'berfsk' I want everybody to cheer and applaud." Dave arrives while I'm doing a guitar number, and all of a sudden I stop playing, lean close to the mic and say, "Berfsk." Right on cue, everybody stands up and faces him, clapping and cheering and calling his name as he's walking into the room. Garroway never got applause like that in his life, and he can't figure what the hell has happened. He's got the most bewildered expression, and the whole house is falling down laughing. He was in shock. But he was a wonderful, talented person, very successful in his own career, and a dear friend who helped me many times.

Breaking the Dress Code

For our first performance, Mary wore just a simple dress, the kind you would wear around the house, nothing fancy at all. Warren wore an open collar shirt, no tie or anything, and I had on loafers and was dressed very casually, and we went on and did the show. And after one night, we were axed.

There was a pay phone located right beside the stage, and the manager of the place, a guy named Frank Holzfiend, placed a call to General Artists, the booking agency in New York. We were right there on the stage and could hear him saying the act Garroway had recommended was no good and he was firing us. He said, "Here's this gal playing all the wrong chords and she's got a gingham dress, and Les Paul is making phone calls with his shoe. I gotta get rid of them quick because they're terrible. Who can you send to take their place?" And they said they could get Louis Armstrong, but it would be at least a week before he could get there.

So that night, after the show was over, Frank told us what he didn't like about the act. It was the fact that we didn't dress as he thought professional entertainers should dress, that we didn't wear matching uniforms, that we were far too casual for a swanky place like the Blue Note. He was used to groups coming in wearing tuxedoes, or Dixieland outfits, with their singers in evening gowns. We were just too different, and it was quite a shock for him to see how relaxed we were on stage, and how we just joked around with the audience and had a good time mixing jazz standards with country stuff. It was a whole new thing for him, and since he didn't buy it, he assumed the audience wouldn't either. He told us the least we could do while waiting for Louis Armstrong to arrive was to dress up.

Mary and I talked it over and decided we should satisfy Frank by getting some flashier clothes. So we went out the next day and bought Mary a gown, dressed Warren up with a shirt and tie, and got a tuxedo and some new shoes for me to wear. In the meantime, the reviews of our opening night had come out, and they were all fantastic. Billboard said we were refreshingly different and bound to be one of the biggest club acts in the business. All the important Chicago reviews were very positive.

So that afternoon, when we returned to the club with our new duds, Frank Holzfiend throws his arms around us and says, "Where the hell have you guys been, I've been trying to find you." And I said, "We've been out buying the clothes you want us to wear." And he says, "Well, don't wear 'em. Wear what you've been wearing 'cause you're a hit!" He had all the reviews from all the papers laid out for us to read, and was very happy to have been proven wrong. So Frank did a complete turnaround, we kept our act the way it was, and we all had a big laugh about it.

Sound-On-Sound

As soon as we finished our opening night performance, we went back up to the room and went right to work with the tape machine. We were up all night putting a new radio show together, which I sent off to NBC the next day in order to meet our deadline.

NBC at that time had a rule that no tape machines could be used on the air. All the networks had that rule in the early going because tape was too new and its reliability had not been proven. So we produced our shows on the Ampex and shipped the tapes back to NBC, who then transferred them to disk for broadcast.

After years of being anchored to the two disk recorders, the tape machine was a great advancement, but the sound-on-sound was very tricky. The extra playback head enabled us to hear what we had recorded on the previous pass. And as we heard it, we sang and played along with it, and the whole thing combined was recorded as a new track on the same tape.

Let's say take one is Mary singing a harmony part with me playing rhythm. Now, we're going to play that first take back and add other parts to get take two. When you press record, you hear the playback of the previous take before it gets to the erase head, so you have the privilege of hearing what you did on the first pass and adding what you want as the second pass is made. But there's a catch. You now have the two takes combined on the tape, but in the process of recording it, the first take is erased and is now a generation down on your new take.

It also meant that Mary had to lay down her vocal parts in a backwards order, and I had to do the same thing with all the instrumental parts. In other words, the most unimportant parts went on first, and the most important parts, the lead vocal and guitar, went on last so they wouldn't get buried in the mix. Mary had a tremendous talent for being able to do this, and it was not an easy thing to do. I wouldn't even try it now.

Now the plot thickens because with the tape machine, if you made a mistake on the third pass, you couldn't go back to the second pass like you could on a disk. With the disk method, if you made a mistake on the disk you were cutting, you only had to re-do that one part because everything else was saved on the previous disk. But working with just one tape machine, there was nothing to go back to. Whether you blew it on the third pass or the twenty-ninth pass, when you made that mistake, you were done. You had to go back to one and start the whole process over again. This happened to us a few times, and it was very frustrating. So we learned you just don't make a mistake, and the discipline required turned us into professionals.

Goofus

The first Capitol release recorded on the Ampex was *Goofus*. Mary and I heard Wayne King's band playing it at the Aragon Ballroom, and then went up to our room at the St. Lawrence Hotel and recorded it for one of our radio shows. Capitol pulled my recording out of the show and released it, and *Goofus* was another Top Twenty instrumental hit in the fall of 1950.

When we recorded the radio shows, I made sure each song we recorded was clear at the beginning and at the ending. There was no talking or anything else over the intro or ending of any song we did for the radio show. We made each song record length so the recordings could be used later for phonograph records. And Mary said, "But half of this stuff just has to do with the radio show." And I said, "That's why we don't interfere with the music when we mix it into the radio show; so we can take it out and use it as we need to for any other purpose."

So I put in the bits about the gas-powered guitar, the Les Paulverizer and all those other things, and they were cute as hell for radio, but at the same time, we were cutting records to use with Capitol.

In recording *Goofus,* I used what I called the 'pucka-pucka' sound. It was a simple technique of using the right wrist and heel of my picking hand to mute the strings slightly so when you picked the string, it went "thuck." I'd been fooling around with it for several years, and had used it previously on *Dry My Tears*, but this was the first time I used it on a hit record. In no time, every guitar player in the country was doing it, calling it 'chicken-pickin' or pizzicato, but my name for it when I introduced it was 'pucka-pucka'.

We went on to have a terribly successful run, packing the house every night, and Frank Holzfiend said he'd never seen such a mixture of people in his club. There were jazz hipsters and country fans mixed in with all the high brows, and everybody got along and had a great time. It was a wonderful way for Mary and I to launch our career together, and to start putting the accident behind us. We left the Blue Note feeling confident about our act, and our future.

211

CHAPTER EIGHTEEN

Back To New York

After the Blue Note, when Mary and I decided to tour our way to New York, we lost Warren Downey. I was sorry to see him go because he'd been with us since the beginning at Club 400, and the three of us had become comfortable with our act. Warren was one of my first musician buddies, going all the way back to childhood days in Waukesha, and he loved what we were doing, but he had plenty of work in Chicago and didn't want to leave his family to go on the road. So Warren left the group and was replaced by Ed Stapleton, another Chicago bass player.

Our first engagement after the Blue Note was in Rock Island, Illinois, and one night a drunk in the audience kept asking for *Rock Island Line*, the old railroad song. When I told him we didn't know it, he said, "Well then, play anything with a rock in it." And I said, "The only thing I know with a rock in it is *Little Rock Getaway*. It's an old piano number and I've never played it on the guitar, but I'll give it a shot."

So I played *Little Rock Getaway,* and the Rock Island audience loved it. After the show, we went back to our room and recorded it, and used the recording to finish the radio show we were working on. The tape was sent to California for broadcast on NBC, and later, *Little Rock Getaway* was pulled out of the show, released as a single, and became another of my instrumental hits for Capitol. And it came from an audience request in Rock Island, Illinois.

Minding The Audience

The informality of our act allowed for spontaneous interplay with the audience, and after starving as a jazz musician earlier in my career, I had learned to pay attention to what made them happy. If they liked a song, we kept it. If a song didn't get a good response after we tried it a time or two, we ditched it. I would never have given a thought to *Little Rock Getaway*, but when it went over so well in Rock Island, we kept it and ran with it.

We often worked out arrangements for new songs while we were performing, and I would sometimes involve the audience by asking if what we were doing should be faster or slower, higher or lower or whatever. It added humor to the show, and also helped me cover for my weak arm, which was still causing problems. But more importantly, learning what the audience wanted and then giving it to them taught me how to make better commercial recordings for Capitol. And this wasn't being done by chance. Mary and I were doing it by design, based on an idea that came to me back in Chicago.

The Blue Note Realization

One night after a set at the Blue Note, I said to Mary, "Let's go take a walk and get a breath of air." The Blue Note was a downstairs club, so we went up and out to the street, and right next door was a liquor store. I took Mary by the hand and pulled her into the place and told the counterman I wanted to buy a little bottle of whiskey. And he said, "What brand and what size?" I said, "I don't care. See that tiny little bottle there, that sample size? Give me that bottle right there." We went back out and Mary said, "What in the world are you doing?" She was puzzled because neither of us were whiskey drinkers.

There was an alley there between the buildings, and we walked back into it with this sample shot of booze. And then I said, "We've got a problem." She said, "What's our problem? Is it awful?" I said, "Yeah, it's awful, and here's why. I think *How High The Moon* is a hit song, but not the way we're playing it." Mary was trying to follow me, but she wasn't there yet. So I uncorked the little bottle and said, "You take a good swig of this, and I'll take a good swig, and then I've got some news for you."

Mary couldn't take the drink without holding her nose, so that's what she did. She held her nose and took a belt, then handed the little bottle to me and I took one. And then I told her, "We're celebrating. I've found the secret to making a hit record."

How To Make A Hit Record

Over the years of performing and observing, I had realized there's a difference between the audience on a Monday night, a Tuesday night, or any night of the week. No matter where you might play, each night there is a different response to the same song, and it was while we were playing the Blue Note that I figured out what to do with it.

I said, "When we play *How High The Moon* on Monday night, it's great and the crowd loves it. On Tuesday night, it's still pretty good; Wednesday, it's just fair; and by Saturday night no one pays any attention to it. We need to play it so it grabs the audience every night of the week, and I now have a plan to create the arrangement to do that. When we do that, we'll have a hit record."

With a record, the audience is in their own world and listening with their ears. But when the performance is live, they're in your world, and they listen with their eyes. So there's a difference. And what I wanted to do was make sure what you hear is also what you see, and what you get anytime you hear the song. That's what's going to make any particular song a hit. So when we left Chicago and went to Rock Island and beyond, the plan was to take *How High The Moon* and play it three different ways to prove my point of arriving at one arrangement that went over as well on Saturday as it does on Monday.

So we're in Rock Island, we're in Terre Haute; we're in Detroit, St. Louis, and Milwaukee. We're touring all over, any place we can get a job, and everywhere we go, we're playing *How High The Moon* in as many different ways as we can think of. I'm doing it solo, the trio's playing it, we're doing it fast, we're doing it slow, we're changing keys, the whole nine yards. And after playing one way and then another over a period of time, we condense it down to three different arrangements, all with instrumentals and Mary's vocal, but all with different tempos and all played differently. And everywhere we go, we're trying these different versions of *How High The Moon* on the audience, and I'm watching their reactions very closely.

The Call To New York

While we were playing in East St. Louis, we got a call from New York with an offer to play a club there called Bop City. This was good news because the job was to pay well, and Mary and I had just a few bucks between us. The medical bills were still piling up and I hadn't worked for a year and a half after the accident, so we were still in a deep hole financially. The good pay at the Blue Note had been very helpful, but that money was already gone and we were just barely getting by living on the road.

We were finishing up our engagement in East St. Louis and getting ready to go to New York when Ed Stapleton suddenly resigned and said he was through playing bass and was now going to study to become a clarinet player. So I was committed to a trio job in New York, and stuck with no bass player.

Bop City Flop

We drove to New York to open at Bop City, and the night we got there, Louis Armstrong went up to the microphone and acknowledged we were there and scheduled to open the next night. And then he said, "But the sad news is, tonight is Bop City's last night. After tonight, it's closing and will be no more. It's the end."

So the place closed down the night we got there, and now we're stuck because we had no other engagements booked. And Mary said, "What are we

Mary and I look like we're having fun here. Wally Kamin is the bass player.

going to do?" And I said, "Well, the best thing to do is get a newspaper, and I'll look in the classifieds and see if there's anything available out where I used to live." I was talking about the old Electra Court neighborhood in Queens. I knew that area, so it would be easier for us to camp there than anywhere else. And sure enough, I found a little furnished apartment in Jackson Heights for $40 a month. So we parked the '42 Caddy and moved into this two-room basement apartment. We had no jobs to play, but we still had the radio show to do, so we set up our equipment and started concentrating on making recordings.

Lovers Hideaway

This was the first of three different times Mary and I lived in Jackson Heights, and when we got there at the end of the summer, we were damn near broke. We had less than five hundred bucks between us and had to be careful because other than the small amount coming in from the NBC radio

215

show, it was all we had.

The basement apartment had a bed that folded down out of the wall, and a little half-kitchen where Mary cooked. There was a place up the street where you could get groceries and beer, and we didn't really need anything else. Mary and I loved our beer and we loved to record, and that's what we did there. We just worked on our recordings and enjoyed being together and living on love in that little private place. We were so much in love that the rest of the world was way back in second place. We had no telephone, so there was no one calling, and very few people even knew we were there. Louis Armstrong, who I knew from Chicago, lived just up the road and would sometimes drop in when he was on his way home. But other than Louis showing up once and a while, it was just the two of us, and the world left us alone. It was the honeymoon we never had, and some of the happiest days we ever knew.

The Power Of Love

So that fall, we holed up in our little basement hideaway, turning out a new radio show every week, doing lots of recording and just trying to survive while I learned to play again. My arm was getting better and I was adjusting to having a frozen elbow, but it was still one day at a time, and very slow going.

This time provided an important beginning for all the music and invention ideas I'd stored up during my long recovery, when my mind was going all the time with the synthesizer, electric guitar experiments, recording experiments and a million other things. I was thinking, "Oh boy, I could do this, I could do that, and when I get my hand back I'm going to have to learn to pick a different way because it isn't going to be like it was." The long recovery period was quite a challenge, and also a blessing because it gave me a chance to think, and read, and plan, and dream. And with a lot of balls, you could do it. It wouldn't be easy, but it could be done.

And Mary asked the question right there in that little apartment. She said, "Hon, what makes you think these things and do these things? Where in the world does it come from, and how does it happen?" And I said, "It's because of two things: God, and being in love." And it's true. If you have belief in God, then He decides whether you live or die. And if you believe God will help you, then all these breaks come your way, and some of them, like the accident, you don't understand. And if you're fortunate enough to find true love with a girl whose God-given talent made her sing like an angel, then you can actually do what you dream of doing. So this was a very special precious time in our life together. We were totally dedicated and committed to each other, and to everything we were doing together.

CHAPTER NINETEEN

Love And Marriage

Our little world was hit with a shock when a telegram arrived with the news that my Dad had died suddenly from a brain hemorrhage on October 2, 1949. We dropped what we were doing and hurried back to Wisconsin for the funeral and to stay with Mother for a few days. Besides his wife and family, there were many in Waukesha affected by his sudden death. My Dad had been a well-known character there all his life, and was only 67 when he died. The Club 400 had become a popular gathering place because of him, and now my brother Ralph was on his own.

After he remarried, my Dad gave up the gambling and carousing that took him away when I was a kid, and we had patched things up not long before he died. He was very proud of my success and felt bad that he hadn't been more interested or supportive when I was a curious brat driving everyone up the wall with all my questions and crazy stunts. He was also terribly fond of Mary, and didn't approve of the fact that we weren't married. And he got on to me about it, saying he didn't want me to make the same mistakes he'd made. I didn't see it his way at the time, but after he was gone, the talk we had stayed with me.

Marriage In Milwaukee

We went back to Jackson Heights and continued with our recordings and the radio show until early December, when we went back to Milwaukee to play an extended engagement at Jimmy Fazio's nightspot called the Town Club.

During our long run at the Stage Door, we had developed a loyal following in Milwaukee, and they came out in force when we came back. This was now after the instrumental hits with *Lover* and *Brazil* and *What Is This Thing Called Love*, so there were a lot of new faces, too. We were only 20 miles from Waukesha and had some great times with Mother and Ralph and our friends there, and we also drove down to Chicago to appear on Dave Garroway's radio show a couple of times. Warren Downey rejoined us as our bass player, so the old gang was back together again.

This was again a situation where having a fresh audience every night was a tremendous tool in helping us improve our act. We were continually adding new songs, experimenting with different arrangements and adding the numbers that proved to be popular to our play list. This was also a time when Mary

Mary and I are married by Judge Cannon on December 29, 1949.

made great advances with her guitar playing. She had the ability to learn quickly, and whether it was a vocal part or something on the guitar, once she knew where she was supposed to be, she never wandered. This was one of the great strengths of her talent.

We had formed friendships with some of the Stage Door regulars, and it was great to be able to play for them again. Among them were George and Bertha Miller, who had become special friends. Dr. Miller used to record our performances so we could listen to them later, and many times brought his young son, Steve, to hear us play. This is the same Steve Miller who went on to have a great career as a guitarist and recording artist, and we've been close friends ever since.

We worked through the holiday season, packing the Town Club every night and recording during our free time. We stayed busy and were having a blast, but my Dad's words kept coming back to me. There was also the certainty that as we kept going, Mary and I were going to be more and more in the spotlight. And these things led to the decision that it was time for Mary and me to tie the knot.

Several of our Milwaukee friends were involved, and much of the story took place in the club, but we didn't actually get married there. Dr. Miller came by one afternoon and administered the blood tests we needed for getting a marriage license. After the waiting period, we went to the Milwaukee County Courthouse where Judge Cannon, another friend, married us. This happened on the afternoon of December 29, 1949, with George and Bertha Miller as our witnesses.

When we got back to the club, the place was all decorated with balloons and banners put up by our friend Fred Miller of Miller Beer Company. So we got married in the afternoon, and our performance that night became a celebration with all our Milwaukee friends, sponsored by Miller Beer.

Marriage To Mary Made Sense

When I married Virginia, it was because of Jimmy Atkins and his wife, not because I wanted to do it. It was back in '38, when we were getting ready to go find Fred Waring, that Jimmy said, "You mean you're going to go to New York and leave your gal behind in Chicago?" And I said, "Well, it's a problem. If we want to live together, that's okay, but I don't want to get married." But Jimmy and Wilma both put pressure on me, saying, "If Virginia is going to follow you to New York, you gotta do right by her and get married."

So I let myself be talked into it, but it wasn't what I wanted. And it wasn't because I didn't love Virginia. It was because I knew my first love was always going to be the guitar, and that first love is very selfish. I knew it wasn't going to be a fair situation for her because I was focused on my music and ideas and where they could take me, not on marriage and being a good husband.

It was this understanding that made me think marriage wasn't for me, but with Mary, it made sense because we were so madly in love and committed to our music. But there's a lot to consider when two people are together 24 hours a day, no matter how much you're in love, no matter what the conditions are. Take any two people who work and live together all the time, and rarely do you find they can manage it successfully. My good friends George Burns and Gracie Allen were able to do it, but Fibber McGee and Molly had tough, tough problems. And so did most of the people I knew who attempted it. It's just very hard to do, and it eventually caught up with us.

220

Meeting Chet

I had an appointment with Dr. McKeaver, and there were things pending with NBC and Capitol, so we returned to Hollywood after playing New Year's Eve at Fazio's. As we were making the drive, again in January, again on the same highway where we'd had the accident two years earlier, something memorable happened.

I'd told Mary the stories of how I started at KWTO with Sunny Joe, the programs we were on, hunting arrowheads and the whole nine yards. So now we're driving through Missouri listening to my old Springfield station, and who do we hear but Red Foley doing a live show. And I'm jumping up and down in the car because it's amazing to hear this national star I've known since my early days performing on the little Ozarks station Sunny Joe and I had opened years earlier.

So we're listening to Red's show and I'm telling Mary stories about our days back in Chicago, and suddenly I hear this great guitar sound. It grabs me, and my mind immediately goes back to what Jimmy Atkins told me when he bought my L-10 to give to his kid brother. And of course, we're talking about Chet. Jimmy said, "You know, my brother plays like you, he plays like Merle Travis, he plays like Django. He's got you guys down. He's pretty good, Red. He's got something." But up until this time listening to the radio with Mary, I'd never heard Chet play. I'd only heard what Jimmy said about him.

So we're driving into Springfield listening to this guitar player who sounds like Les Paul and Merle Travis at the same time, and I say to Mary, "I'll betcha that's Jimmy Atkins' brother." And sure enough, when the song ends, Red Foley says, "Thank you, Chet Atkins." And I said, "Come on, we're going straight to the station."

So we drive over to KWTO and go upstairs, and nothing has changed. The lobby is just like it always was, and I look through the soundproof window and there's Chet playing his ass off on the air. He's got that Travis thumb thing combined with a bunch of my licks and his own stuff, and it's a great sound, a knockout.

When they take a break, our eyes meet and we're staring at each other. I'd never seen Chet before, but I knew it was him. He'd seen pictures of me with his brother, so he recognized who I was immediately. He put his guitar down and came out and said, "I know who you are. Hello, Les." Then we talked about Jimmy and the trio, Fred Waring, the L-10 and everything else. Mary was there with me, and that's how Chet and I met for the first time. It was the beginning of a very special friendship.

We'd been gone from California for several months and didn't waste any time once we got back. We were immediately back in the garage studio contin-

221

uing with our recording work, and I welcomed the opportunity to try out new ideas with my electric guitar and recording experiments. In no time, our little place was again like Grand Central Station, with engineers and musicians and singers coming and going at all hours. Mary and her sister, Carol, were devoted to each other and loved to spend time together, so it was a natural that Carol started spending more time at our house to help Mary with all the things that needed to be done, and also to free Mary up to spend more time with me in the recording studio.

Wally Kamin

I needed a new bass player, and was delighted to hook up with Wally Kamin, an old friend who had been playing with Art Van Damme. Wally and I had jammed often back in Chicago, but we went further back than that. We'd known each other since we were nine years old back in Wisconsin, so there was already a built-in connection. I might've found a better bass player, but I wasn't going to find a better friend.

So Wally joined us as our new bass man and we started rehearsing, getting him acquainted with our material and the way Mary and I did things when we performed. He and I were old buddies, so from the beginning he was spending a lot of time with Mary and Carol and I. The four of us had a natural chemistry, and it wasn't long before Wally and Carol paired up. It was the most natural thing in the world, and it fit in perfectly with what I wanted to do, which was to get back to New York as soon as possible.

We didn't stay in California very long. Hollywood was great if you were involved in the movies, but there wasn't enough performing work to keep us going. For performing and touring, you had to go back east. This was 1950, and there was something else picking up steam in New York and Chicago. It was called television, and I was terribly interested in it.

So I had my visits with the doctors, with Capitol and NBC, and then we took off for the Midwest, where Mary and I had bookings arranged. And this is where Wally and Carol became an important part of what we were doing. This time, more instruments and audio equipment went with us, and we needed a second vehicle. So we loaded up Wally's station wagon and my Cadillac, and the four of us hit the road together, touring across the country until we arrived back in New York. Once again, we went to Jackson Heights, set up our recording equipment and settled in.

Nola

I had been working on recording *Nola* since 1946, and it's an interesting little story how I finally finished it. Zeke Manners was one of the top disk jockeys in Los Angeles and a major supporter of *Lover* when it first came out. We were good friends, and he came by the studio one night to show us his new accordion and get a recording of it.

When Zeke crashed the studio, we were recording *Cryin'*, an instrumental I'd written which made Mary cry when she first heard it. Since she liked it so much, I wrote lyrics for it so she could sing on it. So I said, "Zeke, we're trying to make a record here." And he said, "Well, take a little break and just let me record one quick song." He wanted to hear how his new accordion would sound recorded with the delay effect. So I said, "Okay, step up to the mic and play something." And he plays *Nola*, the old piano solo piece. I cut the recording on one of the disk machines so he'd be able to play it back, and then gave it to him. So Zeke's got what he wants, he leaves, and Mary and I are back to *Cryin'*.

Late that night, we've gone to bed, but something is bugging me about Zeke's take of *Nola.* And I finally realize what's bothering me. He played it too fast. It's a piano solo piece, and everybody wants to play it fast because it's very catchy, but you can't dance to it that way. So now I'm out of bed and back in the garage working on my own recording of *Nola,* and I'm slowing it down. I take it down to the tempo of a guy walking to the rest room, and now anybody can dance to it. The slower tempo made all the difference in the world.

I worked all night finishing the recording and took it straight over to Capitol the next morning. Jim Conkling wasn't there, so I laid it on his desk with a note that said, "Here's your next hit!" Then I went back home and started working on the next thing and forgot about it. I didn't give another thought to *Nola*, and Mary didn't even know I'd recorded it.

This happened in California, and it was maybe two months later, after we were back in Jackson Heights, that I got a telegram saying, "Congratulations for being Number One." And I thought it was a joke. Then, Jimmy Atkins comes knocking on our door, and we're very glad to see each other. And he says, "You don't have a phone so I had to come and ask how it feels to be Number One." And I say, "You're the second guy to say that. Now what the hell is going on?" And Jimmy said, "You don't know?" And I said, "Know what?" And he says, "Your recording of *Nola* just hit Number One."

This was a complete surprise to me, and even more so to Mary. We were overjoyed at this unexpected news, and hadn't heard about it because we were just holed up in our apartment recording and trying to survive.

Tennessee Waltz

My instrumental hits had created great interest in the New Sound, and the techniques of overdubbing we invented in the garage were sweeping through the recording business. And who picks up on it but Patti Page. She hears about this new thing and people around her say, "Hey, look what Les Paul is doing." So Patti picked up on it and made a record harmonizing with herself on *Tennessee Waltz*, and it became a number one hit. So Patti Page is jumping in ahead of us doing the thing I invented, and I wasn't going to sit still for it.

Now the most peculiar thing in the world happened. I immediately made a record of *Tennessee Waltz* with Mary, delivered it to Capitol Records, and said, "Get this out right now." And nothing happened. The president of the company was out of town, so my record just lay there and nobody else took action on it. Weeks passed with everybody in the business talking about Patti's recording, and then I got a phone call from Capitol suggesting Mary and I do a cover of *Tennessee Waltz*. And I said, "Look on the president's desk; it's been there for a month."

So Capitol put it out, and what happened? Patti's record went all the way to number one; and our version came following after and went to number six. So our *Tennessee Waltz* was not as big as hers, but now people are listening and comparing the two and saying, "My goodness, they both sound so good, it's like Russ Colombo and Bing Crosby." You've got two people now that are almost like each other, they're very close in the way they sound and both doing the same thing—singing along with themselves. And here's where the catch came, and I knew it was going to happen.

I said, "Patti doesn't dare put out another record right now because she's at number one, but we can." When you've got the number one record and you know it's going to stay up there a while, you don't create your own competition. So I said, "Patti's locked in, but we're not. Let me look for a good song for Mary to follow with."

So I was listening to song after song, and when I heard *Mockin' Bird Hill*, I said, "That's it. That's the song we're going to do. And Mary said, "That's an awful song." I said, "No, it's the right song because you'll sound great on it, and it's going to force Patti to follow us. I started it; they stole it, and now we're going to turn it back around and run with it so they'll have no choice but to be following us." So we put out *Mockin' Bird Hill*, and it goes straight to the top.

Now Patti is saying, "What am I going to do? Am I going to kill my *Tennessee Waltz* by putting out another record?" And they made the decision I knew they would have to make. "Yes, we're going to have to cover Les Paul and Mary Ford and make *Mockin' Bird Hill*." So she did, but her version didn't catch up with ours, and suddenly we were the leaders, just that fast.

Mary and I did our share of big TV shows like The Ed Sullivan Show, often working with other guests. Here we are with Patti Page.

And Capitol said, "Now what are you going to do?" And I said, "I've got it under control now. We'll do *How High the Moon* and Patti would have to be totally insane to go anywhere near it. She won't touch it and neither will anybody else. It's all ours from now on."

CHAPTER TWENTY

How High The Moon

1950 was the best year yet. I had three instrumental hits with *Goofus, Nola* and *Little Rock Getaway*, and we closed out the year with *Tennessee Waltz* going all the way to number six around Christmas time. Then it was a monster number two hit with *Mockin' Bird Hill* to start 1951, and we were on our way to the top.

This was a wonderful thing for us because we had now established Mary's popularity as a vocalist, and it was a sign all the work we'd been doing for so long was going to pay off. One hit followed another, and the royalties started rolling in a few months later, building as the hits piled up. It was an amazing thing for us to realize our financial worries were over. I was able to take care of the remaining medical bills, and later in 1951 buy a second Ampex 300 tape recorder. And we were now in demand, with job offers coming in from everywhere.

The Final Arrangement

So things were definitely going our way, and now it was time to prove my point about how to make a guaranteed hit. We had been working on three different arrangements of *How High The Moon* for over a year, and I had settled on the one I believed would work. It was not the most up-tempo of our arrangements, but it was the one in the upper key, and when we hit upon it, I knew we had the nucleus for our hit, and now it was time to fill in the details and record the song.

It was wintertime in Jackson Heights, and Mary was asleep in the fold-down bed. I had been up all night thinking about *How High The Moon*, and decided to go down to the White Castle hamburger stand and get something to eat. So I went out and got nine little hamburgers and some beer. My intention was to go back to our apartment and wake Mary so we could have breakfast together.

While I was getting the hamburgers, I saw a guy watering down drinks in a tavern right across the street, and I recognized him as an old buddy. So I went over and knocked on the window, and the guy opens the door and says, "Red! Where the hell have you been?" And I said, "California, but I'm back in New York now and I've got a new thing. I'm making sound-on-sound recordings for Capitol and doing a radio show on NBC with Mary, the gal I married.

This is the exact setup I used to record How High the Moon: *klunker number one, the Ampex 300 with added head, and my "Wally box" mixer.*

227

I'm gonna go wake her up so we can eat, and then we've got to record another broadcast." And he says, "Well, stick around a little while and have a drink."

So we pulled up a couple of bar stools and ate the hamburgers and drank the beer. And while we were talking, I picked up a little round coaster lying there on the bar and wrote out the arrangement of *How High the Moon* in just the way I wanted to record it. Then I put the coaster in my coat pocket and said, "Well, now I gotta go get nine more hamburgers and another quart of beer and go wake Mary."

I went back with the food and beer and woke Mary, and she said, "What are you doing up so early?" And I said, "I never went to bed. Now let's eat these things and then we're going to make *How High the Moon*."

We started laying down the tracks playing our guitars in the G position, but tuned up to a higher pitch. And we did that because whenever you perform anything on stage, you're more wound up and you punch it out, so you're naturally going to go up a tone or a half tone higher. A person in the recording studio may go down and sing real low, but belting it out live with a band behind you, you need a higher pitch. We kept it in the G position because otherwise, the open string harmonics wouldn't be there. You want that same sound, but in a higher key, so you tune your guitars up to get there.

The Les Paulverizer

It took hours and hours of work to build our recording of *How High The Moon*, and during a break, I went out to a phone and called Zeke and Bea Manners, our California friends who were now living in New York, and invited them over to see what we were doing. So they came to our little Jackson Heights place and sat there listening and observing while Mary and I continued work on the recording. As we worked on *How High The Moon*, we were also putting our next radio show together, and it was then and there the Paulverizer got its name.

I needed to come up with something to tell radio listeners that would explain why they were hearing more than one Mary, and multiple guitars, and a glee club and an orchestra. And rather than try to explain it all technically, I wanted to make something up we could use as a running gag from week to week in our show. And that's when it happened. All four of us were kidding around shooting one-liners back and forth, and suddenly out of my mouth came, "the Les Paulverizer." I said, "There it is, that's it!" And it immediately became a part of our radio show.

So I named it the Les Paulverizer, which I described as a little black box that allowed me to do all those things. And it was a complete hoax, just an imaginary running bit on our radio show, until 1956 when I ended up actually building it for Mary and I for our live stage shows.

Capitol Balks

When I first went to Capitol and told them I wanted our next release to be *How High The Moon*, Jim Conkling, objected. He said, "You're making a big mistake. There are already 85 records on *How High the Moon*, and none have made it. You think you're going to be the one to hit with it, but we don't agree. *How High The Moon* will never make it."

Jim Conkling was my friend and I didn't want to argue about it, so rather than try to change his mind, I just went ahead and recorded it. And when we finished it, I sent it to him with a note that said, "Here's your next number one."

As soon as he got it, he called me up and said, "You've still got this thing for *How High The Moon*? What in hell makes you think it's going to be number one?" And I said, "I just know." And he said, "Don't even tell me. You've been right in every damn thing you've done. Whatever your secret is, don't tell me. Just do it."

And I never told him I had a jury. And traveling from city to city, we'd listen to the jury and the jury never knew they were the jury. But they were right, and so was I. Capitol released *How High The Moon* around the end of March 1951, and in two weeks it was our first number one hit as a duo, and it stayed on top for many weeks. After Billboard named it the number one song of the year, I received a telegram from Capitol. It basically said, "Les, I was wrong. Jim

229

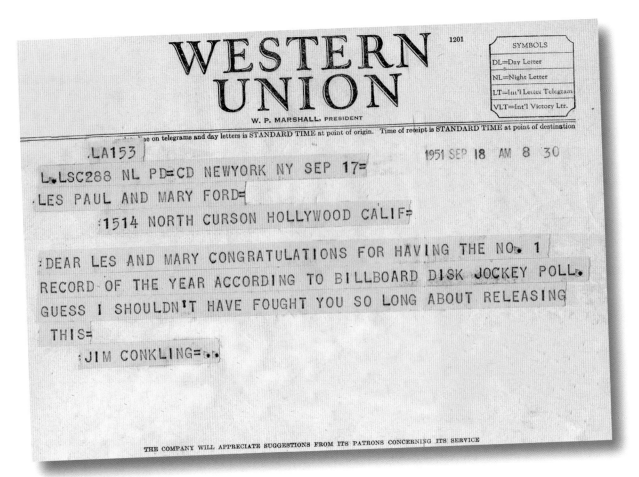

Conkling." I still have it in my scrapbook, and it's one of my favorite souvenirs.

Flying High

When *How High The Moon* hit number one, *Mockin' Bird Hill* was still holding at number two, so for several weeks, we had the top two songs in the country, and now things really took off. Our records were literally selling faster than Capitol could make them. We were doing Bing's show in Hollywood, the Garroway show in Chicago, the Ed Sullivan TV show in New York, and playing somewhere almost every night as we dashed back and forth across the country trying to meet the unbelievable demand for our little act. One week we'd be headlining at the Paramount in New York, the next in Nashville appearing on the Grand Ole Opry, and the next breaking attendance records in Reno or Las Vegas. It was craziness, but we loved it. It was what we'd worked so hard to achieve, and now that we had arrived there was no slowing down.

It was when we did the Crosby and Sullivan shows that I first began to engineer the multi-layered sound of our records into our live performances. This was not the real Paulverizer I built later, but that's what I called it as a way of explaining the multiple voices and guitars, just as we had done on our radio show. For Mary's vocal harmonies and my additional guitar tracks, I had the tape recorder loaded with the extra parts we needed to make it sound like the record. Wally couldn't operate the equipment because he was playing bass, so it took repeated rehearsals with the audio engineers of the various shows to pull it off. But we did it and the audiences were continually amazed.

Bing flipped when he heard *How High The Moon* and invited us to debut it on his coast-to-coast radio show a week before Capitol released it. His show was the most popular weekly broadcast in the country, with millions of loyal listeners, so his endorsement was a tremendous asset in launching the record. Bing knew *How High The Moon* was going to sell more Ampex tape recorders, but he was also genuinely happy for us because he knew it was going to be a smash. He played along with me on the Paulverizer bit to help sell it to the audience, and then sang harmony on *Mockin' Bird Hill*, which was an enormous boost for Mary. Nothing could have confirmed her arrival as a major talent more strongly than singing with Bing Crosby on his national radio show. So once again, Bing proved to be a great friend.

Down Beat

By the end of April, *How High The Moon* was the number one selling record in the country, number one in radio airplay, the most played selection on the nation's jukeboxes, and number one on the rhythm and blues charts, which was a first for a white act. It was also number one in England, so now we were an international hit, and newspaper and magazine reporters from London and all over America were following us around doing stories and putting us on the cover. So we were flying high, but not everybody was happy about it.

After *How High The Moon* had been out maybe a month, *Down Beat* magazine, which was devoted mostly to jazz and swing, put a headline on one of their covers saying, "The National Anthem Is No More." *How High The Moon* was a sacred song in the world of jazz, *the* song that all jazz players had in their repertoire, and rarely did anyone do a commercial rendition of it. And the *Down Beat* critic was beating us up because we had made it popular with the masses, and that ended it for jazz lovers. So, according to him, we sank the ship and destroyed the jazz national anthem.

The jazz world had been putting me down ever since I decided to quit starving and start playing what most people wanted to hear, and *Down Beat* was speaking for those who thought I had sold out jazz in order to become a commercial success. And the terribly interesting thing is that it only served to make us more successful, and to bring recognition to Mary. It took Patti Page making *Tennessee Waltz*, and then us making *Mockin' Bird Hill* to make Mary popular. Then came *How High the Moon*, and now Mary is famous and everybody is looking our way.

231

Re-Labeling With Capitol

After *How High The Moon* was released, Jim Conkling left Capitol and it was time to renegotiate my deal with them. One of the things I insisted on was to change the way our records were labeled. Our earlier records were tagged, "Les Paul," with "vocal by Mary Ford" getting second billing. The first pressings of *How High The Moon* were labeled that way, but after we re-signed, it was "Les Paul and Mary Ford" from then on.

At this point, we were writing our own ticket with Capitol and they were glad to let us because they were cashing in like nobody's business. They didn't have to pressure us to go out and promote our records because we continued to travel and perform relentlessly. Hell, they couldn't stop us or keep up with us! After *How High The Moon*, we scored continuous hits with *Josephine, I Wish I'd Never Seen Sunshine, Whispering* and *The World Is Waiting For The Sunrise*, all in 1951, and all recorded with our own equipment while we were on the road. By the end of that year, we had sold over four million records and were making up to $20,000 a week performing.

From our beginning, Mary and I had always enjoyed listening to the radio while we traveled, but now it was an even greater pleasure because so much of what we were hearing was our own music. And we'd make bets as to whether or not we could scan the radio dial from one end to the other at any time, day or night, and not hear at least one of our records. And excluding newscasts and non-musical programs, there was no way. All you had to do was turn the radio on and scan across the dial, and you would hear *How High the Moon, The World is Waiting for the Sunrise, Lover, Mockin' Bird Hill, Nola* or one of the others on the air.

That's how powerful the situation was at that time.

The Team

To manage our heavy schedule of traveling and performing on the road, the four of us, Wally, Carol, Mary and I, formed what we called The Team. After Carol and Wally got married, we were a team at home as well. Carol and Mary were sisters and so happy to be working together they became almost inseparable. It was good for Mary to have someone who matched up so well looking after her needs. Mary loved to cook and Carol loved to shop so the two of them just naturally worked out who was going to do what in those departments. And Carol was just the right lady to take care of Mary's shopping because they were the same size. Carol could go to New York to try on gowns and dresses and bring them back to Mary knowing they would fit. This was a

What a team we were! Mary and I, with her sister Carol and Carol's husband Wally. I wish I had a nickel for every mile we logged together back in the crazy days of the early 1950s.

tremendous help because Mary had no desire to go shopping in New York or anywhere else. She much preferred to stay home when we weren't traveling.

When we were on tour, Wally and Carol would drive on ahead in the station wagon to make arrangements and get things ready at our next venue, while Mary and I followed in the Cadillac. Let's say we're going from New York to Chicago. It would take them two days to get there. Me, it'd take 12 hours. I drove very fast, and Mary and I were always zooming. So Wally and Carol were in one vehicle, Mary and I were in the other, and we often ran on different schedules to get where we were going.

It was during this time that Carol became Mary's unseen harmony voice. When we played a network radio or television show, qualified engineers operating the equipment allowed us to use pre-recorded tapes for supplying added voice and guitar parts. But when we were playing club dates or other non-broadcast venues, that wasn't possible. My solution was to have Carol sing into a microphone offstage or behind the curtain, providing the multiplying vocal effect of the imaginary Paulverizer.

Wally was in charge of all our gear, and most of it went with him in the station wagon. We traveled with three guitars, a bass, three Ampex tape recorders, speakers, amplifiers, microphones, the mixer, cords and cables and all the stuff that went with it. To meet our needs for live performing and recording on the road, we carried 1,100 pounds of equipment. As soon as we finished a job, the equipment would be broken down and loaded into the station wagon, and Wally and Carol would be leading the way to the next gig. Carol took care of Mary, Wally took care of me, and we worked together perfectly, so it was a very efficient, well-organized operation.

Tuning In

Mary and I were constantly visiting radio stations as we traveled across the country. Wherever we went, we'd find the radio stations, the little ones out in the sticks, the big ones in the cities, all of them. We'd just show up and walk into a station at any hour, day or night. And there was a routine in the way we did it.

We'd go in and introduce ourselves and usually go right into the broadcast studio and go on the air with the disk jockey. We would talk about our records and where we were going to be playing, and kid around with the deejay and do plugs for the radio station. And while we were doing this, Wally would take a picture of us with the disk jockey, or whoever happened to be there. Then he would go into another room and put his hands inside a film-developing bag, which was completely dark inside, and develop the picture. As soon as the photograph was ready, we'd autograph it and put it on the control board console, shake the guy's hand and be on our way. And the whole thing took maybe twenty minutes.

So the guy has met us, we've plugged him on the air, he's playing our records, and he's with us in the picture we autographed and gave to him right there on the spot. Each time we did this, we made a new friend, and Wally would enter all the information into a file he kept. Every time we hit a radio station, when we left, we had the disk jockey's name, the names of his wife and kids, the station we were at and what we did there. Wally had it all sorted out with a system and could come up with the information when we needed to be reminded.

After *How High The Moon* and *Mockin' Bird Hill* both hit at the same time, we were traveling all the time, constantly making unannounced visits to radio stations, record stores, charity events, hospitals, dancehalls and clubs, private parties, any place we could find to generate more interest in what we were doing. In the spring and summer of 1951, we visited over fifteen hundred radio stations and record stores in three months. And we left every one of them with an autographed, original picture.

Moving at such a rapid pace produced an ungodly amount of information, and managing all the details was one of Wally's great talents. He could carry on a conversation with you and type a letter to someone else at the same time and never lose track of either thing. He'd be smoking a cigarette, typing, and talking to you, doing two or three things at the same time that were absolutely independent of each other. He was slow, but very thorough and always tried so hard to do everything just the way I wanted it done. He was the only person I could ever trust to write a letter for me.

After the hits started coming, mail was pouring in like you wouldn't believe, and it was Wally who handled it. He would type an answer for each letter, enter the information about it in our info book, and then give it to me to read and sign.

Say a disk jockey writes and says, "We're playing the hell out of your *Alabammy Bound* and we just want to know that you're well taken care of here in Pittsburgh." The letter comes addressed to me, but it goes to Wally to be answered and then a note about it goes into our traveling info book. So the next time I'm heading for Pittsburgh, I've got all the information I need about this particular disk jockey, including the dates of his letter, Wally's reply, and everything I should know to make the guy feel appreciated.

Every time Wally brought me a batch of letters he'd written, I'd read them, sign them, and pass them back for mailing. And there were no fake signatures. I hand-signed every one so whoever was to receive it would have an original autograph.

It was a very effective system for maintaining contact with all the people who were helping us succeed. Thanks to Wally, wherever I was going, all I had to do was look in the book and I'd have a running sheet on everything I needed to remember to make everybody happy and keep things moving along. And on top of everything, he was my bass player and a very loyal and dedicated friend. Wally was one-of-a-kind, just a super friend who absolutely could never be replaced. He was great, just an invaluable guy.

CHAPTER TWENTY-ONE

Hooking Up With Gibson

One of the stories most often told about my early experiments with the solid body guitar is when I took the Log to Gibson in Chicago in 1941 and was laughed out of the room. That did happen, but it wasn't the end of the story. I remained very close with the Gibson people even after they rejected my idea, and while I was developing and playing my Epiphone klunkers. And in California, during the concentrated time in the garage studio before the first big hits, something very interesting took place.

Two friends who used to hang out in my back yard all the time were Leo Fender and Paul Bigsby. Both of them were deeply involved in their own electric guitar experiments, and we spent a lot of time together talking about our various ideas and pushing each other to keep looking for a better sound. And this one particular night, Bigsby comes over and brings me a guitar. And it's a prototype of one of Leo's early design models, an original Fender solid body guitar. It had "Fender" on the headstock, but there was no model name for it. And Bigsby brought it to me in Leo's behalf with the message that he wanted me to look at it and think about it.

Then, the next thing, Leo came to see me with an idea. And the idea was for him and me to form a partnership and start making the Fender Les Paul guitar. He said, "How about you and me join up and start the whole thing together, and we'll put out a solid body guitar with both our names on it." This first hit me as a swell idea, but after I thought it through, I told Leo, "Geez, you know I've had a great relationship with Gibson all these years, and it's part of the biggest instrument company in the world, and I'd like to take another shot at doing a guitar with them before I make a move." Leo knew all about the Log and my ongoing talks with Gibson, so he was okay with me not wanting to abruptly jump into something new.

Right after this happened, I called Mr. M.H. Berlin, the head of Chicago Musical Instrument, the company that owned Gibson, and told him about Leo's guitar, and what he was planning to do. And Mr. Berlin said, "Come to Chicago and bring one of those things with you, and bring that broomstick of yours along too."

So I went to Chicago with the Log and the guitar Leo had given me, and met with Mr. Berlin. After he looked them over, he asked for my opinion. I first told him what I'd learned about sustain and the controllability of the pure electric sound, and then I said, "I believe the solid body guitar is going to be very important, and if you don't do something, Fender is going to rule the world."

With the Fender Company now in its early infancy, the solid body guitar was no longer being thought of as an oddity. Now it was something that could be and was being done. It was bound to happen, and Mr. Berlin recognized it.

A sit-down meeting was held that included Mr. Berlin, a guy named Carlucci who was his right hand man, some of the Gibson people, myself, and Marv Henrickson, a lawyer who worked with CMI and also represented me. We talked for hours about how my endorsement deal was to be structured and various details concerning the guitar's design. It was a very positive discussion, and afterward, Mr. Berlin said, "I think we're going to make this thing happen. Start thinking about it and get your ideas together and I'll call you when its time to start."

Less than a year later, he called and said, "Come on back. We're ready to do something." So I went back to Chicago and met again with Mr. Berlin and the Gibson people, and the first thing they said was, "Well, what would you like? How do you want this guitar to look?" I had drawn out some simple plans, which I showed to them, and I had a list of specifications concerning the frets, the bridge, and having more of the fingerboard clear of the body so it was easier to play higher up on the neck. Gibson had ideas too, so we put everything together and started closing in on a prototype.

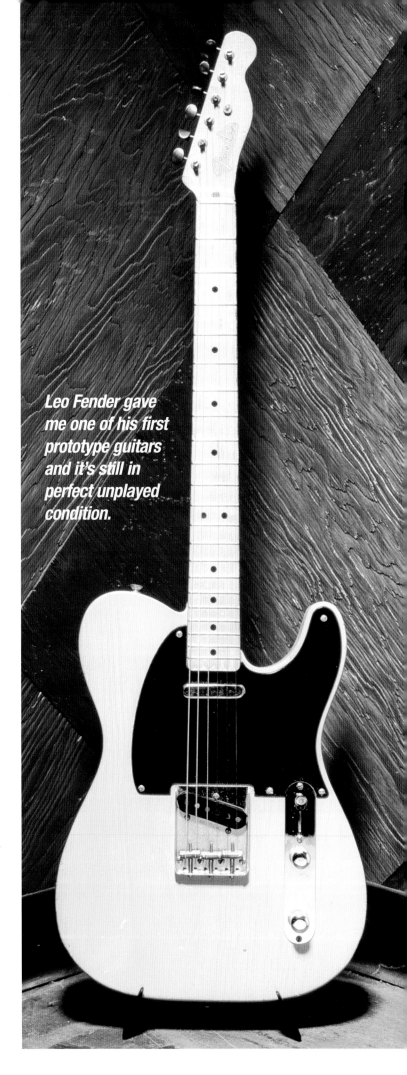

Leo Fender gave me one of his first prototype guitars and it's still in perfect unplayed condition.

The Golden Archtop

In my visions for this guitar, I had imagined it as a flattop because the neck was going to be one solid piece of wood from the top of the headstock to the butt end. We were discussing this when Mr. Berlin suddenly said, "Do you like violins?" And I said, "I love violins. In fact, I'm nuts about violins." And Mr. Berlin said, "I am, too. I've got a whole vault full of violins, and I think we should go take a look at them."

So we go to the Chicago Musical Instrument vault, and it's packed with beautiful violins, some of them priceless. We're looking at them and admiring

the skill it took to build them, and he says, "There's just something lovable and warm about the shape of the violin. Would you consider making your Les Paul guitar with an archtop?" And I said, "Oh, I'd prefer it. I just thought it would be much more expensive to do that." "No," he said, "It won't be because we're tooled for it. It will be easy for us to do, but the other companies aren't tooled for it and won't be able to do it, so an archtop will make our solid body instrument by far more beautiful, and they won't be able to touch it." And, of course, he was right. We both wanted to aim for an instrument that would have a classic shape and be beautiful to look at, and giving it an archtop was the key.

So we were in immediate agreement on that point, and then Mr. Berlin said, "Now, what color do you want?" And without hesitation, I said, "Gold," just blurting it out without a thought. "You mean gold like a wedding ring?" "Yeah, gold like rich." And Mr. Berlin said, "I like it. You got it." But a guy in the room with us didn't agree. He said, "That's the worst damn color in the world because it'll turn green on you. Pick any color but that." And Mr. Berlin said, "You heard what the man said—gold." So gold it was. Then he said, "What's the other color going to be?" And I said, "Oh, I hadn't even thought about another color." Mr. Berlin explained that we would sell more guitars if we gave people a choice because not everyone was going to want the gold. So I said, "Okay, the other color is black." And everybody immediately wanted to know, "Why black?" And I said, "Because you can see your hands move when you're on the stage, and it looks good with any outfit you wear."

So we decided on making a gold guitar and a black guitar with a single-cutaway mahogany body, the archtop, two bar pick-ups and a 22-fret neck, to be called the Gibson Les Paul Standard.

And Mr. Berlin and I reached an agreement on how all this was going to be handled legally.

239

Ted McCarty And The Prototype

After the meeting in Chicago, Mary and I went back to recording and touring and doing our thing with Capitol. This was during the time when *How High The Moon* and the following releases were hitting one after the other, so we were terribly busy playing an endless string of dates and promoting our records.

As our popularity went crazy, it became more and more difficult to find the time and quiet and privacy we needed to do our recordings. So along in the summer of 1951, we decided to take a break. Wally, Carol, Mary and I drove down to Stroudsburg, Pennsylvania and rented a secluded place that belonged to Ben Selvin, the bandleader. It was just a few miles from Fred Waring's big resort on the Delaware River, and perfect for what we wanted to do, which was get away from the world and the road so we could record and rest and enjoy ourselves for awhile. And it was there we recorded *Bye-Bye Blues* and several others.

We had been there for maybe a month when Ted McCarty, the president of Gibson who worked under Mr. Berlin, came down from Kalamazoo to show me the prototype for our solid body guitar. I liked it, but there were problems that needed to be identified and resolved, which is exactly what prototypes are for. One of the biggest problems was with the bridge, which wasn't set properly. There were no proper tools available, so with Wally's help, I took a screwdriver, heated it up on the stove and used the hot tip to burn and gouge out a channel in the wood for the bridge to sink down into. That guitar has gone through so many changes since then you wouldn't be able to recognize it as the original, but I've still got it.

It was while Ted McCarty was with us in Stroudsburg that we came to terms on my endorsement deal. It took all night, but we finally reached an agreement that specified royalties to me for every Les Paul guitar Gibson sold, in return for which I was to play my signature Gibson guitar exclusively when appearing in public, and be their advertising spokesman.

240

This is the first Les Paul guitar, the one that Ted McCarty brought me. Look under the bridge and you can see where I had to carve out a quarter-inch-deep hole to lower the bridge and make the guitar playable. I guess I should have kept this one all original, but I sent it back to Gibson and they refinished it a different color and put in low impedance pickups. It was originally a gold top, the very first one.

McCarty went back to Kalamazoo and had the design corrections put into play, and things began to pick up steam. We made the first pair as a test, then four more, and then a hundred or so of them, some of which were sold before we got bugs like the original trapeze tailpiece worked out of them.

The next two Les Paul models I got from Gibson were experimental flat-tops, a black one and a white one, and then I got some of the archtop models, including the original gold top prototype Gibson sent to me back in '51, which doesn't have a serial number. I love the look of the archtops, but for some reason, those first two flattops have always been my best guitars, and I still prefer them to all others today. The Les Paul Standard went into full production in 1952, and that's when my endorsement deal kicked in and we started using them for all our performances.

But the agreement I considered to be the foundation of what I was doing with Gibson came before the legal specifics of the endorsement deal, or any

other deal. And that was the verbal understanding I had with Mr. Berlin in the very beginning.

When the original agreement between Mr. Berlin and myself was made, there was no one else involved except the lawyer, and he didn't come in until the agreement was already made. And we specifically understood that the agreement was between Les Paul and Mr. Berlin, representing CMI, and that he would instruct Gibson what to do based on what he and I decided.

One of the things we discussed was ownership of the copyrights, patents

and everything connected to this new guitar. And Mr. Berlin said, "What would make you comfortable?" I could've asked for more, but I chose to say, "What about splitting it even, 50-50?" And he said, "Fine. Agreed." We'd already picked the color and shape of the instrument, we knew what we wanted to do with it, and now we had a working understanding. And when it was agreed upon, the Gibson people were to apply for the design rights and patents on the Les Paul Guitar.

Based on my agreement with Mr. Berlin, those rights should have been

divided equally between Les Paul and Gibson, but it never happened. What did happen is that Mr. Berlin called me years later and said, "We have a problem. I'm going to have to fire Ted." I said, "What did he do wrong?" And Mr. Berlin said, "He did two things. One, he bought a company called Bigsby, which is a conflict of interest. And worse than that, he tried to register the patent on the Les Paul Guitar to himself, personally. So I'm firing him."

This was shaping up to be a Hatfields and McCoys thing, and with everything we had going, nobody wanted that to happen, especially me. So I shrugged my shoulders and said, "What's our problem?" And that ended it right there. No one ever made an issue out of it or said anything more about it. McCarty made his move, I continued to do what I was doing, and the case was closed.

The Mini-Les Paul

At the beginning of our endorsement agreement, Gibson custom made two miniature gold top guitars for me, approximately the size of a mandolin and the only two they ever made. I used them when we did live performances of *Lover.*

When I recorded *Lover*, I sped up a guitar track artificially to get that very fast, high-pitched track you hear on the record. And there were critics who said I couldn't perform the song live because nobody could play that high and fast without a gimmick. To prove them wrong, I started including a mandolin in our performances of the song. At a certain point in the arrangement, I would hold the mandolin close to the mic and rip through the fast, high riff just like on the record.

The mandolin worked for this because it's a very high-pitched instrument, but when I hooked up with Gibson, I had them make the little guitars for me and used them for the same purpose by tuning them an octave higher. And it was a surprise to everybody when I went out on stage and played *Lover* live like it sounds on the record. In Pittsburgh and a few other places, I stopped playing the regular gold top and used the mini to pick the sped-up high part. I toyed constantly with ideas for how I was going to do on the stage what I was doing on the records. You could easily build an act on the records you couldn't follow in person, and I was working my ass off to avoid doing that.

From 1952 on, Mary and I always played Gibson Les Paul guitars when we performed, promoting them everywhere we went, but I continued to use my klunkers in the recording studio because I had labored over them and built them and that's where my sound was. And Mary was the same way. She loved the old klunkers and didn't like the new one at all. She wanted to refuse to play it altogether, but I said, "You've got to play it. This is now a part of who I am."

CHAPTER TWENTY-TWO

The Whirlwind of '51

Getting involved with Gibson in designing and launching the Les Paul solid body guitar was just one of the amazing things that happened in 1951. Everything was happening at once, and all we could do was keep on going and try to keep up. Looking back, I could say I pushed too hard, but at the time there was only one way to go, and that was straight ahead. This was the year we visited fifteen hundred radio stations and record shops in three months time. This was the year we sold six million records with seven big hits in eleven months; the year we had our first number one hit as a duo and had the number one and number two songs in the country at the same time, and on and on.

With the success of *Little Rock Getaway* and *Tennessee Waltz* at the end of 1950, followed by *Mockin' Bird Hill* and *How High The Moon* in early '51, the world opened up to us like never before. We had our pick of the best venues all across the country, and we formed the Team to go find as many of them as we could. We started touring with no thought of when it would end, and before it did, we had played in 49 states, Europe, and South America. We broke attendance records headlining in Las Vegas, San Diego, Chicago, Washington, D.C., everywhere we went, and we didn't back up from anything. We took as much work as they wanted to throw at us and kept on going, sometimes playing six shows a day.

It was also in 1951 that we started doing the very successful jingles for Rheingold Beer, which became another trademark for us. We would be playing a show, and one person would be shouting for *How High The Moon*, and another for the beer jingles. It was just a crazy, wild time where commercials we made were in demand just like our songs. And Capitol complained to me that the popularity of our jingles was hurting the sales of our records, and the radio stations were complaining because the disk jockeys were getting requests for them and playing them when they weren't scheduled, so the stations couldn't charge for them. Of course, Rheingold loved it because their business was booming, but to keep the peace, we eventually had to quit doing them. I still take pride in the fact that we were one of the first big name acts to start doing creative endorsements, and that the ones we did were originals we created.

In October, we played a series of dates at the Paramount, which had a special meaning for me. This was where I'd played with the Andrews Sisters and met Django Reinhardt back in '46. And back in the Fred Waring days, I'd always thought of the Paramount as the top of the line, the place where the most important acts played. So to be featured at the Paramount was an important personal accomplishment. We were on the bill with Frankie Laine, but his fans had a hard time finding a seat because ours turned out in mobs and filled the house every night.

They Think They Own You

When the big hits started coming one after the other, we became so popular it became a hindrance. No matter where we were or what we were doing, there were always people wanting to do something for you, or wanting you to do something for them. It became unbearable at times, especially for Mary.

Once, when I could see she was at the end of her rope, I said, "Come on, we're going to Bear Mountain. Wear your old clothes and put on a bandana and we'll spend a few days up there where no one will notice us." So we drove up there, and as we're getting out of the car, someone walks up and asks Mary for her autograph. And, of course, she gave it to them because every fan is important and we didn't want to disappoint them. But you just wished they could understand you were there because you specifically didn't want to be signing autographs.

Another time, we flew to Brazil, and I said to Mary, "Wear your old Levis, and I'll register under a phony name." So I sign us in as Les Polfuss, and no one knows we're there. We get settled in our room and come back out with our old clothes on, and a guy walks up and says, "Are you Les Polfuss?" I say, "Yeah." He says, "Well, can I speak to Mary Fordus?" He thinks it's funny, and Mary says, "We can't hide."

Looking back on that part of it, I think I was too nice. If the fans caught up with us, we always accommodated them, when maybe I should have yelled at them and told them to leave us the hell alone. But we never did that because being good to your fans is a part of being successful in show business.

Snowbound

There was another retreat we found by accident, and it turned out to be one of the best experiences we had before we left California permanently. It was late fall of 1951 when we finished a date in Buffalo, New York, and headed for Cedar Grove, New Jersey, where we were booked to play an extended engagement at Frank Daley's Meadowbrook club.

Meadowbrook was a big dancehall and well known for the musical broadcasts that originated there. It had been a big name venue since before the war, and I used to hear those shows in Waukesha. Glenn Miller, Tommy Dorsey, Harry James, Tex Beneke, Sinatra, all the big names had played there, and now it was our turn.

As we were leaving Buffalo, I called Frank Daley and said, "There's four of us and we're headed your way, and I'm bringing a lot of sound equipment for the recordings we're going to be doing." Frank knows nothing about recording, so he has no idea what I'm talking about, and I'm trying to make him understand we're going to need extra room. I said, "Whatever lodging you normally provide, we're going to need twice that much. Half for our recording set-up and the other half for our living quarters while we're there." And Frank said, "Don't worry about it. You're gonna come in here and do your thing, you're gonna have Buddy Morrow's band, you're gonna do shows and broadcasts for a couple of weeks and then you're gone." It was like talking to a foreigner because he just didn't get it.

So we're on our way to this important two-week engagement, and from Buffalo on we were in a terrible blizzard that stretches all the way to New Jersey. And the further we drive the worse it gets till we're up to our necks in snow. Anybody who has ridden with me knows, if I'm not doing at least 80, I'm looking for a place to park. For better or worse, I am and have always been a very fast driver.

A publicity guy from Capitol, Dick Linke, had been traveling with us much of the time and had become a good friend. My driving always made him nervous, and now, he was in a panic. He spent most of his time on the floor praying because I was still driving very fast, even with the snow. He's literally on the floor behind the front seat, and we can hear him praying. And, of course, Mary and I are in the front seat laughing because this is just everyday stuff to us. I was raised in Wisconsin, so snow is my middle name, but Dick Linke was from California where they never see snow, and he was terrified because we're driving up into the Catskills in a blizzard going 80 miles an hour. It was ridiculous, but we made it.

No Vacancy

When we arrived at Meadowbrook, Frank Daley wasn't there. He had gone to Las Vegas and left no instructions with his people concerning our accommodations. Nothing had been arranged, so here it is midnight in the dead of winter and we've got no place to stay. So I asked, "Where's the nearest hotel or motel?" And they said, "There are no motels, and hotels don't exist around here. And if they did, they'd be closed for the winter."

With no offer of assistance from the Meadowbrook people, we did the only thing we could do. We got back in the car and started driving, looking for anything we could find. We drove and drove and drove, and finally, I see a sign that says "Summer Cabins." It's a seasonal resort for summer tourists, and it's in the sweet little town of Oakland, New Jersey.

So I'm knocking on the door in the middle of the night, and after a while, this little lady comes to the door in her nightgown and says, "Yes?" And I said, "We're looking for a place to stay." And she said, "Well, I don't have anything because we're closed for the winter and all my cabins are shut down." And I said, "I understand that, but this is a special situation because we are specifically looking for a place that's closed during the winter. We want a place where no one disturbs us and we don't disturb them, so we can set up our machinery and do what we need to do."

So I explained it to her about our recording equipment and Meadowbrook and the whole nine yards, and then she said, "Well, you can have the upstairs of the house here for $40 a month." This was in the main house, where she lived on the ground floor, which was the only building heated during the winter months, and there were enough rooms on the second floor to easily accommodate Wally and Carol, Mary and myself and our recording set-up. So it was ideal for us, and that's where we settled.

Otto's Floral Manor

So we moved into Otto's Floral Manor and took over the upstairs and everything just fell into place. We were very comfortable being more or less snowed in there. Wally and Carol had their room, Mary and I had ours, and it gave us a little bit of heaven to be able to unpack and stay in one place for awhile.

Frank Daley's nightclub was not that close, maybe an hour's drive, but once we got there we didn't even consider staying anywhere else. And we were now glad Frank Daley had forgotten to make the arrangements because it led us to this great place. So for as long as the Meadowbrook engagement lasted, we were glad to make the drive.

When we were snowed in at Otto's Floral Manor we recorded *Tiger Rag*, *Smoke Rings*, *and My Baby's Comin' Home*.

We set up our recording equipment in the kitchen area because it gave us the most room. Then there were the sleeping rooms we could choose for certain purposes, as we needed to. I would have Mary sing a certain part while standing in the hallway, and other parts in different rooms to give each track its own sound. I'd also sometimes move my recording equipment to one of the other rooms to accomplish a particular effect. We had different sized rooms available and were willing to do whatever it took to get the sound I wanted to hear. We had the bathroom, which produced an echo-like sound, and once I determined exactly where to position Mary and the mic, the hallway was a great place for natural reverb. We only had mono to work with, so we had to make the best use we could of our surroundings to give depth to the recordings. And we were fortunate that the natural acoustics of the old manor house allowed us to do that.

There was extra room, and we needed it because we were getting massive amounts of mail every day and we had to store it somewhere until we could get to it all. We now had a string of smash hits, and with Capitol promoting the hell

250

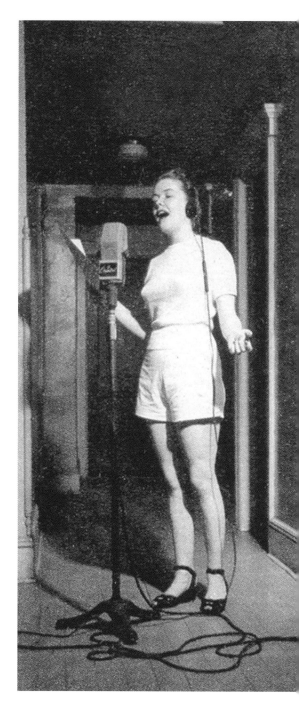

out of us, the volume of mail was such that we were asked to pick it up at the little post office in Oakland rather than having their guy deliver it. So that's what we did. One of us made the post office run every day, and Wally stayed very busy with his typewriter trying to keep up with the thousands of fan letters that kept coming in.

The four of us were a family, and we developed a way of life built around the cabin resort and the little town of Oakland. We'd make a haul from the grocery store about once a week, and it made Mary happy to have her kitchen set up to do the cooking. Carol took care of the trips and errands, Wally kept his typewriter clacking writing letters, and I worked on the recordings with very good results. And other than a few reporters and other special friends, there were almost no interruptions. So it was very relaxing, but we were accomplishing things, too. It was a lot of fun while it lasted. And we got all this for forty bucks a month.

Held Over By Popular Demand

The remote broadcasts were a hit and the crowds loved us, so Frank Daley extended the engagement beyond the original two weeks. We played for about a month before we finally closed it out. By that time the snow had been cleared and we were free to move on, but the four of us liked what we had at Otto's Floral Manor so much, we stayed on for a time longer. We were there a total of three, maybe four months, and many wonderful things happened during that time. Everything important in television was coming out of

251

We used a Hollywood movie tiger for this Capitol publicity stunt. Mary was petrified. The guitar is a Gretsch they stuck in my hand for the photo.

New York, which was only 45 minutes away. So we did another Sullivan show, the Como show, and a lot of different guest shots on various programs while we continued to live in Oakland.

Tiger Rag

We recorded a mess of hits at Floral Manor, which we sometimes called the Haunted House because it had so many rooms you could just wander around and get lost. We did *Smoke Rings* there because there was a place up the road called Glen Gray Camp, which reminded us of Glen Grey's theme song. We did *My Baby's Comin' Home* there too, which became a hit late in 1952.

I can't begin to remember all the songs we recorded while living at Floral Manor, but one of the biggest hits was *Tiger Rag*, and there are several interesting parts to that story. For one thing, it was one of the first recordings where Mary and I used the new Gibson solid body instead of my klunkers. Gibson had sent me six flattop prototypes, two each in gold, black and white, so Mary and I would each have a full set, and we put them to use on the recording of *Tiger Rag*.

This was not my first go at recording *Tiger Rag*. I had done an instrumental version while Mary and I were living in the basement apartment in Jackson Heights, sometime in '49 probably, and when Capitol heard it, they wanted to release it on the spot. But I wasn't satisfied with it and wouldn't hand it over. And while we were at Floral Manor, I finally realized what was lacking, and it had to do with the vocal, not the instrumental parts. We began to approach the song from that angle, adding Mary's tracks, and when I came up with the "here pussy, pussy, pussy…here kitty, kitty, kitty" line, we had it cinched.

We finished *Tiger Rag* near the end of 1951 and I immediately sent it to Capitol. It was released soon after, and hit the top of the charts like a rocket in January. So 1952 was starting off just like 1951, with another smash hit.

Traveling constantly and taking our portable recording studio with us was something remarkably new, but turning out one hit after another from hotel rooms, basements and New Jersey resorts was absolutely unheard of. In fact, many people didn't believe we were really doing it. The critics and doubters thought it was another hoax, a gimmick to attract attention because it didn't seem possible for us to be getting the sounds we were getting on our records without being in a permanent recording studio with all the modern facilities. But it was the truth, and we were getting better at doing it all the time.

When it was finally time to leave Oakland and Floral Manor, we all agreed it was a wonderful neighborhood, a beautiful part of the world we were terribly glad to have discovered. And this again is fate because it had nothing to do with planning. It just happened and we went with it. We stumbled upon the place, which led to us falling in love with the area, so it was a case of one

thing leading to another. Mary was not from the east, so to her it was all delightfully different. To me, it was like Missouri, it was like Wisconsin where I grew up, and familiar to me. And less than a year later, we got the Mahwah house and were living full time not ten minutes away.

Going Back East

We still had the house and garage recording studio in California, but with all that was now happening for us, it was getting harder and harder to find the time to get back to it. And during those long periods of time when we were away touring and performing, we had learned several things.

Our time at Otto's Floral Manor and Ben Selvin's place in Pennsylvania had shown us we no longer had to live in a big city to maintain our career.

After I finally recovered from the accident and no longer needed to make repeated visits to Good Samaritan Hospital, it was the garage studio more than anything else that had anchored me to California. And now, with the Ampex and all our success from recordings made on the run, the garage was no longer a necessity because we had proven we could supply Capitol with hit after hit from anywhere in the world.

And there was more. Our radio show with NBC had run its course and we decided not to continue it because we knew bigger things were ahead and didn't want to get tied up in another contract for that sort of thing. Also, after our appearances on the Sullivan show, I was more and more interested in television; and for that, you had to be in New York. So the writing was on the wall when we finally got back to Hollywood in early 1952.

CHAPTER TWENTY-THREE

The Move To Mahwah

It was harder for Mary than for me to think about leaving our little bungalow and studio, but we were both very attached to it. It was where we met and fell in love at first sight, and where we started out on our amazing life together. We had made it our own little paradise right there in the heart of Hollywood, where so many of our dear friends were located, and knowing it was time to move on didn't make it easy to do. We kept talking about the hard decision we had to make, and then one day the phone rang.

It was Martin Block calling from WNEW in New York, where he had the most popular radio show in the world. He was a disc jockey who had become famous doing a wildly popular show called *Make Believe Ballroom*. His bit was to pretend he was broadcasting from a big swanky ballroom, creating the illusion that the records he played were live performances. We had appeared on his show a number of times, and he was another radio guy who had helped us by repeatedly playing our records.

He was contacting us to tell me about a phone call he had just gotten. What happened is that a bigwig with the Listerine Company was driving down from Connecticut listening to Martin's show, and heard one of our recordings for the first time. I'm not sure which record it was, but when he heard it, he pulled off the road and called WNEW and got Martin Block on the line. And he said, "That song you were just playing, what is that?" And Martin said, "It's Les Paul and Mary Ford, and everything you heard was just the two of them. They're on Capitol Records, and they're good friends of mine." And he said, "Well, I would love to get in touch with them because I have an idea."

So Martin passed this on to me, and I got in touch with the Listerine people to find out what they wanted. And I find out the president's idea was for Listerine to sponsor us on a television show. And I'm immediately very interested because this is 1952, and other than Ed Sullivan and Lucille Ball, there were very few shows making any noise. This was at the beginning, just before all the big names on radio started jumping ship, so the ground floor was wide open.

The Plaza Powwow

The next step was a couple of very serious meetings in New York. We first met the president of Listerine and a couple of his people at the Hampshire

House to basically introduce ourselves to each other, and then we had a big meeting at the Plaza Hotel which included, the brass from Capitol, the Listerine people with their attorneys and advertising agency, and Mary and I with our manager and our business manager. So there was a group of ten or twelve people involved, and Mary and I sat at this enormous conference table while all these bald heads and smart-thinking people proposed this and that and talked about what we were going to do.

The idea they had was to do a weekly show called *The Les Paul and Mary Ford Special* and model it after *The Ed Sullivan Show*, which was by far the number one variety show. And in discussing it, it was realized that the variety show format was right for the Sullivan show because Ed was not a talented performer himself, so it took all kinds of different acts to keep the show interesting. And I said, "If you think about it, what's being done with the Sullivan show is to take what's left of vaudeville and put it on television. And it's working great for him, but we're two entertainers who do have talent, with a completely new way of recording and performing our music, so we don't need jugglers and dogs. We just need to do our thing."

So the meeting went on and on, and the idea for our show changed from an hour once a week to three half-hour shows a week to however many 15-minute shows a week. Mary and I were sitting there not saying anything, and these ideas were bopping around the big table as all these guys took their turn saying what they thought should be done. And out of nowhere, I suddenly blurted out, "Why don't we do a five-minute show, five times a day, five times a week, and do it on both radio and television?"

I don't know where the idea came from and I had no logical reasoning for it, but that's what I said. And it got the biggest laugh you ever heard. All the bald heads are laughing, and I'm thinking, geez, I'd like to have an opening line for my show that would get a response like that. And then the president suddenly sobered up and said, "Wait a minute. Why did you say that?"

And my reply was something to the effect that you'd catch the listeners and viewers at all hours of the day, so if they missed you in the morning, they could still catch you at noon or around quitting time or in the evening. With five shows a day, we'd be there during the drive-times, before the news, after the news, anywhere you wanted to go. And with the shows being only five minutes in length, you would have the flexibility to sandwich them into many different places. I was winging it like hell but it was making sense, and then Mary said, "But radio is dead!" I could've wrung her neck!

So then came a big discussion about how radio was changing because television was taking over, but that it was still very important and useful for what I had proposed. And we beat that horse for another hour until there was finally an agreement that doing a five-minute show five times a day five days a week was the smart thing to do because of the nationwide exposure all parties involved would get at every hour of the day or night. And we're talking about Capitol, Listerine, and Mary and I.

We decided to call it *Les Paul and Mary Ford At Home*, and it was specified that our last show of the day would always be immediately following the news at 10:00pm, when the majority of the people go to bed. That way, the person going to bed who turned off the TV or radio would hear us again next morning when they turned it on again. So we put them to bed and we wake them up, we catch them leaving us and again when they come back. That was the marketing theory I made up on the spot, and they bought it.

When we began to discuss where the show was going to be produced, they said," Would you consider doing it from your home?" And I said, "Not the home I've got out in California. It's just a little two bedroom bungalow with a boarded up garage that I bought for $15,000 furnished, and surely not suitable for a television show. And they said, "Well then, would you consider moving to New Jersey?" And I said, "Why New Jersey?" They said, "Our home base is in New Jersey, and it will be much more convenient if the show is produced near us so we can work closely together. There would just be many advantages to doing it in New Jersey."

So Mary and I talked it over, and we were both thinking the same thing. So I said, "It's fine with us. We'll move to New Jersey, but we have some specifications." And what we wanted was to be in a place where the public couldn't easily get to us. And we weren't speaking just of our fans, who we loved. We had become so popular that everywhere we went, we were overrun with publishers, songwriters, agents, promoters, you name it. The constant interruptions were killing us, and as we kept getting bigger, the problem just kept getting worse.

I said, "What we need is a place that's far enough away from New York to have quiet and privacy, but still less than an hour from Broadway." And then I told them about our recent experience of living in New Jersey and how favorably impressed we were with the area. So we took a map and calculated what areas would be 45 minutes away from Broadway, and then they started looking for a place that would meet our requirements. And the place they found was in Mahwah, in the very neighborhood Mary and I had fallen in love with when we were snowed in at Floral Manor. So it was perfect.

You Can't Take It With You

In most cases, throughout my life, when the time came to make a move, I kept the bare essentials and left the rest behind. Just went out the door and left it there, and that was the end of it.

I was always determined that dealing with the dead weight of a bunch of stuff was not going to slow me down, and it will if you let it. I'm not so happy about that tendency now, but back then, when I had somewhere to go, something waiting to be done, it was more important to keep moving than it was to stay behind and deal with every little thing. So in leaving California, I kept the important things like my recording lathes, certain guitars and pieces of equipment, but a large part of it, I just let it go.

Oddly enough, much of it has come back to me. It's either you get a letter from somebody, or someone picks up the phone and calls you and says, "Hey, this has been sitting in my garage for the last 20 years. You forgot it and it's still sitting here." I got a letter from the guy who's got my first speaker, the one I used down in Nashville in 1951. He says, "You gave it to your friend, and your friend gave it to my father, and my father gave it to me. It's a flowerpot now. I got a beautiful bouquet." So he's got a flower garden coming out of my old speaker. He sent me a picture of it to autograph it for him.

Eventually, I sold the North Curson house, and the garage with it. When we were cleaning out the house, I pulled a drawer open and a check for $7,000 fell out that I hadn't cashed. And it was no longer any good because so much time had passed. I had forgotten it completely and it had been stuffed in that drawer for years. When we found it, I just laughed because it showed how busy we were during that whole time.

And you're not going to lug all these guitars around, so I kept the special ones, my klunkers and a few others, and just gave the rest of them away. I even gave a guy my original console out of the garage. And now, someone will say, "How could you do that? That was history, that was important." But what was I going to do with it? I had no place for it, no use for it, and couldn't see hauling it all the way across the country. So I gave it to this guy, and he put it in a cellophane wrapper in his garage and it stayed there.

Finally, many years later I run into him somewhere, and he says, "You know that thing is still in my garage. Would you like to have it?" I say, "Oh, I'd love to have it." And it comes back to me better than if I had saved it myself. He's got it all wrapped up so the dirt doesn't get to it. It's odd how these things work.

Pro And Con

As much as I loved it for all the important things that happened there, I was glad to be free of the garage. There was no end in sight to what I was doing with the tape machines so letting it go wasn't such a loss, but leaving

California cost me in other ways. Making the big move to New Jersey to start a whole new chapter was terribly exciting, but it meant I would no longer have Leo Fender sitting there in my back yard, or Bing Crosby dropping in to see what's going on, or the Andrews Sisters, or the important people nobody ever heard of who provided so much input and gave me so many ideas. So you cut your own water off. The guy that says, "Hey, I'm bugged with so much stuff I don't want anybody around me." He finally gets it where nobody calls him, nobody bothers him. Isn't this wonderful? But if the phone doesn't ring, unless he gets a letter from somebody, he's not going to learn anything.

And there are certain things you don't realize you're borrowing or are being given to you that are terribly important in what you're doing with your life. But I didn't have time to miss all my California buddies because now, I'm in Vegas, I'm in New York, I'm in London, knocking around with a whole new group of friends learning tons of things I wouldn't have learned if I had stayed put in my California back yard. So you lose one, you gain another, but they're different worlds. And wherever you are, it's your life and you're living it, and all you can do is your best. And that never changes.

Mahwah House

When I told Listerine I wanted to be 45 minutes from Broadway but still out and away from everything, I already had this particular part of New Jersey in mind. Mary and I loved the area, and we knew from our own experience the drive could be made to New York in less than an hour. So we expressed to Listerine that this neighborhood was our preferred choice, and they went out and found the house and seven acres that was to become our permanent home. It's still secluded and quiet today, but when we arrived in '52, everything around us was just farms and cows, and our house on the mountainside was one of the first in that immediate vicinity.

The house was built into the side of one of the Ramapo Mountains near Mahwah, with lots of trees and big windows that had a great view across the lit-

Our beautiful new home near Mahwah, New Jersey, tucked into the side of a mountain.

tle valley. It was less than two years old, one story with seven large rooms, designed in the modern architectural style that became popular after the war. And from the first moment we saw it, Mary and I loved it. We thought both the house and the location would work great for the television show, and there was just enough room for Wally and Carol to live with us, so it was a perfect fit.

When we first moved into the place, we took the approach that we were going to live there only as long as the Listerine show lasted. And, of course, we had no idea how long that might be because doing television was uncharted territory for everybody involved. We were going to give it our best shot, and if it worked, we'd stay in the house and keep going. If it didn't, we'd just leave and carry on with our career as before.

But what we didn't account for in our early plans was the fact that we were a growing family, and that's where our concept of the house began to become more than just being the set for our television show. I had two kids from my prior marriage who now wanted to come and live with Dad. And Mary and I would soon have two children, three actually, but one passed away, and that meant the house had to be bigger.

Also, as the Listerine program became more and more successful, there was an increasing need for additional space to store the props, scenery and equipment that were a necessary part of doing the show. And I personally needed more room for my recording equipment and all the different electronics inventions I was working on, including the eight-track machine, while at the very same time we were launching the Gibson Les Paul guitar.

With all this happening, we were continually enlarging the house with one building project after another, until it had grown to 22 rooms. And it had to happen fast, so there was no time for developing and debating the plans. I would just say, "See this space right here? Come in with a plow and plow it out and build a room right there." And this was not easy to accomplish because the back of the house is up against granite. It's notched into the mountainside with the ground dropping away below, and could only grow in length.

When the need developed for a sitting room, I brought my builder into the house and pointed out the window and said, "See that area? That's where we want a sitting room." And he looked at me like I was crazy because we're looking at nothing but big boulders and a steep hillside. And I said, "Just come in here with a bulldozer and plow it all out and level it up and build me a sitting room, and make it two stories high."

So they go to work on the sitting room, and at the same time, at the other end of the house, I'm saying, "Now here's where I want my recording studio, and I want a big hole gouged out of the granite behind the house so I can make a live echo chamber in the side of the mountain." I had always wanted my own live echo chamber, and now, thanks to Listerine and Capitol, I finally had it.

Union Rules

There was building and bulldozing going on all the time for the first several years, and somewhere in '53, after this thing was on its way, I took my bulldozer guy out back and said, "I want you to level out and extend this whole area behind the house because we need room for parking the trucks they're going to bring up here." We needed a much bigger parking area, and there was a reason for it.

The reason had to do with legal problems concerning the performance unions and whether an artist can work in his own home. With the big studios and networks, you couldn't change a light bulb or throw a switch unless it was done according to strictly enforced union rules. And the unions were watching us very closely because what we were doing was very unusual and they wanted to control it. But they couldn't get to us because the driveway up the mountain to our house was considered a private road, and as long as the technical people needed to do the show were on it, we were free of union jurisdiction. So that's why we needed a parking lot.

An Uninvited Guest

When I told the contractor what I wanted done, he tried to talk me into doing it in front of the house. And I said, "No, no, no. I want it right where I said, right here in back. Just go do it." He was still very reluctant, but finally he did it. And I could tell there was something odd about his reluctance, but once the job was started, I forgot about it.

The parking lot was built, and it was two, maybe three months later, on New Year's Eve, that he came to me and said "Les, I've got to level with you. There's something I need to tell you." And then he tells me an amazing story.

The person who owned and originally built the house was a doctor, and he loved a particular dogwood tree that was on the property. And when the doctor passed away, they secretly buried his ashes under it according to his final wishes, and the contractor was the only one who knew about it other than his widow. So the doctor was buried in the ground behind our house the entire time we had been living there, and I now knew why the contractor had been so reluctant to plow up that particular area.

And here's the kicker. The reason the contractor came clean about it at the New Year's Eve party is that he had a problem. And the problem was that when they plowed and leveled the parking lot, they had to dig the doctor up, and then they couldn't put him back. So the contractor put the remains in the back of his truck thinking he would contact the widow to arrange for burial elsewhere. But they couldn't make contact with her because she had gone to Europe and no one knew when she was coming back.

So the contractor tells me all this, and then he says, "And the hell of it is, I've still got this guy and I've been dragging him around in the back of my truck for two months. We gotta do something." If there was ever a time where you didn't know whether to laugh or cry, this was it. It was just the oddest thing in the world, and very disturbing because there are serious legalities involved with an unauthorized burial. So we did what we had to do to find the widow, she retrieved her husband, and that ended the story.

263

The Listerine Show

It took over a year of work enlarging and wiring up the house to get ready to start doing the television show. In the fall of 1953, after going back to Paris a second time to help with Django's affairs after he died, it was finally time to take it on the air. *The Les Paul and Mary Ford Show* debuted on television in October, with five five-minute shows a week, just as we had planned. And to make it clear, the same show ran all five times each day, and then the next day another show would air five times, and so on. So in a week's time, five separate shows would air a total of 25 times.

The schedule we had called for 36 shows to be produced in 15 weeks, and it was hell to keep up. We did it by working together, and the show was a success from the first episode.

The format of our TV show followed the pattern we had established a few years earlier with our NBC radio show, but the work was much more tedious because the timing had to be absolutely precise, down to the second. So everything had to be scripted, and the fun of ad-libbing was all but gone. Even though things weren't computerized like they are today, if you were one second too long, down came the guillotine. So our goodbye at the end of the show had to be on time if we didn't want to get cut off at the knees.

The five-minute show actually went four-and-a-half minutes to allow for the commercials. And in that four-and-a-half minutes, we had to play our theme song, make our entrance and say hi to everybody, and then immediately move into whatever the situation was for the particular episode. Mary might be in the kitchen cooking, or the living room looking at a magazine, whatever the vignette was, and I always had one of my Gibson guitars. We'd exchange a few words to set it up and then weave a couple of songs together with the bit we were doing according to the pre-timed script. This was a far cry from the anything goes fun we had with our Rhubarb Red and Mary Lou radio show back in Hollywood, but we eventually got used to the restrictions and made the best of it. After we had established the television format, the TV audio tracks were edited for the five minute radio show, which aired all over the country following the same programming schedule as the television show.

What Listerine did which kept us in tow was establish the policy that "You can take as much time as you want but you pay for it." So they paid us a great amount of money, but in receiving this great amount of money, we had to accept the responsibility that if we blew lines and made mistakes, the cost of the extra time it took came directly out of our pockets. So it didn't take me

Our TV show for Listerine was filmed right here in our new house. The flagstone floor in this picture can be seen in many of the new photos in this book.

long to realize that everybody was going to have be very disciplined in how we approached doing the show. This was very much a learning experience for me because I've always been an ad libber. So if I wanted to ad lib, I now had to make sure they were timed.

The Drawbacks Of Fame

It wouldn't be truthful for me to say I didn't want to be known. I wanted to be famous, and at the time we're talking about, to be famous you had to be on television. We had our big hit records, and our names were known, but being on television means you're being seen, and you have to be both seen and heard to become a household name. So if what you want to do is achieve fame, you have to work very hard and make sacrifices to do it.

And I know I was pushing everything to the max, and kept on pushing when the ones I loved the most were getting exhausted and worn down. They couldn't keep up because no one has ever been able to keep up with me, and Mary kept saying, "We have more money than we can ever spend. Why don't we take a break and just be us again?" And I wanted to do it, but then the phone would ring and there would be something else to do, more people to please, somewhere new to go, and I could never say no to more work. And this was exactly what my Dad had foreseen when he shook his head no at the Club 400. No matter what was put in front of me, I'd say, "Sure. I can do it." There was nothing I couldn't do or would not want to do. If someone said, "Would you do this tomorrow at midnight?" I'd say, "Okay."

This was going to be the downfall because it wasn't Beekman's Barbecue I couldn't say no to. It was the fact that the phone would ring and someone would say, "President Eisenhower would love to have you perform for him Sunday night." And Mary would say, "Les, no. I don't want to go and I don't want to do it. There's just too much work." And I would say, "But Mary, we can't turn the President down." And she would agree, you can't turn the President down. Nobody should do that.

So we'd pack up and go play for the President, and maybe we'd have a good time, but it was overtaking us. I was feeling it. Wally and Carol were feeling it. We were all feeling it. But how do you stop it? How do you lay it down when it's what you've worked for your whole life? And what do you say to yourself when you've become so well known and so popular that even playing for the President of the United States is a drag? And Mary was the one who said, "I can't take it. I just can't take all the hard work anymore." It was extremely hard work. It was relentless, and it was tearing us up.

266

CHAPTER TWENTY-FOUR

Overdrive

If 1951 was a whirlwind, then '52 was a hurricane, and now it was no longer a matter of being in control, it was hanging on for the ride of our lives. We started the year in California with *Tiger Rag* at number one, playing two-week engagements in Hollywood, San Francisco and Las Vegas, with every performance sold out. In the annual *Down Beat* magazine poll, I was again voted the number one guitarist in the country, and Mary and I were also named as the number one recording act by the radio industry. It was absolute craziness, and everybody in the world wanted a piece of us.

We'd had seven big hits in '51, and we topped ourselves with eight more in '52. And they were all recorded on the road because we never stopped. I now had the biggest Cadillac they made, a new Fleetwood, and we drove the wheels off running back and forth across the country more times than I can remember.

I approached those cross-country drives like a race, and we would make New York to Hollywood in less than three and a half days. And this was long before interstates and loops around cities; this was old 66 and two-lane highways that went through the middle of every town along the way. When I drove, I had one speed: flat out. Every time we got back east, we'd go to Mahwah to check on the building progress and lay up for a couple of days, and then we'd be gone again.

Showing Off The New Baby

Gibson worked the kinks out of the Les Paul guitar and turned it loose on the public with a massive advertising campaign in the summer of '52. Ads featuring Mary and I with the new solid body guitar began appearing in the magazines and trades, and we made sure every disk jockey and reporter we came in contact with knew about it. We performed with the new guitars for the first time in June, during a two-week engagement at the Paramount, and Gibson was soon selling them as fast as the factory in Kalamazoo could turn them out.

We had by now perfected our stage act, which included Carol singing harmonies off stage and a limited use of pre-recorded background tapes to get the fuller sound, and we made full use of it in marketing the guitars. The Les Paulverizer gag was still the running bit I used to explain all the multiple effects in our act, and if people didn't realize it was a hoax, I wasn't going to tell them any different because it added to the mystique and popularity of the instruments we were putting my name on. And the Paramount engagement was a great success. This time there was no Frankie Laine sharing the bill. We

The day we opened in Chicago, my old friends the Atlass brothers had their friends at City Hall declare it "Les Paul and Mary Ford Day." We entered the city on a yacht crossing Lake Michigan, escorted by fireboats squirting their hoses in the air.

were the headliners and the huge crowds were all ours.

A couple of months later we were back in Chicago for an extended engagement as the 1952 presidential election was coming up. Both the Democrats and Republicans had held their national conventions in Chicago that summer, and the campaigning for Stevenson and Eisenhower was going strong in the press and on the radio. We never took sides in politics, but what did mean something to us was that on our opening night, a group of our fans showed up in front of the Chicago Theatre wearing buttons and carrying signs that said, "Les and Mary for President!" So Mary and I went out front and mingled with them and signed autographs and just enjoyed the situation. And to top it off, we were being paid $18,000 a week.

The summer and fall of 1952 was a whirlwind for Mary and me. This large group of fans met us at the Chicago Theater.

London Triumph

Our sound had really caught on in England. In fact, some of my early instrumental releases that didn't hit so big in the States had done very well over there, so there was a definite awareness and appreciation for what we were doing. And shortly after *How High The Moon* hit the top on both sides of the Atlantic, we received an invitation to play a two-week engagement at the London Palladium. This was a great thrill for us because the Palladium was the top of the line in London, like Carnegie Hall and the Paramount put together.

So we made our plans and cleared our schedule, and in September, Wally, Carol, Mary and I took a 12-day sail across the Atlantic on the *Queen Elizabeth*. The voyage was an interesting experience, and an enjoyable, restful break once we got used to the motion of the ship. But it was a very slow pace, and I kept wishing I could be driving my Cadillac across the ocean because then we would get there damn quick.

273

Meeting The Royalty

When we arrived in London, a mob of reporters was waiting for us at the boat dock. This was unexpected, and it was then I began to realize just how popular we had become outside America. All our Palladium shows were sold out before we got there, and the reception we received from the public and the press was tremendous.

We got there just a day before we were to open and went to the Palladium that night to see Bob Hope's closing performance. There was a tradition there that the headliners who were going to be the next act would sit in a special reserved box on one side of the balcony, and any royalty or other bigwigs who might be in attendance sat in a balcony box on the opposite side. So that night, Bob Hope introduced us from the stage to confirm we would be opening the next night. When we stood up to take a bow, there was a huge round of applause, and Bob Hope made a joke that he hoped the same crowd would come back the next night. And this was because Palladium audiences were famous for being very critical and tough on even the most respected entertainers. If someone was having an off night, or the audience sensed they weren't as good as their press notices made them out to be, they would crucify them.

After the show, Mary and I were backstage with Bob Hope and a number of other famous people, including Betty Hutton. The performance had gone very well, and our merry little group was laughing it up and having a few drinks when I was informed that members of the Royal Family wanted to meet Mary and me.

We had earlier been told the Queen might be attending Bob Hope's performance that night, so now we're in a dither thinking the Queen of England is about walk in and catch us with our hair down, and Betty Hutton passed out on the dressing room couch from too much booze. So we're hiding the liquor bottles and buttoning our shirts, we're dragging Betty off the couch and into the closet to get her out of sight, and we're laughing like hell because it's like the Keystone Kops or the Marx Brothers. And then the royalty shows up, and it's not the Queen. It's the Duke of Kent, a boy in his teens, who is very interested in show business and in music.

We were all being very polite and trying to behave, and the Duke was telling us of his desire to play the accordion when he suddenly turned to Mary and said, "You make a beautiful noise!" We thought Mary was being insulted until it was explained that the British sometimes use the term "noise" to mean music. We realized it was intended as a compliment and had a good laugh about it. As soon as the Duke and his group left, we looked in the closet and Betty Hutton was still out cold, so she missed the whole thing.

During the day, Mary and I spent time seeing the sights, and it led to

Backstage at the London Palladium with Bob Hope.

another little incident. There was a song associated with a popular British stage production, which I'd heard and recorded earlier in 1952. I didn't know the name of the tune when I recorded it, so when I sent it to Capitol, I titled it *Meet Mr. Callaghan* after the name of the guy in the show. And this little tune was another instrumental hit for me at the same time we were in London. So we looked the guy up just to meet him and thank him for the song, and explain why I had gotten the title wrong. So that was good for a little adventure and a laugh, but there was someone else on my mind while we were there, and it was someone very important.

As Recorded by LES PAUL on Capitol Record #2193

MEET MISTER CALLAGHAN

By ERIC SPEAR

PIANO SOLO

40¢

LEEDS MUSIC CORPORATION · NEW YORK · CHICAGO · HOLLYWOOD · LONDON

In Search Of The Master

I hadn't heard anything from or about Django since the time back in 1946 when we met and spent so much time together while he was in the States. We had gotten to know each other well during the Ellington tour, and had also shared a lot before that, indirectly, because of my work with the AFRS producing programs for the troops.

During my time in the service, I played guitar on damn near everything that went out. So everywhere Django went in Europe during the war, it was Les Paul, Les Paul, Les Paul. And, of course, he had an ear for it, so he knew everything I had done, and I sure as hell knew everything he had done. So there was a mutual admiration thing going on even before we met, and now six years had gone by without any news of him at all. So I had it in mind to look him up while we were there because he was my friend and I was concerned about him.

And I know I've said it before, but I'll say again that in my lifetime, to this day, Django is probably the one individual who impressed me the most as just one hell of a creator and a true genius with a guitar. He was a big influence on me, and I was about to find out that I had become the same to him.

While we were in London and had the time, we decided to go across the channel and look for Django in Paris. Because I had completely lost track of him, we decided to try and find Stephane Grapelli, thinking if anyone would know where Django was, it would be him. So we went looking for Stephane and saw a sign at a place on the boulevard there that said "Stephane Grapelli."

We went into this tiny little club and sat there and after about an hour we gave up because no one we ask speaks English and there is no sign of a violin player, just this guy playing the piano. We're getting ready to leave and Mary says, "Why don't you go over and ask the piano player. Maybe he knows where Stephane is." So I went over to the piano player and make like I'm playing a violin and say the name, and he says, "I am Stephane." I had never seen him before so I had no way of knowing, but here was Stephane Grapelli, playing the piano instead of the violin.

He spoke some English, so I introduced myself and said, "We are friends of Django and we want to find him. Where is he?" Stephane was aware of who I was and very cordial, but he couldn't help. He said, "If you find him, you're a better man than I am. We've been looking for over two years and no one can find Django anywhere. We don't know where he has gone." And now I'm remembering how sad and downhearted Django was when he left America, and now feel we really must do something to find out what has happened to him.

When Mary and I walk outside the little café, we see a couple of taxicabs parked there. And I was immediately reminded that when you need to find something in a strange city, you rely on the cab drivers to know where everything is. So I took two twenty-dollar bills and tore them both in half. Then I went to the first cab driver, handed him one of the halves, and said, "You get the other half when you find Django." Then I did the same thing with the second cabbie, and told them both where we were staying. So for forty bucks I've got two cab drivers on the hunt for Django.

The next morning, Mary and I are in our hotel room when the phone rings, and it's Django down in the lobby. So one of the cab drivers had found him. When we went downstairs, I gave the cabbie both the twenty halves and he became our friend for the rest of the time we were there and took us everywhere we needed to go. He also spoke English, which was very helpful because Django and I needed an interpreter to be able to talk.

Django's Change of Style

We were very glad and excited to see each other, but he was terribly depressed. We're all riding in the cab together and the driver is interpreting for us and Django is telling us everything. He had gone to playing electric. He said, "I love your guitar," meaning the electric sound he had heard in 1946. And I said, "Forget about it. You stick to your guitar and your sound. It's your trademark, and if you change it you can only go down, you can't go up. You leave my guitar to me, and your guitar to you. That's what makes you so special."

I'm sitting in the front seat and he and Mary are sitting in the back, and he doesn't agree with me. He says, "No. I like your guitar and that's what I want. I want that sound." And that's when I began to realize how much I had influenced him. A few minutes later he pokes me in the back and says, "Can you read music?" So I told him, "No." And he's jumping up and down with glee in the back seat. He's the happiest guy in the world because he's thinking if Les Paul can't read music then it's okay that he can't either.

We ride along a little further and he pokes me in the shoulder again and says, "Do you like be-bop?" I say, "Not particularly." He says, "Well, I like it." And then a few minutes later he's asking me another question. "I don't play bad, do I?" And that told me for certain he had never gotten over bombing with Duke Ellington in the States, that it had been eating at him all those

277

years. He had not been recognized and accepted and it still bothered him terribly. And now I find out he'd been hiding out for two years and not playing in public because he was changing his style completely. He thought if he started playing be-bop using an electric guitar and amplifier like mine, he could come back to America and everyone would love him. This was his thinking, and this is what he had done. And by the time he accomplished what he wanted, his whole way of playing had changed so much you couldn't recognize the Django you knew and admired.

With my guitar hero, Django Reinhardt, in Paris, 1952.

We jammed while I was there, and it was just so disappointing to hear him sound so different and foreign. In fact, you would actually go looking to find something you could recognize that was coming from his gypsy soul, the thing that had meant so much to everyone who heard him, and it just wasn't there. And you had to marvel at the fact that a guy can change that much. It's like he had taken a big eraser and rubbed out everything he'd ever learned. He had removed it completely, and when I understood why, it tore a hole in my heart.

Tragic Misconception

Django made his only trip to America to do an extended tour with Duke Ellington as a featured special guest, and had come with no guitar, no pick, nothing; just the clothes he had on. Soon after he came to see me at the Paramount, Lou Levy came one night and said, "Come on, we're going to see Django."

So we went over to Café Society and watched Django roll over and die. Lou and I sat at the table and were just stunned at how awkward it was because we knew how great Django was and how misplaced the whole scene was. The Duke Ellington group didn't play well behind him, didn't fit him at all. It was a terrible mismatch, and Django was a fish out of water. It was just a bad performance, and a very sad situation. And what's worse, the experience made him think there was something lacking in his music, that he had to change in order to be well received. And little did I know that Django was so impressed with my electric sound and what I was doing on the guitar that he made a decision to change his whole way of playing, which was very hard for me to believe or understand until he told me and I saw it for myself.

Incidentally, I once asked if he had ever listened to Eddie Lang and Joe Venuti. And he said, "Yes, of course, that's where the idea came from for me and Grapelli." He loved

Django had laid down his acoustic guitar and was now playing electric .

what Eddie Lang and Venuti had done with the guitar and violin. He learned from it and then took it far beyond everyone else. And this was terribly interesting because Eddie Lang was my first mentor for jazz guitar, and then, years later, I discover Eddie Lang was the beginning for Django too.

The Last Goodbye

That visit in Paris was the last time I saw Django. We'd had a wonderful time, but there were so many things waiting for us back home that we couldn't stay a day longer. Mary and I got back ready to conk out because it was a long, rough journey, and we were very glad to be back home. And we no more than got in the house when the phone rang and someone said, "Django has died." He'd had a massive stroke and the light just went out. So I turned around and flew back for his burial and to help take care of his family because without him, they were lost.

Back in France, I went to his home to gather up his things, his papers and belongings. This was in the spring of 1953, and it was then I found out how old he was. He was 53 when he died, 15 years older than me. We took his wife and kids shopping for things they needed, and arranged for a gravestone, but the best thing we did for Django, and probably the smartest move I could have made for his family, was asking, "Who's been taking care of his songs and stuff?" Nobody had an answer, so I had a friend of mine do a search on it in Paris and discovered there were a number of business people who had profited from Django's music but hadn't taken care of their obligations. So I

279

said, "Get all those guys together and have them cough up some money for this gypsy woman and her son." And I got them $50,000, which to them was a fortune. It came from back royalties and other things these people had just nonchalantly failed to account for to Django.

Django Reinhardt
1900-1953

How many people do you think Django Reinhardt has changed in the world? I think he's probably touched as many guitar players as ever known to man, and through all those thousands of guitar players, he's reached millions of people. And he's still reaching them because it doesn't end. It keeps on going every time somebody hears what he did. I asked him once where he learned to pick like that, and he said, "From a little old gray-haired man that used to sit around our fire. When I pick up the guitar he'd say, 'No, no, no— like this, like this!'" So Django's way of playing came from his surrounding people, from the gypsy culture he was born into. They are a fiery people, intensity is their natural thing, so the passion was already in him from his genes. He had tremendous energy, and when he played, it all went right into his guitar. This gypsy fellow just came along and what he did is uncanny, unreal. He is the source of so much. And he did it all with a crippled hand.

This is the pick Django used when he visited me backstage at the Paramount in 1946.

The way I understand it, he was in a caravan wagon and a lantern got kicked over. There was a fire and his hand was badly burned. It crippled his fingers so that the little finger on his left hand, his fretting hand, was frozen in a certain bent position, and the finger next to it was also frozen in a locked position. I listened to his records for 12 years before I ever met him, so I was accustomed to how fast and sharp he played without knowing of his condition. After we met, it was amazing to see what he was able to do with that handicap. The interesting thing is that you don't really need five fingers to play what Django played. Django found the things that fit what he had to work with, and that's exactly what I've had to do. And maybe it's not so surprising that we both landed in the same boat.

Django had a son named Babik who I knew since the day we held hands after his dad died. I saw him for the last time in 2001 and we had a wonderful time. He was a great kid, but he had problems. He had a stroke just like his dad, and now he's gone too. Thanks to him, I have Django's guitar. It's his acoustic guitar, not the later electric thing, and I'm so glad to have it because it keeps Django with me, and it reminds me of what can be lost trying to please people who don't understand you. This is where Django went, and then he died, never having the chance to come back to America to prove his point. I never again used that little pick he borrowed the night we met, and I keep it with me to this day.

CHAPTER TWENTY-FIVE

Vaya Con Dios

We finished 1952 appearing in the Hollywood Christmas parade. Capitol's float was like a big three-layer cake, and they put us on the very top because we were their top-selling artists for the year. And 1953 started off just like the previous two years, with a big hit in January. This time it was *Bye-Bye Blues,* a song we recorded while on retreat in Stroudsburg, using one of my klunkers. *I'm Sitting On Top Of The World* was another top ten hit early in the year on which I used one of my Gibson solid body prototypes. We had another seven hits in '53, including the one that topped them all, *Vaya Con Dios.*

We had gone up to St. Paul to play for a big auto show, and Don Forman, one of the Capitol guys, was traveling with us. Anita O'Day had just released an up-tempo recording of *Vaya Con Dios,* and Don kept suggesting that we should cover it. Then we heard it on the car radio, and I realized he was right. So we got a copy of Anita's record on the way home to New Jersey.

We went straight to work on recording the song, and in the process, I changed the lyric. Anita's version used English, which was, "May God be with you, my darling," but Mary sang it, "Vaya con Dios, my darling, vaya con Dios, my love." We both thought it carried more feeling that way, and just sounded right, so we went with it.

Capitol had already pressed half a million copies of *I'm A Fool To Care,* which was to be our next release, but I called them up and said, "Stop the presses, I've got something more important!" When I told them I had a new recording of *Vaya Con Dios* I wanted to do a rush release on, running it in ahead of *I'm A Fool To Care,* they didn't want to do it. Even though they owned the song, they thought *Vaya Con Dios* was a sure bomb and told me to forget about it. It took some persuasive tactics to convince them to go along with me, but they finally did and the record was released in June.

Right after its release, *Vaya* was doing okay, but it wasn't taking off. And here's the interesting thing. The B-side was *Johnny Is The Boy For Me,* a song I owned publishing rights on, and my disk jockey buddies all over the country were playing it instead of *Vaya* to help me out. And Capitol was saying, "See? We told you it was a dog. It's the B-side that's hitting." And they were right. *Johnny* was number one in seven cities, while *Vaya* was getting the B-side treatment.

So Mary and I flew to California, convinced Capitol to help us pay for a chartered plane, and we flew to those seven cities to personally convince the disc jockeys to turn the record over.

When they did, *Vaya* took off and became a nationwide number one hit. It stayed on top for weeks and weeks, and was our biggest record ever.

Incidentally, on both *Vaya* and *Johnny*, I played my gold top prototype. *I'm A Fool To Care*, recorded with an early black archtop while we were in Stroudsburg, was a top five hit in the summer of '54.

Reality TV

I keep hearing about today's so-called reality TV. I haven't seen any of it, but I don't need to because we lived it for real. And I'm talking about our TV show, which hit the airwaves in the fall of 1953. And by now the house had expanded from the original seven rooms to 24, with eight of those rooms devoted to audio recording and producing the television show.

We shot the show on 35 millimeter black and white film, with the same high-grade equipment used for shooting movies in Hollywood. When you look at those old shows today, you can see the quality of the picture is very sharp and clear. We had an excellent staff of professional technicians, the same people Jackie Gleason used. When they weren't camped out at our house, they'd be with him, doing his show. Our production schedule called for 36 five-minute shows to be produced in 15 weeks, and we would shoot one right after the other until they were done. This meant our house was full of cameras and lights and cables running everywhere, and all kinds of outside people coming and going. The cameras weren't following us around all the time, but they were there and we were stepping around them. So we were living in the middle of a movie set for three or four months at a stretch.

During the years our TV show was on the air, we produced a total of 170 episodes. After the first couple of years, it became very challenging to continue to come up with ideas and bits that could be worked into the four and a half minute format. When we needed a storyline, we'd just start pitching ideas back and forth, looking for anything we could take off on. The scripts were timed tight, but for our material, we were winging it most of

283

the time, and sometimes it got pretty wild.

And it was more than just the acting bits. We also did all the music, which had to be timed down to the second, and we were producing the five-minute radio shows at the same time. It was very tedious, demanding work, and to stay on schedule, there could be no letting up.

The Eight Track

It was 1953, while filming the TV show, when I got the idea for the first multi-track recorder, the eight track. Working with film audio inspired me to want to build an eight-track recording machine where the heads were all evenly aligned, what we call sel-sync. We'd had multiple heads before, but there were limitations because they were always staggered, so you couldn't edit or do stacked multiples where each track was independent of the others. And my invention was to stack the heads one on top of the other so they were all aligned in the same place, and you could use the same multiple head for recording and playback, and everything would be in sync.

The big name in film sound was Westrex, so I took my idea to them first, but they weren't interested. So I turned again to my friends in San Francisco, Ampex, and they immediately got very actively involved and agreed to build the thing for me.

They worked on building the big beast for about a year, and then delivered

In this closeup you can see how the eight tracks are stacked into a single head.

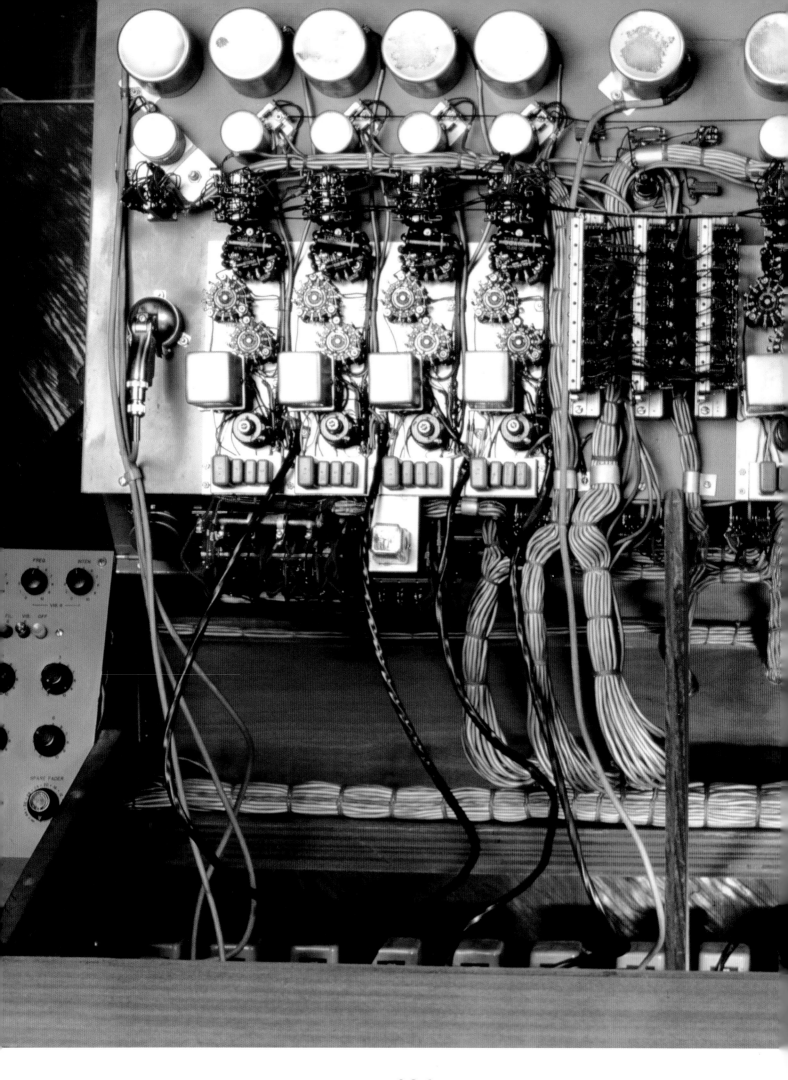

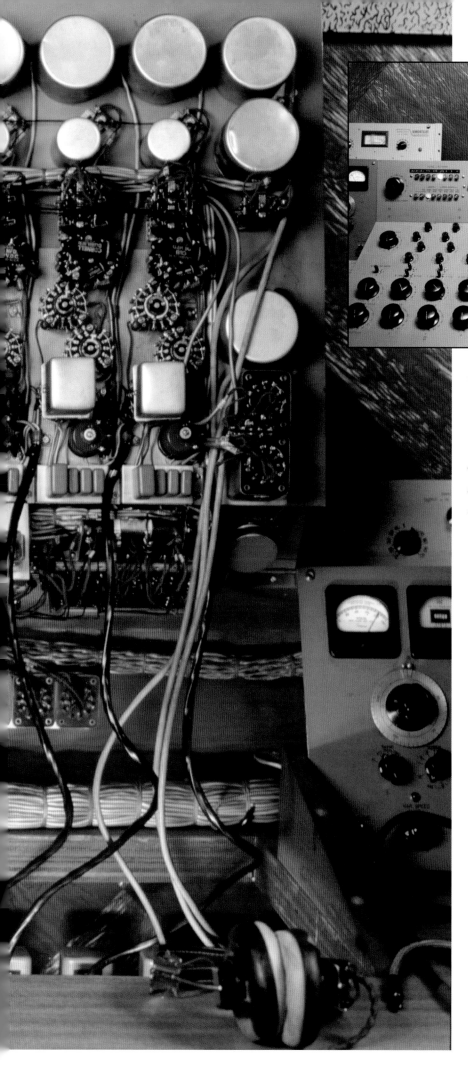

(above) The control panel for the Eight Track Ampex.

(left) Lifting up the control panel shows the circuitry designed by Rein Narma. The beautiful wiring job was done by Bob Flint.

the prototype to Mahwah with a bill for $14,000. I paid them, but I was very disappointed because there were many problems. The speeds were off, the EQ was unacceptable, and there were a million other bugs that had not been worked out. So I sent it back to California with my suggestions and requirements. You'll see in the pictures, this thing is huge, and shipping it was not easy. We'd have to lug it out to the airfreight terminal and fly it back to them. Then they'd try to fix and send it back again.

With so many variables, it was terribly temperamental and had to be constantly maintained. It didn't really become functional until 1957, when we finally redesigned it ourselves to get it right. And when my design guy, Rien Narma, finished it, Ampex admired his work so much they hired him and he became their vice president. I worked on it four years and it cost me about $36,000 total before I ever recorded the first song on it.

The Team Breaks Up

Just before we began filming the first series of Listerine shows, Wally and Carol decided to move back to California and it was a terrible loss for both Mary and I. Mary lost the company of her sister, who was also her best friend, and I lost the trusted faithful friend who did such a wonderful job of keeping everything in my life in order. He had the patience of a saint and did everything for me, and when he passed on, we lost the key to the whole thing. After Wally left, John Mack, another good friend, came in and took over. He did a great job, but it wasn't the same.

I didn't want to see it at the time, but during those days, I was not the easiest guy to work for. With so many pressures and demands coming from so many different directions, you had to be on your toes, and sometimes it got a little rough. But I don't know of anybody involved in all the incredible things we did that didn't look back and say how great it was, how much fun we had doing it, and how proud they were of what we achieved. We set a standard that was very high because when you walk out on that stage, you're putting yourself on the line, and you want to do your best. And for that, everybody around you has to care as much as you do. And if they don't, there's going to be a problem.

At my age, I've had a lot of friends I hated to see go, but it's just absolutely impossible to imagine ever finding anybody that could do what Wally did, or replace him. We'd been friends since nine years old, and never had an argument in our whole life. From the beginning and on through our careers, he knew me and I knew him, and we loved each other very much.

After Carol left, I remember once when I was lying on the floor soldering something under the eight track, and Mary said, "Nine-tenths of the time you're under that machine working on it or trying to fix something." She used to kid around and say, "For Christmas, I want to take away your oscillator." And what she was really saying was that we were working too much and too hard and not having enough time for each other. And she was right because for years, we worked night and day, and we worked harder than anyone else we knew.

I remember when were playing in Las Vegas and recording in our hotel room with the Ampex, and a lady came knocking on our door at 3 in the morning. We were working on a recording, and she said, "I'll be glad when you finish that thing. I love what you're doing, but I'll sure be glad when you're done with it."

So this lady in the nearby room had been hearing us work on the song, and we had been repeating it so many times it was driving her crazy. And Mary was looking down from our balcony, and right below us, just hanging out around the pool were Frank Fontaine and Lucille Ball. And Mary said, "You know, we're up here and we work so hard. And they're down there just goofing off, doing nothing." And I probably said, "Yeah, they're goofing off and they're not getting anything done. Now come back over here to the microphone and let's try this again."

I loved my work, and I needed Mary for everything we were doing. And for Mary, it wasn't her career she cared about, it was the music.

We suffered the most terrible blow of all in 1954. That spring, we were overjoyed to learn Mary was pregnant with our first child, and as she got further along, we began to slow down our schedule of touring the country when we weren't filming the TV show. On Thanksgiving Day, 1954 the baby was born a month premature, and died five days later. This was devastating to both of us, but for Mary, it was something she could never get past. It haunted her from then on, and we were never the same after that. It was the beginning of our breakup.

We'd had four solid hits in 1954 before the tragedy of losing our child, but afterward, the hits became fewer and further between, and *Vaya Con Dios*, our biggest hit, was to be our last number one. In 1955, we had three hits, but only *Hummingbird* cracked the top ten. In 1956, with rock and roll now dominating radio and pop music, we charted two minor hits, in '57 only one. When our contract with Capitol expired in 1958, we moved over to Columbia in hopes of reviving our recording success, but it wasn't in the cards. Our run was over, and we'd had a damn good one. From *Lover* in 1948 to our last charted hit in 1957, we had 40 singles, a number of gold albums, and sold over ten million records.

The Real Paulverizer Debuts

Despite our problems, we continued to play engagements and make recordings. And in 1956, I debuted the real Les Paulverizer, which consisted of two tape machines placed off stage. One machine was set up so I could vary which cut I wanted to select on the tape, while the other machine's order was fixed and couldn't be altered on the fly. I operated both machines by a set of controls I mounted on my guitar. So I had one with a fixed routine and one that had cue marks so I could chase around on it. From my guitar, I could control whether it automatically wound to cut one or eight or ten, whatever I wanted, and it would automatically cue itself up. We traveled with our own PA, which also served as our monitor system on stage, and I operated the whole apparatus from my guitar.

I had just finished building the Paulverizer in 1956, when Mary and I were invited to play for the President. So I planned to use it for the first time on that occasion, but wanted to give it a test run first. So I went to my neighbor, Mr. Wehren, who had 500 acres of farmland near our home, and told him I was looking for a place to test my latest invention, the Les Paulverizer. I asked if I could put up a temporary stage in his field and run some AC current down to it. And he said, "Why in the world would you want to do that?" And I said, "So Mary and I can play a show for all the Boy Scouts." We needed a live audience to test the Paulverizer, and I didn't want to haul it any great distance to conduct the test. There was a Boy Scout Camp up on the mountaintop behind our house, so I had a built-in audience.

With Mr. Wehren's approval, hundreds of Boy Scouts came down to his field to listen to Les Paul and Mary Ford play on an outdoor stage. We didn't have enough AC current to do anything more than power the tape machines and our sound system, which meant we couldn't have any stage lighting. But the Boy Scouts came through for us. We got our lighting from several hundred of them shining their flashlights on us.

So it's no longer just a gag, now it's real, and that's how I used the Les Paulverizer in a live performance for the first time. And there were several problems during the performance, which was exactly why I wanted to do a test run. For one thing, one of the tapes broke and went flying all over the stage, and there were other electronics glitches that became apparent in an actual performance situation. This was just a few days before we were scheduled to play for President Eisenhower and Vice President Nixon, and it gave me a chance to get the bugs worked out, but it also caused Mary to further doubt the whole concept.

This was the time when Mary said she would rather stay home than go play the White House. And after the Boy Scout performance, she said, "And

290

we're going to play for the President with this thing?" And I said, "Yes. It's all done, and the problems are all simple to fix. It'll work just fine." But Mary said, "No, I don't want to play for the President, and I'm not going to go."

This was not the first time this had happened. After our baby died, Mary was very depressed and her personal problems became more pronounced. I tried everything I knew to help her overcome it, but nothing worked. There were several times where we were scheduled to perform somewhere, and when it came time to go to the venue, she wouldn't come out of her room or be persuaded by me or anyone else to open the door. When this happened, I would do the only thing I could do, which was go on and perform alone. I would tell the audience Mary was ill, which was true, and then do the best I could without her. It was a terribly difficult situation.

Mary was adamant in her refusal to play for the President, and I was packing and preparing for the trip assuming I would again have to excuse her and go it alone. When the day came to leave Mahwah for the drive down to Washington, after all the equipment was packed into the car, I went back into the house to tell Mary I was on my way. But I couldn't find her. I walked all through the house looking for her so I could say goodbye, but she was nowhere to be found. Finally, I gave up and went back out to the car to leave, and there she sat in the front seat. And I said, "I thought you weren't going." And she said, "Well, I thought I might as well come along just to be there and watch."

So we drove down to Washington and went to the White House, where we were to play for President Eisenhower, Vice President Nixon, their wives and a bunch of Washington brass. After we got all the equipment set up and it was time for us to perform, I announced from the stage that this would be the first time anywhere, anybody had ever seen or heard the real Les Paulverizer, and explained how the running gag for the radio and television shows had finally become real. And Mary did play the show with me, as I hoped she would.

To play the show, I had five numbers set up in a pre-arranged order on the tapes. And just before we were to go on, Nixon came over and whispered a request in my ear. And the pitch was, Nixon wanted me to ask President Eisenhower if he had a favorite song he'd like to hear. Now I was ready to kill Nixon because I was stuck with the order of the songs as I had them on the tapes, and this was going to put me in a corner.

There was no way out, so I asked President Eisenhower if he had a request. Ike scratched his head and turned to Mamie, and she said, "The first time we ever heard Les and Mary do *Vaya Con Dios*, we pulled off the road and listened, and it made us both cry. I know we would both love to hear you do it now." And I said, "You've got a deal!"

I was very relieved because by sheer blind luck, her request just happened

to be the very next song on the tape. So we did *Vaya Con Dios*, Mary sang it beautifully, and the Paulverizer worked like a charm. And when we finished our show and left the stage the President, the Vice President, everybody thought I was a genius. And Nixon later wrote a letter to me that said, "I don't know how you do it, but it's magic." So they were impressed, but it wasn't magic, it was luck. I don't know what I'd have done if any other song had been requested, and I'm glad I didn't have to find out.

It wasn't long after our appearance at the White House that Mary said to me, "Either quit the music or I'm going to leave." And her reasoning was very logical. We had all the money in the world. We needed nothing. We could be with our family and we could retire. And I could go nuts. And I said, "Mary, I would have to do something. I can't just sit around and do nothing. I just couldn't do it. I've got to play. I'm just too wound up." And Mary said, "Well, then I plan to leave. I don't want a career."

Mary was very frightened of the stage, always. She could do her part and put on a good show, but she never got over the problem of stage fright. It didn't matter that we had played hundreds of performances in every imaginable situation; she never got over it, and the problem persisted. She was just very frightened of being around people, and after the tragedy of losing our child, it

293

got worse. So consequently, the problem was, are you just going to hide and isolate yourself from the world? Is never going on stage again an acceptable answer to the problem? This is what she wanted me to agree to, and it was going to be very difficult.

End Of The Road

There aren't words to express how painful this was for both of us because the love never died. It was always there, so this wasn't happening over love being lost. It was simply a matter of coming to a fork in the road, and one of us had to go one way, and one another.

I tried to get Mary's mind off the negative things by taking her to Europe around the end of '54. There were no performances, no publicity stunts, nothing like that. It was just the two of us, and I hoped a different culture a world away would get us away from all the stress and sad memories that were eating away at her. We went to Spain, Germany, Sweden, all over the place, seeing the sights, but when we got back home, the problem was still there. The next step came in 1958 with the adoption of our beautiful infant daughter. Colleen brought comfort and joy to both of us, but Mary's problem with stage fright and withdrawal from public life was not resolved.

In thinking of how I could stay involved in show business without having to go on stage, I thought about going into the business of managing others. If I retired from performing to do that, then the pressure would be off Mary and she could stay home with our family, but I'd still have to travel all the time to be a successful manager. And if I was going to be on the road, I might as well be playing my music because that's what makes me happy. So it didn't make sense. And the inventing, the music, and all the other time consuming things that caused Mary to feel neglected, that's just me. That's who I've always been, and I couldn't just stop doing it, even if I wanted to. It's like I told Jimmy Atkins back in Chicago. He was telling me I should marry Virginia because I loved her, and I said, "I'm already married, to the guitar."

So we were stuck with a serious problem, and it festered to the point that lawyers got involved and determined it could only be solved by divorce. But it wasn't because of ill feelings or loss of love. It was a standoff of career versus no career, of working versus not working.

And I was hesitating to answer the question, "Were you tough to work for?" But I will answer. You bet your ass I was tough to work for, but who wouldn't be? You're doing five TV shows and five radio shows a week from right where you live. Plus, you're on the *Perry Como Show*, you're on the *Ed Sullivan Show*, you're performing live at the Paramount Theater, you're making

This photo was taken in Tampa, Florida, in the early '60s. Our daughter Colleen is dancing and son Gene is on the drums.

records for Capitol and jingles for Robert Hall, all at the same time. You may have five things going at once, and they're all important, and the only way you can keep it all going is to constantly be going a hundred miles an hour.

And then add all the interviews and hype, all the PR work with the disc jockeys and record stores, all the guest appearances and charity work, and it's a tremendously hard schedule. I had to be tough to carry the load, but never was I blaming Mary for wanting to say, "Hey, let's stop. I've had it." I understood how she felt, but to cut if off completely was something I couldn't honestly do.

CHAPTER TWENTY-SIX

Gibson Resurrection

The Les Paul Standard solid body guitar came out in 1952, based on my agreement with Gibson for a total endorsement period of ten years. In '61 or early '62, the ten-year term was up, and with the contract expired, there was nothing more to be done until we made a new agreement. Mary and I were then involved with the divorce, and we all agreed to stand pat until the divorce was over, and then we'd go back into business.

So Gibson sat and waited, and the divorce thing was dragging on and on. And finally, they called and said, "We have the solid body SG model, and we need to get it out there to hold on to our market share. Would you mind if we put it out without your name on it?" And I said, "All right, leave my name off the SG and go with that until the divorce finalizes." So that's where it stood with Gibson and from 1962 through most of 1965, there were no Les Paul Gibson guitars manufactured.

The Offer From Fender

During the last stages of the divorce process, which was 1964, it happened that CBS bought Fender. Meanwhile, word had gotten around that I had not renewed with Gibson. And the next thing I know, CBS has contacted my lawyer and they're paying me a visit. And the purpose of the visit was to offer me a new endorsement deal with Fender. They wanted me to walk away from Gibson and become the Fender guy, and they were offering a tremendous deal if I would do it.

My business manager studied their proposal, and said, "It's a very lucrative offer and I recommend you go for it." And I said, "Well, I'm not comfortable with it because I've got a verbal agreement with Gibson to wait until this standby period is over." And due to my close relationship with Mr. Berlin from the beginning, and my long history with their instruments going back to the L-5s, I felt a loyalty to them.

So I called M.H. Berlin in Chicago and told him the situation, and he said, "Les, we're planning to sell all the electronics at Gibson. The electric guitar is extinct. We're going to discontinue them." And I was shocked. I said, "Mr. Berlin, there's a lot of things happening that you may not know about." He said, "That may be true, but we're not the only ones having trouble selling the electric guitar. Fender is hurting too, and that's why they want you."

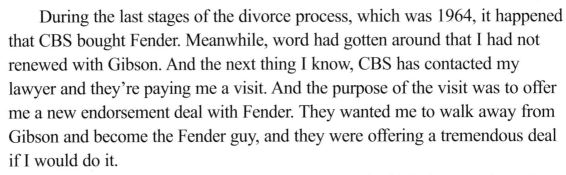

And he was right. This was the time when folk music became the big thing for a few years, and if you look into the records, you'll find that Fender was in trouble. All the electric guitar makers were starving, and Gibson was ready to junk the whole line because they had lost faith in it. There was just a big hole electric guitars fell into there in the early '60s.

But during this same time, I'm going down 48th Street seeing youngsters like Steve Miller, Jeff Beck, Jimmy Page, all these hot young guns looking for Les Paul guitars and paying huge prices when they can find one because they're out of production and getting harder and harder to find. So I said, "Mr. Berlin, before you make this decision, let me come and talk to you." And he said, "Well, come on then. Come to Chicago and tell me what you see."

Crucial Meeting

So I went back to Chicago and met privately with Mr. Berlin, and our meeting went on for 20 hours. And this expresses how willing Mr. Berlin was to seriously consider what I had to say because he was a very methodical person with an established schedule that never varied. He would always say, "Don't bother me at night because if it's ten o'clock, I'm in bed."

We sat up together all night talking about how far we had come with the electric guitar and considering the pros and cons of Gibson staying in the business of making them. And I put the whole thing in front of him with everything I had because my reputation, my future, and so much that was important to me was on the line. And really, when they agreed to sell the electrical parts inventory, the decision had already been made. They intended to sell out the few electric guitars still in stock, and then it was lights out.

Mr. Berlin told me they had agreed to a bulk sale of all the pickups, pots, wiring harnesses and other electrical stuff that goes into manufacturing electric guitars, but the deal was still very fresh and the inventory had not been removed from the factory in Kalamazoo.

And I said, "Well, I think you're making a terrible mistake. And if I were you, I would just do the opposite and hit this thing hard because I know it's going to turn around. The folk music boom isn't going to last because it's digging up the past, and the younger generation will never stay interested. There's nothing in it for them. But the kids own rock and roll, and it's just getting started."

I was very passionate in believing this, and the surest proof was all the young guitar players going crazy trying to find our guitars. And I told him; "They're showing up at my house and pounding on my door trying to buy them from me." And Mr. Berlin said, "Well, maybe that's just because they're hard to get, maybe it's just the status of having a rarity." And I said, "Oh, I'm

297

sure of it. They're hard to get because we've quit making them and the people who already have them are hanging on to them."

And finally, after 20 hours of talking and thinking and looking at it in every possible way, Mr. Berlin said, "Les, I'm going to do it. We'll hang on to the electronics division and we'll start making Les Paul guitars again just as soon as we clear a new deal with you. And don't let anybody change your mind. It's your baby. You take it and go with it. I believe in you."

And when he said that, I almost cried because this is the kind of thing you dream about but never expect will happen. To have someone as powerful as M.H. Berlin willing to trust you that much is a terribly great honor, and also a huge responsibility. He said, "I'll point out the different people you can have as president to work with you, and you pick the one you want." In saying this, he was being sensitive to the misunderstandings with the patents ten years earlier.

And I said, "Thank you very much, but no, I don't want you to do that. I can work with any of these guys and I'd be more comfortable with your preferred choice." And he said, "Well, I was asking because I want to be sure it's someone in harmony with you, otherwise there will be problems." And then he picked Stan Rendell to be the new president of Gibson, a choice which I very much approved. Stan Rendell was a damn good foreman, a tough, beer-drinking guy who had the respect of the Gibson workers. He had risen up through the ranks and was definitely not a man who could be pushed around or persuaded by slick talk. I knew he would honor Mr. Berlin's intention that this comeback for the Les Paul Gibson guitar was to be done according to the way I wanted it done.

My divorce was at last finalized in December of 1964, I signed a new endorsement deal with Gibson, and Stan Rendell and I took the bull by the horns. Stan did a great job, and we worked together like brothers to get the thing rolling again. And it's still going strong today.

The Precious Few

I've always been a sucker for a guitar, and ever since I signed the new deal with Gibson and they started producing Les Paul guitars again, the factory has been sending them to me. Every time a feature is changed or added on one of the models, they always send me one or two as a sample. Or if I call them up with an idea I want to try, they do it and send me two of them. Multiply this by 40 years, and you've got a houseful of guitars.

Still, with that many fine guitars stacked up by the hundreds in the hallways and closets and all over my house, there are just a few older instruments I really have feelings about. Django's guitar, Sunny Joe's L-5, the L-5s Joe helped me buy on the way to Missouri so long ago, the trio of klunkers I built my soul into, the first two Les Paul solid body flattops I got from Gibson; and a few others that got away from me, like the Gibson Nick Lucas model I had in my early Chicago days and the little cheapie archtop that put me and the electric guitar on the map with Fred Waring. Those two and a few others I don't have anymore, but they're still a part of me, just like the guy who lost his leg will tell you he can still feel it there. These are the guitars my life's story is wrapped all around, that made the trip with me.

__Two of my very favorite Gibson Les Paul models are these two very early flattops which Gibson made for me. I still prefer playing the flattop version to the archtop version.__

Too Much Stuff

You know the old saying, 'them that has, gets'? Well, it's true. I'm a somewhat well known person, and it just happens that a lot of my fans may also be involved in some part of the performing and recording business, or the guitar making business or some kind of business where they feel I would like to have something they can provide. Like last summer when I opened the door one day and there sat seven big boxes of new audio equipment from somebody who has come up with something they want me to have. Maybe they want me to try it out and give them my opinion, maybe they want me to show it to somebody who might help them along, or maybe they just want to give me something so I'll know and recognize what they've done. Whatever the reason, stuff keeps showing up all the time, and it's not anything I've ordered or asked for. It long ago reached the point where the sheer volume of things coming at me all the time is almost crippling.

There's hardly a month goes by that someone doesn't come into the Iridium on a Monday night with an instrument they want me to have. They're always sincere in giving it, and convinced I'll love it and be so happy to have it, so rarely do I turn them down.

And it's not always guitars. Sometimes it's like a photograph someone found of Mary and me with Mickey Mantle. I remembered the picture but didn't have it, so am I going to throw the picture away? No, I'm not. So…I bring it home. And another guy comes into the club, and he has a guitar. And he says, "I want you to have this." Now, I need another guitar like I need another hole in my head, but how can I refuse such a gift? The guy traveled a great distance to come and give it to me, he's been planning to do this thing for years, and I'm not going to hurt his feelings. So every Monday, I come home from the club with more than I went in with because people are always bringing me things, and I can't refuse them. So where does it end?

It's crazy, and we're going to have to stop bringing it all home because pretty soon, there won't be room left

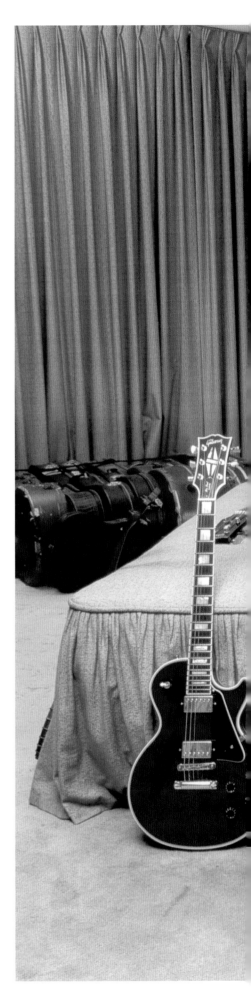

300

This bedroom on the second floor of our house was mine and Mary's. Now it's filled with guitars.

for us to live in. It's not
a complaint. It's just
that I've got this big
house here, with so
many rooms, and still
you can barely move.
And there's no way of
filing it. It's just not
possible to stay on top
of it now because it's
piled up for too long
without being properly
managed. And then
you fall in love with it,
so when you do try and
deal with it, you wind
up standing there say-
ing, well, I can't throw
this away, and I can't
throw that away, and I
don't want to sell it, so
you're stuck and that
just makes it worse. It's
a problem because
somehow, all this stuff
has to be dealt with,
and when you look at
how much there is, the
sheer mass and weight
of it all, it's over-
whelming. And this is
where I miss Wally
again and again
because this kind of
thing was right down
his alley, and as long as
he was here, everything
was in perfect order.

303

Lifelong Affair

I have loved the guitar ever since Pie Plant Pete let me hold his and showed me a chord or two back in my earliest days. And later, when I was getting my first experience as a professional musician, before I went to bed at night I would first take my guitars out of their cases, rag them down to a shine, and position them so when I opened my eyes the next morning, they would be the first thing I saw when I woke up. I loved that. I went to sleep thinking about them, woke up thinking about them, and dreamed about what I was going to do with them in between.

Guitar players love their instruments for more than the sound they make. We invest something of ourselves into them until they become like an added

part, an extension of who we are. So it becomes very personal, and it stays with you. It's been more than 70 years since I lined up my little family of instruments so I'd see them waiting to greet me when I woke up, but I remember it like it was yesterday.

And if somebody came along and invited me to choose one thing out of my career to put into a time capsule for the future, it would be the Gibson Les Paul guitar. Sure, I'd like the recordings to go in too, but if it were a matter of picking a single thing, it would have to be the guitar. After the hits ran out in '58, our relationship with Capitol came to an end, Mary left, and my hands went south, but the one thing that's remained constant with me is the guitar. Before I married Virginia, and Mary knew this too, I told her, "The guitar comes first and you come second, and that's it." I always told anyone who was close to me they weren't first. The guitar was at the head of the line, and they came second.

CHAPTER TWENTY-SEVEN

The Last Tango

I decided to retire in '65, after Mary and I split. I said, "Let the young guys play the hot guitar now because I've had it." I had done my thing and had success. I didn't have to work any more, so I thought I'd find another career, some other way to satisfy the use of my time. But before I could retire, I had one more contract to fill, and that was to make one last album for London Records. So I made the album, and one of the songs on it was *Whispering.*

Of all the records I ever made, *Whispering* was Mother's favorite. It was one of her all time favorite songs, and I made the original record especially for her. After the album was released, I visited Mother to get her opinion, and she said, "Lester, don't go away now, stay right there." And she came back with two records, the original *Whispering,* and the new one. She put the London recording on and let it play for about 16 bars, then stopped it and played the Capitol recording. And when it was over, she said, "Why? Why did you change it when the original was perfect?" And I said, "Well, Mom, they wanted me to do new recordings, so I had to play it differently." In her opinion, I'd made a mistake re-doing it because I was never going to top the original recording.

On that same album, I also re-made *How High The Moon*, and actually played better on it than I did on the original. But it wasn't as good either because Mary wasn't on it. Even though I played better, cleaner and more precise, it didn't have the feeling, it didn't have the magic, it didn't have the love that was there when I did it with Mary.

Les And Mary

Mary and I had the kind of connection every person dreams of having in their life. And I've said a thousand times, I had what I had and did what I did, but without Mary, it would never have happened the way it did. Mary had everything. She worked hard and did her job well, she was the prettiest girl you would ever hope to see, and she had a great ear, which you recognize immediately when you hear her sing. I worked side by side with Peggy Lee, Ella Fitzgerald — that's really the top comparing her — Rosemary Clooney, Doris Day, Patti Page, all of them. And none of them could approach what Mary could do as a recording artist, much less play the guitar. We're talking about sheer talent, and the difference between her and the others was just unbelievable. As a singer, she was probably the most underrated for her time.

I think where I came into it and got it right was recognizing where her talent was and bringing it out. It's like the group I'm working with now on Monday nights. They're all great players, but I know their limitations. I know what's difficult for them and where they really excel, and from that, I know what to throw at them and what to avoid when we're performing. Mary was talented beyond belief with her voice and rhythm and sense of pitch, but she was not creative. She had to be led to the arrangements because it didn't come naturally to her. Understanding what the phrasing needed to be to create a sellable product was a gift I had, and when Mary and I put our gifts together, the result was sensational.

Mary had a phenomenal ability that was critically important to the success of all the sound on sound recordings we did, but there was one drawback. We would work on a song until I figured out just what I wanted her to do, and then she would do it perfectly, time after time. But once she did it, it was stamped in her mind and very difficult for her to change. So if I later wanted to move a part or alter something, it was tough for her to do. It's just the way she was, and much more a strength than a weakness.

I remember one recording where maybe a year had gone by since we first did it, and then I got an idea and had to redo one of my guitar parts, which required re-doing her vocals. We'd been through dozens of towns and a lot of water was under the bridge when I asked her to re-do it. She re-did her parts, and when I compared them to the original, it wasn't just close, it was identical. It's scary because I don't know of anyone else who could've done that so precisely, and she didn't even have to try. It was just naturally there for her to be able to do that. With me, it's exactly the opposite. Whatever I did back then is long forgotten. And my attitude has always been that what I'm going to do tomorrow will be better than what I did today. I'd want to throw up if I had to do the same thing over again.

Mary's Guitar Playing

Mary's ability to hear and learn the vocal parts quickly and then have it down for keeps also extended to the guitar. Again, she was not an innovator, but if there was something she needed to do on rhythm guitar, I only had to show her how to do it one time. After that, it was there and no reminding was necessary. She learned quickly and never forgot anything, and she had a great sense of rhythm. She played just excellent, solid rhythm guitar, which was an important part of our sound. And it was another gift. Lead guitar players are everywhere, but good rhythm players are very rare.

307

Neither Mary nor I had perfect pitch, but we were damn close. We might be driving along listening to the radio, and I'd say, "That's E flat." And Mary would say, "I don't think so, it's an F." And I'd say, "I'm telling you it's an E flat." And this would go back and forth until I'd slam on the brakes, get a guitar out and check the note. And either one of us might be right or be wrong. Neither of us had true perfect pitch, but we both had a very good ear for music which served us well during our recording days. And all I had to do was tell Mary what we needed her to do, and it was there. It took a special kind of talent to do what we did with the recordings, and Mary had it big time.

A Guitar In The Hand

The one problem Mary always had and could never overcome was stage fright. It didn't matter that we were successful, that everywhere we went the crowds all loved her; the problem never went away. If anything, it got worse as we got bigger and the pressures to keep hitting increased.

When she was one of Gene Autry's Sunshine Girls, she stood in the center so she could hold each of the other two girls' hands, and it helped her be less afraid. But the Sunshine Girls were just a minor feature, not the main attraction. It's an entirely different thing when you walk on stage at the Paramount and you're the reason the audience is there and you've got no one's hand to hold. And playing guitar was something that helped her get through it because it gave her something to do with her hands. It was something she could concentrate on while we performed, so it was like a defense.

And the odd part is that it wasn't obvious to the audience. After a show, someone would usually say something like, "You looked a little nervous out there tonight, Les." I was always too busy thinking ahead to be nervous, but before and during a show, Mary would be just terribly anxious, to the point of being sick. But when she did perform, it didn't show. In her singing style and in the way she presented herself on stage, she had a very calm demeanor, but inside she was churning.

The Missing Tape

Something regrettable is the fact that, as far as I know, there is no recording of Mary and me performing live. With all the recording we did, and the countless number of live performances before and after the Paulverizer was put into use, it's just a ridiculous thing that I don't have a recording of a single live performance. And every time we did a show with the Paulverizer, a recording was automatically made, but they weren't saved.

As a part of the live show set up, I had a smaller tape recorder which was used to produce an echo effect, like a slapback. It held a full reel of tape, and that tape would be running during the show, recording everything that went through the PA system. But we were running it for the purpose of creating the sound effect, not for making a recording. So each time we did a show, the tape would be re-wound and whatever was on it from before would be erased.

After we played for President Eisenhower, it occurred to me that it was historic, so I spoke to the President's office. I said, "I recorded our perform-ance on my echo machine, and I have a beautiful tape here of the President and the whole thing. Am I free to keep it?" And the answer came back, "The President is very appreciative of what you did for him, and the tape is a gift to you. You can do with it what you wish."

This was wonderful news, and I was thinking about what to do with it, and definitely had every intention of preserving that reel of tape. Then we go to Scranton for our next performance, and Earl Davis, our sound engineer,

309

Even though my Les Paul solid body was doing great, I couldn't keep from cutting up guitars to experiment with the sound. Here's a nice Gibson L5, serial no. A9204 (1951).

rewinds the tape as part of the normal set-up routine. We do the show, and the performance for the President is completely erased because I forgot to take it off the machine. And that was just a tragedy because you can't retrieve it or go back and do it over. It's gone forever.

Other than that lost recording, if I ever had another of Mary and I doing a live performance, I don't recall it. I have the background tapes that ran on the Ampex machines, but not a recording of the whole show. And it's just ridiculous because we played coast to coast and all over the world, and tape was my thing! Now I'm searching for them in museums and collections, hoping somebody will turn up who has one.

And here's another odd kicker. While I don't have any live recordings of Mary and I when we were in our prime, I now have a recording made at the Club 400 the first time Mary and I ever played together. Some guy with a recording machine of some kind was there that night and recorded our very

Here's another L5 (serial no. 62143) that I cut a back door into. I used this guitar on my recording of Golden Earrings.

first performance. Years later, he contacted me, and said, "I've got something, and I think you're going to like it." He sent it to me, and when I heard it, I nearly fell over because there we are, talking about just getting the cast off my arm, and here we come, back playing again.

For The Record

If you read what I've said about Mary in other books, in the magazine stories, the interviews, whatever, you'll see I haven't really told much. I will say she was a great talent and a good cook, she was pretty, I couldn't have done it without her, and then I'm on to the next thing. There are things we went through that will always be painful to recall, and I don't see any good purpose in digging it all up because some of it would be shocking and hard to accept, even now.

But I do want to go on record about our relationship while I have this opportunity because there has been so much written that only tells one piece or another

311

of our story, and then is presented as the whole truth. And there are so many pieces that would have to be understood to get it right, too many for me to bring together now. The thing I want everyone to know is that it wasn't career or ambition or the desire for money and fame that carried us so far and kept us going as long as we did. It was love.

We loved each other from day one, and not because either of us wanted it to happen. It just was. It was there, and it took us in together. So if you want to talk about Romeo and Juliet, or Frankie and Johnnie, okay, you can put Les and Mary right up there with them. We had our high times, and we had our rough times. And yeah, our marriage broke down and Mary moved out and we finally got divorced in 1964. But we never stopped loving each other. We got divorced legally, but that's all. In fact, after the divorce was finally settled and the pressure was off, we became very close again.

Vaya Con Dios

After we had gotten over all the legal fighting, Mary remarried and was living in California and we would talk on the phone almost every day, sometimes for hours. Nobody will believe it, but we once talked for 30 hours. Yes, 30 hours. We would lay down the phone to get something to eat or go to the bathroom, and then keep going. It was

excessive, but we did it because our bond was so strong. She knew me like nobody else, and I knew her. And she told me, "I don't know my husband. I just got married stupidly to get away from you. We should have worked it out."

She called me on a Friday in the fall of 1977, and said, "My vision is blurred." She had a serious drinking problem and had developed diabetes, and I said, "From what little I know about it, you better give your doctor a yell and find out about it because the eyes are closely related to the symptoms of diabetes." And she said she would do that after the weekend, on Monday.

We talked for probably eight hours that day, mostly about all the great times we had, remembering funny things that happened that only we knew. We even talked about getting our act back together, but I don't think either of us thought we really would. We just both enjoyed knowing the other would consider it and still want to do it. This was on a Friday, and they found her the following Sunday in a diabetic coma, and that was it. Mary passed away September 30, 1977.

This was, of course, a very sad time, made much more so by the fact that

These two Guild flattops were custom made for Mary and me.

Bing died two weeks later, and during this same period, Jimmy Atkins and Ernie Newton had also passed. I was listening to the radio when Bing's sudden death was announced, and when they started playing one of his records, I ran into the bedroom and bawled like a baby.

In time, the burden of grief lifted, and what stayed with me was a very deep appreciation for how fortunate Mary and I were to have what we had. Very few in this world are that lucky. There were things between us, regrettable things we both did that hurt, but with a love like ours, the bad things go with time, and the good things are there forever. There's nothing better than the happiness you feel when you're in love, and we were blessed to have loved each other so much. She was my partner, and we had it all. I'm not a religious man in the sense of being Baptist or Catholic or any particular church, but I believe whatever I've been given came from Somewhere, and that includes Mary. She was such a wonderful gift in my life.

313

CHAPTER TWENTY-EIGHT

Back In The Swing

Retired from performing and life on the road, I stayed busy working on various inventions, and design ideas for the new line of Gibson Les Paul guitars. And it was an amazing thing when the revolution in rock music erupted in California because our new guitars were right on time. Just as Gibson got up to speed with getting the new Les Paul line on the market, a creative outburst swept across the country resulting in thousands of young musicians latching onto our guitars. We couldn't have scripted it any better. So Gibson started selling record numbers of Les Paul guitars, and Mr. Berlin's faith in me paid off for both of us.

An Earful Of Bad Luck

I was very fortunate with my new Gibson deal, but my luck went the other way when an old friend who came to visit playfully cuffed the side of my head with his open hand, saying, "Les, you old dog, how are you?" He didn't hit me hard, but his open palm just happened to clap over my right ear, and the sudden pressure popped my eardrum. And it was very bad because an infection got started and developed into mastoiditis, which creates a lot of rotten wood and swelling that puts pressure on the brain. So I've got this mastoid swelling in my ear canal, right up against the temporal bone, and I wind up in surgery in bad shape.

When I woke up in recovery, the doctor was standing by the bed, and he said, "Les, can you hear me?" And I said, "Yeah, I hear you." And he said, "Well, I'm glad because I almost lost you." I didn't understand how an operation on my ear could be life threatening, so I asked, "You almost lost me? How come?" And the doctor said, "I was drilling against your temporal bone to clean that junk out of your head, and all of a sudden I had gray matter on my drill. And I damn near lost you." He was admitting his drill had pierced my brain sac, and it scared the hell out of me. I'll never understand why this happened, never understand it in my life, but his error resulted in two more operations because, first of all, it wouldn't heal and kept draining, and also, I was left with a constant pounding, like I had Buddy Rich's bass drum in my ear.

This was driving me mad until I found relief by putting my finger to my ear and pressing in a certain place. In doing that, I stopped the blood flow to the vein causing the pounding, and as long as the pressure was there, the

Gibson made this double-neck guitar for me. As a joke, I added a shower head and walked out on stage with it wearing two pairs of glasses.

thumping ceased. So I went to Dr. Moore, an ear specialist at New York Hospital, who took one look and said, "We're operating tomorrow." So the next day, he went in and snipped that vein, and to my great relief, the constant pounding stopped. Buddy Rich was gone, but so was most of the hearing in that ear, and there was no getting it back.

And then, unbelievably, a very similar thing happened with the other ear when I was in Anaheim. I was there attending the annual NAMM show for Gibson, and a guitar player I knew came up behind me to do the "guess who?" thing. Somehow, his hand slapped over my good ear, and I heard the eardrum pop just like before. I didn't say anything to the guy, never did tell him, but I excused myself and went to my room and just cried because now both ears were blown, and both by accidents where a friend just accidentally hit me in the ear.

The first accident happened in 1969, the second in 1972, and I had to have a total of five operations on my inner ear and eardrums. My hearing was permanently impaired, and I've been dependent on hearing aids ever since. And one of the things I'm working on now is finding ways to improve the hearing aid.

The Call From Bucky

Not long after the second ear surgeries, my old friend, Bucky Pizzarelli, called and said, "Les, I

315

Every guitar player in New York back in the 1930s and 1940s wanted a guitar made by John D'Angelico, who had a little shop where he turned out no more than 3 or 4 guitars a month. I've had this one for a long time, and it's a beautiful instrument, but I still prefer my old L5s.

need you, and I need you tonight." And I said, "Well, my head's in a bandage, arthritis has my hands, and I haven't played in a hundred years. I've retired from performing."

Bucky had a standing gig at the St. Regis Hotel doing a duo thing with George Barnes, so I asked," What's the matter with George?" "Well," he said, "George and I are not getting along these days, and I really need you to play this date with me." And I said, "Well, start getting along because I'm not going to do it."

But that wasn't the end of it. Bucky couldn't find anybody else, so he called me back and said, "Look, I know the policeman on that beat. He'll let you park your car on the sidewalk, and we'll have somebody carry your amp and guitar. All you gotta do is get out and walk up into the place, and I'll be there waiting for you." Then he started talking about what we would do if I showed up, and I finally let him talk me into it.

So that night I drove into New York and went to this tiny little cabaret club at the St. Regis, and the wildest thing happened. I walked in and George Benson was there; Count Basie and some of his guys, Benny Goodman, Roy Eldridge, Ed McMahon and Doc Severinson, all there waiting for me to show up. Bucky had put out the word, and the whole world was in that room by the time I got there. And here I am with a bandage on my head and splints on my fingers, and I'm thinking, "What the hell am I doing here? I'm going to fall on my face."

We were tuning up when Bucky said, "Well, what are we going to do?" And I said, "I'm not going to tell you." And I wasn't kidding around; I really didn't know what we were going to do. So Bucky went out to open the show and played a number on his green Gretsch, and then gave me a very nice introduction, saying, "And here he is, the one you're waiting for…" When I walked on stage, I looked at his green guitar and said, "That's so sad, the thing isn't even ripe yet." The laugh got us off to a good start, and we had a great time playing tunes and kidding around in between. Bucky was great to work with, but the most important thing was being reminded how much I loved performing, and realizing I could still show people a good time, despite the arthritis.

Bucky and I were comfortable with each other and played a little string of dates at the St. Regis, drawing overflow crowds. The applause and laughter was the best medicine I could have had. I wasn't ever going to work like I once had, but I now realized how important it was for me to keep performing. What I had called retirement had been a period of adjustment, and during the time I was holed up, a new generation became very interested in what I had to offer. And I'll always be indebted to Bucky for waking me up and getting me back to the party.

Mid-'70s Blast

After being out of it for ten years, it was energizing to be back doing what I love most: performing for an audience.

Capitol put out a Les and Mary greatest hits album in 1974, which made some noise, and Bucky and I followed it with an appearance at Town Hall in New York. We got rave reviews, and the next thing you know, we're playing the morning show on ABC Television and getting invited on talk shows.

Accompanied by Bobby Sutton or one of my sons, Gene or Bobby, on drums, I started playing a few solo dates, using the Paulverizer. This included promotional concerts for Gibson, appearing at various schools and colleges, and other odd gigs Bucky lined up, including a date we played for Joe Bonano, the mafia boss. I was surprised and honored when a young filmmaker (*Catherine Orentreich*) did a documentary about my life and the importance of my work, and everywhere I played, it was standing ovations and encores. I felt reborn, and it meant the world to know all the years of effort were being recognized and appreciated by a new generation.

Carnegie Hall

In April 1975, Bucky and I joined up with Laurindo Almeida and George Benson to do a concert at Carnegie Hall. It was a thrill to finally headline on that famous stage, but the most memorable thing about the show was what happened with George Benson.

George had come to the St. Regis a couple of times to sit in, and both times I walked all over him. And this shouldn't have happened because I'm positive he plays better guitar than I do. But he had a hangup. Both times, he was so nervous it caused him to bomb. And the Carnegie Hall performance was to be our third time to tangle.

A few days before the concert, I got a George Benson album and listened to it very carefully with the purpose of copying what he does. And that's what I did. I copied all his licks from that album until I knew them frontward and backwards. And I'm thinking, "George is going to have his neck bowed this time, and I'm going to be ready for him."

The night of the show, when George was introduced, he let go with a hot, jazzy run, and his pickup fell out. It fell completely out of the guitar, as though the screws that hold it in place had been removed, and the freeze hit him again. Now his pickup is dangling, he's dropping his pick, and I'm after him like a mad dog, topping him with his own stuff. And after three massacres, George was ready to say, "I don't want to go near Les anymore because the s-o-b will have me for lunch."

Years later, he came to the Iridium on a Monday night, and said, "Well, here I am again, asking for more." And I said, "George, I'm in bad shape. My fingers are gone and I can't play worth a damn anymore. You're home." And George got up on stage and played just great. He played his ass off, and finally broke the spell of whatever caused him to be intimidated. And he shouldn't have been because George is an awesome player, one of the best, and I love him dearly.

Demon Arthritis

I first discovered I had arthritis in 1961, after an incident on the Abbott and Costello TV show. Mary and I had a standard bit in our act that was wrapped around a little hillbilly tune called *Home Sweet Home.* At the end of the song, I'd play the N-B-C chimes, and Mary would repeat the same lick on her guitar. Then I'd play ta-ta-ta-dum, and she'd match it with her own ta-ta-ta-dum. Then I give her a look and let go with a staggering run, and when she starts to mimic that one, I leap over and grab the neck of her guitar to keep her from outdoing me. And, of course, the audience was always on Mary's side, and I'm acting the part of being too proud to let my assistant steal my thunder.

And in doing this on *The Abbott and Costello Show*, when I reached over to grab her guitar, my left little finger hit the hard edge of her guitar neck and was broken by the impact.

Mary and I were playing an extended engagement in Las Vegas at the time, so when we came back from doing the TV show, I went to a doctor and said, "I think I broke my finger." And he said the last thing in the world I ever wanted to hear, "Not only did you break your finger, but you have arthritis."

So in '61, a piece of bone was taken from my hip and used to re-make my little finger, which I had to keep in a splint for a year. At the time, my other fingers were doing okay, but over time the arthritis took them down one by one. And now, the only finger on my left hand I can still bend is that little one that had the surgery. And, of course, the fingers on my right hand did the same thing. So a lot of my ability was gone by the time Chet called with the idea for us to do an album together.

Chester & Lester

In early 1975, I got a call from Chet. We chatted a bit, and then he said, "What are you doing these days?" I said, "Well, I'm not doing much because arthritis has shut me down." And Chet said, "Well, I've all my life wanted to record with you. Would you consider doing an album with me?" And his idea was for me to play banjo and harmonica, him to play violin, and both of us sing, doing old country songs.

So right after the Carnegie Hall thing, I flew down to Nashville with my youngest son, Bob, and got together with Chet. We were going over some country and hillbilly songs, singing them, and I said, "How is this sounding to you?" And he said, "Awful. It's not working, so maybe we better scrap it." I said, "Well, we're known for playing the guitar, so why don't we do what we know how to do?" Chet agreed, and we put together a song list featuring standards we had both recorded in the past.

There's an interesting little story connected to how the album got its name. When Chet called and invited me to Nashville to make the record, he already had the idea of using our two first names for the title, which was very clever. But when he first suggested it, he said, "We'll call it *Lester & Chester*." He was putting my name first as a gesture of respect, which I appreciated, but after I thought about it, I said, "Chet, I think Chester should be first because when you put this record out, people will say, 'Lester who?' But if they see Chester first, they'll think of Chet Atkins because they know you." And he said, "I never thought about it that way. I think you're probably right." So the album became *Chester & Lester*.

We were out getting something to eat when I proposed we record our ad-libbing during the session. I said, "You've got a dry sense of humor and I'm off the wall, and people will get a kick out of hearing us kid around." And Chet said, "Well, I'm not much of a talker, and I don't like to talk on TV or radio." But when we got back to the studio, I'll be damned if a live mic wasn't sitting there between us.

So we made the album, recording the chatter while we were doing it, and it was a hit. Everybody loved it, it sold great, and we both got a Grammy for it. Chet just naturally played a very complementary thing to what I played, and vice versa. It was a great marriage because we were two very different people, probably the two best-known guitarists in the world, and both of us had a lot to say. There's a magnetism and mutual respect in the music and the banter that made the overall package very appealing.

Another reason *Chester & Lester* hit so big is that it made people feel like they were right there in the recording studio, listening to the wisecracks and us winging the arrangements. It felt real because it *was* real, and it was the first time such a thing had been done on a major label. I'm glad it worked, but I didn't lay home thinking about it. It just came to me, like most things come to me, because it seemed like the natural thing to do.

320

Guitar Monsters

So a year or so later, we got back together to make the second album, *Guitar Monsters*. I again went to Nashville and got with Chet, and asked, "Well, what's the plan? What arrangements, or suggestions do you have for what we should do?" And Chet said, "I don't have a thing." So I said, "Then what the hell's going to happen?" And Chet said, "We'll think of something."

We went into the studio and started fooling around, but we weren't getting anything done. The clock was ticking, there was limited time before I had to catch a plane, and nothing was happening. So I said, "Chet, we gotta stop resting here. Something's gotta happen." And he said, "Well, I can't think of anything." So the only thing left was for me to take over and determine what we would do, and that's what I did.

I made a list of songs, going with familiar numbers I already had arrangements for in order to save time, and Chet added a couple to it. One was a song

he had co-written with someone called *I'm Your Greatest Fan,* where we poked fun at each other by claiming to know each others' hits and getting it all wrong.

This reminded me of something that had happened when we were recording the first album, and I said, "Do you remember when you asked me to give you half of *Give My Love To Nell?*" And Chet said, "Yeah, I remember that." And I said, "Well, I'll keep that agreement with you. Now give me half of your song, put them both on this album, and we'll be even." So that's how that little wrinkle was ironed out. The album was released in '78, and our musical energies were again very complementary. There were a couple of points where there was friction between Chet and I, but there was no animosity, no falling out that lasted ten years, as some have wanted to believe. It's true my mood was affected by not feeling well while we were making the second record, but I would never say anything to purposely hurt the feelings of someone else, as was falsely reported. Chet and I barked at each other a couple of times, got over it, and became better friends for it. After the experience of making those two records together, we stayed in close touch with each other until he passed away. *Guitar Monsters* sold well and was very successful. I believe we'd have won another Grammy, but Chet decided to enter it in the pop category instead of the country category.

CHAPTER TWENTY-NINE

Heart Trouble

While Chet and I were recording the second album, I was fighting what I thought was a bad cold, and I wasn't feeling at all well when I left Nashville and went to Arizona to see my old pal and mentor, Joe Wolverton. I mentioned this earlier as the time I gave Sunny Joe one of my solid body guitars, and he turned around and gave me his L-5, the one I had always loved so much.

I had a friend in Phoenix, a doctor, who invited me to have dinner with him while I was there. On the way to the restaurant, I began having serious pain and discomfort in my chest and left arm, and when my friend and I met, I told him about it. He wasn't a heart doctor, but after hearing me out, he said,  "I think we better get you over to Lincoln Hospital. By all indications, you're having a heart attack." So I went to the hospital and had a series of tests, with all the data sent to Chicago via computer. The results came back negative, saying there had been no heart attack, but that didn't make whatever it was hurt any less.

After the hospital visit, I said good-bye to Joe and drove on to California. I went to a friend's house and curled up taking antibiotics, thinking my problem might have to do with my lungs. I didn't move for seven days, and finally the pain went away.

Second Opinion

Time passed, and I didn't have any more pains in my arm and chest. But the arthritis was now twenty years along and had gotten so bad I went to see a doctor to be qualified for disability. The doctor gave me a good going over, and said, "You've got a hell of a lot more than arthritis. You've had a heart attack." A heart specialist then confirmed I'd had a heart attack at the time of the pain, and that's when I learned I had five major arterial blockages. This was at a time when the success rate for surgical treatment of this problem was too low to consider, so the situation was dead serious, and very troubling.

I called Ma, and said, "Well, I have not the best of news. I have an inoperable heart condition, and I'm going to have to take it very easy if I want to stay alive much longer." But Mother interrupted me and said, "I don't want to hear this foolishness. With technology the way it is today, it can be fixed. All you have to do is go out and find the person who can do it. Now, get with it."

She gave me a kick in the pants, and it turned me around completely. I started going to heart clinics all over the country, looking for someone with an idea, and finally, Dr. Robert Levy said, "If I were in your position, rather than roll over and die I would take a shot with this guy in Cleveland. That's where I'd put my money if I were you."

Dr. Loop

The doctor referred to was Dr. Loop at Cleveland Hospital. My close friend, Ralph De Liz, took my angiogram and other medical records there, and the case was turned down, just as it had been at Mayo Clinic, St. Luke's and the other hospitals I had approached. And all for the same reason: the condition was considered inoperable.

But Mother had instilled the determination to keep looking until I found the person who would say, "Okay, we have an idea for how to help you." So I said to Ralph, "Would you consider going back to Cleveland to try again, and this time mention my name because just maybe the doctor plays guitar." I said this half-joking, half-hoping, knowing it was a long shot.

So Ralph took the bus back to Cleveland and went directly to Dr. Loop, and said, "Would you please reconsider the case of this person? His name is Les Paul." And the doctor said, "You mean Les Paul the guitar player?" Ralph said, "Yes, and here are his medical records, and his home phone number." So I'm sitting at home waiting to hear from Ralph when the phone rings, and it's Dr. Loop. And he says, "How soon can you get here?" And I said, "Don't cool off. I'll be there right away." So, lo and behold, it worked.

So Ralph, my son Rusty and I went to Cleveland to consult with Dr. Loop. And the doctor said, "We normally use the Vineberg Method for clearing blockages, taking veins from your leg and using them to bypass the blocked arteries. But in your case, I'd like to try a new procedure which involves connecting your mammary artery to your heart, so you'll have restored blood flow immediately." I said, "What are the odds?" And he said, "About the same as the Vineberg Method." And I said, "Well, my goodness, why don't we try it?" And he said, "Because I haven't thought enough about it." And I said, "I've got all the patience in the world. Just tell me when you're ready."

While Dr. Loop prepared for this radical surgery, we set up a little nightclub scene there in the hospital to entertain the other surgery patients and help us all take our minds off medical problems. Musicians on the hospital staff sat in with us, including a bass-playing doctor who was involved in the surgery done on me. This went on until one evening a member of Dr. Loop's staff came in and said, "Dr. Loop is ready, and tomorrow morning you're going into surgery."

The surgery Dr. Loop wanted to try was one of the latest advances in heart surgery, so there were no guarantees. And, yes, I was scared. As they wheeled me through the corridors to the operating room, I remember looking up at the lights in the ceiling, wondering if they were the last things I would ever see.

The operation took eleven hours to perform. All I remember is being asked to count backwards, and then a voice was coming to me through the darkness, saying, "Are you with us, Les? Can you hear me?" I was in the recovery room, and Dr. Loop was saying, "If you can hear me, don't try to talk, just blink." I couldn't speak, but nodded 'yes' to let him know he was getting through, and the thought kept repeating, "I must be alive because I'm still here." And Dr. Loop said, "We made it, and you're going to be just fine. And now I'm going out on a good drunk." So I had survived again.

Drawing A Line

The surgery was termed successful, but getting back my energy and sense of self was rough. I went to Los Angeles and stayed with Wally and Eleanora Jones for six months, trying to regain some strength, but for the longest time, I felt weak and vulnerable, with none of the old rhubarb in me. Dr. Loop kept close watch during the recovery period, and after doing all he could do, said, "Promise me two things: that you'll work hard and you'll be my friend."

Our friendship was a given and I promised to work hard, but how I was going to go about doing it was a problem. I made the albums with Chet, played a few dates with Bucky and made a handful of appearances on my own in the '70s, but that momentum was gone and there was nothing else going to pick up. Other than my lifetime deal with Gibson, I had no commitments, no prospects on the table, so I was completely free to do whatever I felt like doing.

As a tool to help me think, I took a piece of paper, drew a line down the center, and started listing the pros and cons of everything I'd done in my career. I thought back to the talks Mary and I had about our good old days, when we agreed the times we enjoyed most were not playing big venues for thousands of people, but playing the clubs, where people came to relax and be entertained.

So I'm making my list of what I want and don't want to do, and one thing for sure is I want to play where I can dress casual, and not be pressured. I don't want some guy telling me how to dress, or that I'm on too long, too short or anything else. And I want to be paid, so I want to go somewhere where money isn't an issue. I just want to do what I want to do when and where I want to do it, without any of the old problems. If I want to work once

326

Back when we were touring heavily with Wally and Carol, I had Gibson make me these two identical guitars so I could keep one at home on the East Coast and the other one under Wally's bed on the West Coast. That way I didn't have to lug a guitar with me as we crisscrossed the country.

a week, I work once a week. And if the house is standing room only, that's great, but if it's half empty, I'm not going to worry about it.

I was doing what people often dream about, where you ask yourself, "If I could do anything in the world I wanted to do, what would it be?" And what I came up with is to do just what I'm doing now on Monday nights, playing regularly for a live audience in a little club. Sure, I have to put up with a few people you'd like to get rid of, but that comes with the territory when you're going to play for whoever walks in the door, and it's a very small price to pay compared to the benefits. It keeps your body healthy and your mind young, you make new friends, and keep your old ones, and you make people happy, including yourself.

CHAPTER THIRTY

All That Jazz

By this time, my hands were in bad shape from arthritis, so I had to learn a new approach to playing the guitar. Before, when I played with Bucky, I was just there to have a good time and be a part of the scene. But what I was getting ready to do now was different. Now it would be my show and I would be the featured performer, so keeping my promise to Dr. Loop meant starting over again.

I started out sitting in with friends around the general area, which led me to a place called Molly's Tavern in Oakland, New Jersey, the little town Mary and I fell in love with back in the Otto's Floral Manor days. My friend, Lou Pallo had a standing gig there, and I started sitting in with him on weekends. Lou is an excellent guitarist who happened to be very familiar with my music, and as word got around about the scene at Molly's, people started coming from all over to hear us. In no time, every show was packed, and that was my cue to take our little act to New York.

Fat Tuesday's

Wayne Wright was another guitar player friend I'd played a few dates with after I got back on my feet. Wayne and I hooked up with a bass player, Gary Mazzaroppi, and started looking for a cool little dive as the venue for the new Les Paul Trio. And what we found was Fat Tuesday's, a funky basement joint on Third Avenue.

We made our Fat Tuesday's debut on a Monday night in early 1984, and the response was tremendous. What started out as a limited engagement turned into a standing date that lasted twelve years. Many of my old musician friends from the '40s and '50s started showing up, and the beautiful thing was that

With Lou Pallo and Gary Mazzaroppi at Fat Tuesday's.

many of the young rockers and jazz cats were there too. It was rock and roll that put me out of business, and now they were calling me a living legend.

Awards and honors started coming my way, including induction into the Rock and Roll Hall of Fame in 1988. I was making new friends, and seeing many old ones who had been out of sight for years. I had accomplished what I set out to do when I drew the line on the paper, and it was terribly satisfying to be playing regularly again, and receiving recognition for doing it my own way.

The L-5 Comes Home

Near the end of our run there, a letter came to Fat Tuesday's addressed to me. It was from a person I didn't know, telling me about an elderly lady he was caring for who had a dying son. On his deathbed, the son had stated that the guitar and pair of shoes under his bed belonged to Les Paul, and gave instructions that they be returned to me. So I flew to Chicago, rented a car, and drove to the mother's house. And when I opened the guitar case, there was one of the L-5s Joe had helped me get back in the early '30s.

When Jimmy, Ernie and I left Chicago in 1938, I had given the guitar and a pair of Florsheim shoes to my musician friend, Dick Moran who also inherited my job on the radio. He had kept and cherished them all those years, and now his dying wish was that I get them back. Giving that particular guitar away was something I had kicked myself for many times, and getting it back in this manner was very moving to me. I wasn't able to thank him before he passed, but I would like to now express my gratitude to Dick Moran for his care and thoughtfulness, and for his friendship.

The Iridium

I was forced to take a year off due to ulcers caused by arthritis medication, and the club closed after changing hands in 1995, so that was the end of Monday nights at Fat Tuesday's. Lou Pallo had been a part of the trio for most of that time and wanted to keep it going, so we started

329

When I left Chicago to go to New York for the first time I didn't have room to haul everything so I gave this guitar and a pair of Florsheim shoes to my friend Dick Moran. When he passed away thirty years later he left instructions to return them to me. This is one of the L-5s I bought in Kalamazoo with Sunny Joe.

looking for a new place to play in Manhattan. About a year later, with Paul Nowinski as our bass player, we started filling the Monday night bill at the Iridium Jazz Club, then located across the street from the Lincoln Center. Our regular crowd followed us, so we were packing the place from day one, and the location brought a lot of new faces into the audience every week.

After a couple of years, the Iridium moved to a downstairs setting at 51st and Broadway, just a couple of blocks from the theatre building where the miracle with Fred Waring took place 60 years earlier. So I'm back in my old neighborhood playing in a basement joint, which also happens to be New York's best jazz club.

Something important happened not long after we started playing there. A nurse came in and said, "Mr. Paul, when you have a moment, may I speak to you?" And I said, "I've got a moment right now." And she said, "Well, I'm a nurse, and I know you have problems. I would like to tell you something, and then I'm going to leave." "Okay," I said, "Lay it on me." And she said, "You know, many of the people who come in here never heard you play 50 years ago, so don't be foolish and try to be what you were 50 years ago or think you should be playing like you did then. Just do what you can do now, and if the people like it, you're home."

She was telling me not to compete with myself based on the way I used to be able to play, and she was right on because that very thing was something I was struggling with at the time. I think she had probably seen me play prior to her visit, and realized something about my situation she felt moved to share. And that's what she did. She approached me like a messenger, like it was something she needed to do for me, and basically said, "Relax, kid, and don't beat yourself up for what you can't do. Just do what you can do and you'll be fine." Then she left, and I've never seen her again. But her message made a difference because my antenna was up and I was listening, and I learned something.

Listening And Learning

There is nothing like the joy of jamming, when everybody hits the same groove and flies together. It lifts you off the ground, and there's no other high like it. It's what you live for as a musician, and listening and paying attention to what the other guy is doing is essential to getting there. The sad thing is, it's so obvious, yet so few do it. And it's a terrible problem musically when a person just goes his way with blinders on, without listening to the whole sound.

Most of the people we surround ourselves with and who join us from time to time at the Iridium are good listeners. If someone comes along who isn't, they either get there quick or they're gone. And it's not a mystery. We train ourselves to

331

be that way. Coming up to the seventh and eighth bar, there's an automatic caution because that's the turnaround point where anything can happen. Maybe it's going to be a key change, maybe someone is going to take a solo break, but whatever it is, if you're just sailing along in your own little world and not paying attention, you're going to run through the wall and blow it for everyone.

I know this, and I learned it by making all the mistakes a musician could make. And it's the best way to learn because mistakes make an impression, and you want to remember not to make them again if you can help it. Mistakes are part of the musical process because they tell you what not to do, and sometimes they lead to something unique you couldn't have discovered any other way.

Adapting To Limitations

The obvious limitation on my music is the arthritis, and the way it has slowly but surely become a part of my life is interesting. If it were something that happened suddenly, all at once, like losing an arm or leg, it would be devastating. But the onset and progression of the arthritis has been spread over a 40-year period of time, and as it ate away my old abilities, I had to replace what was lost with what could be found in order to keep playing. The disease moved from one finger to the next until now, the only finger I can bend on my left hand is the little finger. All the others are frozen. But despite this incurable deterioration, and the continual abuse my fingers have taken with all the medications and treatments, the desire to keep going is so strong that I've found ways to play without the movement of the fingers, which would not have seemed possible 40 years ago.

One Good Note

To keep going, you have to ask yourself: if the hands are gone, what advantage do you have? And I can tell you one advantage; you have a choice. You've gone from having the ability to play all the notes very fast to playing just one single note very selectively. So it becomes something new to learn. And if you're only going to play one note, which note are you going to play, and exactly where are you going to put it? That's the challenge, and there are ways of meeting it.

If you have the technique and use it to play two thousand notes when just a few would be a better expression, then your technique is controlling you. So the challenge is to get all that feeling into fewer notes, and this is where you're forced into something that may turn into an advantage. The advantage comes from having to look further and deeper into what you're doing to get the feeling you want because you can no longer fall back on the technique as an easy

out. And this is not something you're consciously thinking about; it's just the natural process of adapting your will to what's available to use.

I know this because when I was young, I was a racehorse and much of the time played too fast. As the years went by and the arthritis progressed, I learned to play less and have it mean more, and now I'm down to playing one note, which is a limitation, but I have all the choices in the world for which note it's going to be and how I'm going to play it. So you give up something, but you also gain something important through the loss.

The last time I saw Count Basie was years ago when he was being given a special Grammy award. They wheeled him out in a wheelchair, and he just sat there with his hand resting on the piano while the band did one of his classic numbers. They were wailing and sounding great, and then, at the perfect moment, boom, his hand dropped and hit a single note, and it was the best damn note I ever heard. That was a very meaningful experience because it showed the way and helped me realize it's not the technique that makes the music, it's the soul you put into the notes, whether it's one or a million.

CHAPTER THIRTY-ONE

Chasing The Sound

When we were making the first Les Paul guitars, Gibson wanted all the klunker electronics to be transferred over to the new line. I gave them some of it, but not all because that sound was my identity, and I didn't want to give it away. Instead, I took the stock guitars they built and continued to modify them for Mary and I. Gibson came at me over and over about this, but I never have exposed the complete information on how I got that big ballsy sound.

In the '60s, when Gibson was starting to make the Les Paul guitar again, the president of the company was in my home, and he said, "Jesus Christ, Les, you gotta tell us how you get that sound." And I said, "No, not yet. I'm still in the middle of it myself." He wanted everybody who bought one of our guitars to be able to get that big beautiful sound, but I was still protective of it. My stock answer was to say it's my trade secret, and I always told them, "When I'm finally done playing and ready to hang it up for good, then I'll give it to you."

During the time before the heart surgery, when I was having life-threatening health concerns, I went to Gibson and said, "Okay, I'm hanging up the guitar. I'm done." They said, "Well, finally, we're going to get your secret." And I said, "I'll go further than that. I'll give you all the drawings and specifications, all the electrical designs and you can make the guitar and put it out there. It's my baby, my secret weapon, and now it's yours because I'm retiring from the business."

So I gave Gibson all my secrets, which elated them to no end, and out came the Les Paul Recording Guitar, which is what I'm playing at the club now. There are no changes in the pots, the capacitors, the wiring, or anything else. It's exactly the same. The guitars Gibson introduced around 1970 were identical to the way I had my own guitars put together, including the low impedance pickups. And when they came out, they were ignored, and finally discontinued in 1980.

The Whole Pie

The Les Paul Recording Guitar didn't sell because the kids were into overdriving the input to get distortion, and to get the pleasant distortion they wished to hear, the pickup has to brutally hit the first stage of the amplifier. But instead of giving you that, my guitar gives you just the opposite. It says, "I'm gonna give you the complete, full tone, and then it's up to you what to do with it." So you can take that complete tone and EQ it, flange it, add highs, add bass, delay and distortion, do any and all variables you want with your

funny boxes, but don't do it at the source!

The source, the signal from my guitar, comes out a complete pie. If you want just part of that pie, Okay, then you cut out what you want and put it to use. But you have to know what you're looking for, and know how to get it. And that has to come from the person, the player. It sure as hell doesn't come from some manufacturer who thinks you can wire balls into a guitar. When that happens, all you wind up with is a dog with a pair of balls hanging out. The player should dictate the sound, not the instrument; otherwise, the instrument is playing you instead of the other way around.

The amplifiers I used were another important part of creating my signature sound. There were two or three of them I fooled with, and each one had its own characteristics, but mostly, I used one particular amplifier that I modified. It wasn't the Toaster or the Fender, it was one I developed myself, so there was no name on it at all. It was my own.

With a Lansing speaker in it, I got the ultimate, best sound I ever had for playing in person, not on records. That amp was the best I ever had for getting my live sound to match the guitar sound on my records, and it wasn't just me who thought so. I worked a special show at Carnegie Hall with Benny

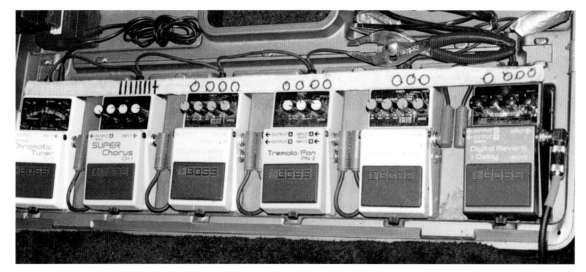

These are the funny boxes I use at the Iridium.

Goodman, Buddy Rich, Ella and Count Basie. A saxophone player was sitting right beside my amplifier, and when I hit just one note, he jumped out of his chair and said, "Jesus Christ! I'd give anything to have that sound."

This was also the amp I used to play the first coast-to-coast broadcast of the Grand Ole Opry, when Chet came out of the band and was down on the floor with a flashlight. It had an enclosed back, and Chet was so taken by the sound he was trying to look inside through the air vents. And it was during a broadcast of Bing Crosby's radio show when Bing got down on the dirty floor, propped his head on his elbow right in front of this amplifier, and closed his eyes.

It got everyone's attention because it was such a big sound, and nothing like it had been heard before. It was just my klunker plugged into my amp, with no other effects, but other things contributed to the overall result. It was the size of the cabinet, the way the cabinet was built and put together, the modifications built into the circuitry, the speaker, the guitar, and it all fit together. It was just one of those wonderful happenings where all the ideas you've been chasing come together and become something more than the parts.

And something important to keep in mind is that this was for live performing, so I could reproduce on stage the sound that was so humongous on my records. But when I was recording, I got that sound by feeding my guitar directly into the mixing board, with no amplifier involved. So to have the same sound playing in person as I got on my records, I had to use a different way to get there.

The final element of my secret is the part I can't do anything about because it comes down to the way you play, and what you're feeling when you play it. I can pick up anybody's guitar, and there it is. It's in your fingers, it's in your head, it's in what you can get out of what you've got. So the guy says, "I'm playing the same guitar you play, I'm playing the same things you play, and I've got the amplifier set just right. So how come I don't get that big ballsy sound?" And I can only tell him, "Well, you're not me. Figure it out."

336

The Right Way To Play

Other than having the will to practice and the gifts of a good ear and rhythm, the most necessary thing in being able to express yourself on the guitar is knowing the instrument thoroughly. If you accomplish that, then you can play whatever's happening wherever your hand happens to be. That's a lot different than having to go to a certain location on the neck to play something because that's where you learned it, and the only place where you know how to do it

The first person to demonstrate this for me was a piano player who would say, "Just show me where the first note is." I'd sit next to him at the piano, and play *it-had-to-be-you*. Then he'd hit *it-had-to-be-you* right after me, and that's all he needed. He knew the instrument so well, he didn't need to know what

Everyone has a good time on Monday nights at the Iridium, including me. Sometimes I crack myself up.

key we were in, or what the chord changes were. All he needed was the location of the first note, and he was ready to go.

I applied to the guitar what I saw him do on the piano, and it led to the understanding that once you truly know your instrument, no matter where you place your hand on the neck, you're home, and you can play what you want to play without hunting it down. And that's something most guitar players don't bother to learn how to do. They can play it great here, but they can't play it there. And to call yourself a guitar player, you should be able to play it anywhere.

Sunny Joe's Teaching Technique

When I was first seriously learning the guitar, Joe Wolverton used to make life very interesting in the way he challenged me to explore the instrument. After I had learned something new, he would remove one or two strings and say, "Now play it." And that's how I learned. I would figure out how to play something on six strings, and then Joe would remove some of them so I'd have to find a different way to play the same thing. Joe taught me to play this way at a very early age, and it proved to be a tremendous asset throughout my career. And it all comes down to knowing your instrument thoroughly and completely, from one end to the other. It's the academic approach, and I didn't always like it, but have since realized how fortunate I was to be exposed to it when I was learning the instrument.

It's like the Julliard student who came into the club. When I asked him how he liked being a student there, he said, "Well, I'm not too happy with it because rather than learning songs and compositions, they have me endlessly doing scales, and it's boring the hell out of me." And I said, "If you don't know your chords and scales, you don't know anything. You've got to have the basics down before you can do anything else." It wasn't what he was expecting to hear from me, but I was agreeing with his instructors because I got the same thing from Joe, and from Segovia.

Segovia

My manager also managed Andrés Segovia. And one day Segovia said to him, "You handle Les Paul. He makes a lot of money, doesn't he?" And my manager, Braunstein, said, "Yes, he does." And Segovia asked, "Well, what does he do that is so successful?" And my manager told him I played the electric guitar and made recordings, both in a unique way.

Subsequently, I met Segovia and had the pleasure of conversing with him when we would attend the same gatherings. He was already hammering and pulling off and doing all those things on the classic guitar that they're finding and using now. But with Segovia, they were already there. He'd say, "If you've got to get from here to there, and the bridge is washed out, then you've got to devise a way to get across." Those are the kinds of questions I was asking him. I'd say, "Well, if you land with this finger on this string on this fret, then how do you get from there to where you need to go?" We would get into deep discussions about the guitar, comparing his tremendous classic technique to my jazz playing.

Segovia was a terribly talented and well-versed individual who studied the guitar with great dedication, and knew how to play all the most intricate, difficult figures. He knew his instrument completely, and would ponder over certain situations where the arrangement, as written and transposed for guitar, called for something impossibly hard to do. The arranger would be willing to alter the notation to make it easier, but Segovia would say, "No, no. Leave it as it is." He welcomed the challenge of playing it the most difficult way, and would consider every possibility for how to accomplish it.

Classic Conspiracy

It was during my time of retirement, I think in the early 70s, when Segovia came to me with a problem. He wanted to amplify his classic guitar so it wasn't so apologetic and hard to hear in the large venues he played. But, he didn't want to injure his guitar in any way, and he didn't want the electronic enhancement to be seen, or discovered, or known.

My interest in amplifying the acoustic guitar went back to the '40s, and at the time we met, I was already occupied with making a pickup for piano and for drums. So I invited Segovia to my house and showed him what I had, and

339

we discussed what he wanted to accomplish. He didn't want to alter his sound; he just wanted to reinforce it. He wanted to find a way to amplify the natural acoustic sound of his guitar so it could be better heard, but not so anyone listening would know electronics were involved.

So I got into the problems of how to accomplish this, and began to study the properties of the classic guitar. Segovia gave me a letter introducing me to his personal guitar makers in Europe, and I went to four different ones – in Spain, Geneva, Munich and one other place – to see what they were doing. And every one of them was trying to make a guitar for him that would project a louder, bigger sound.

In amplifying Segovia's guitar, we were going to have to make it wireless, which was a new thing. The solution I came up with for the amplifier was to build it into the bottom of whatever he sat on when he played on stage. The amplifier would be a box with a chair back on it, just sitting there on stage. Then Segovia would come out with his guitar, sit down on it, and play his concert.

One problem was that a large enough speaker couldn't be used to properly enhance the lowest notes of his guitar. The higher notes were easy, but the lower ones were a problem, and there were problems with the wireless connection and other things. He was very excited about doing it, and so was I, but the answers for the problems he was having were very difficult to find, and we never had a working model good enough for him to try publicly.

Incidentally, the great piano player who just died, Joe Bushkin, made his last album at my home studio using the pickup I made for Segovia, which I applied to his piano.

340

Segovia's Demon

The other thing we talked about was the fact that what bothered Segovia most was to hear his recordings played back. This was something he just despised because all the sliding of the fingers and other extraneous noise would be emphasized in the recording by the closeness of the microphone, which was not the case when hearing him play live. And he never heard a recording of his guitar that matched what he heard with his own ears, and with the vibrations that went through his body when he held the guitar and played it.

The vibrations he felt in his innards were a part of his playing, and there was no way to get that onto a record. When he played, he *felt* that guitar, he wrapped his hands around it and it became a part of him. And when he listened to a recording of that same playing, he heard all the things that shouldn't be there, and none of what made playing the instrument so important to him. So he couldn't get enthused about his records. He would say, "Why can't we make a record that sounds like what I hear when I play?"

Segovia's complaint stated the same problem I had been working on since the garage studio, and which we still have today. Even with multiple microphones, you can put someone in a room and record them playing acoustically until they say, "Okay, I played my best and that sound is me." And you've got a monitor speaker hanging on the wall. It might be a Western Electric, an RCA, or a Lansing speaker, but whatever it is, it colors the sound of the playback. It can be honky, it can be metallic, whatever qualities the speaker creates, and it can be anything but the truth.

When Segovia went into the studio and played something, it was perfection, as good as he could possibly do it. But when it was played back, he did not hear what he had heard when he played it. His biggest disappointment in the music business was the recording, the sound.

Maintaining The Standard

First you find your sound; you create it, and then build your style around it. And no matter where you're playing, you want to have that identity because it's that personal sound that makes you different from the rest of the crowd. So developing the identity of your sound is one thing, but being able to produce it consistently with all the variables that are always going to come up, that's the challenge that never goes away.

And that unique sound is what we work so hard to get because, as far as I'm concerned, the reason people come into the club is not just to see Les Paul, but to hear him. And in order to maintain what my reputation is all about, the sound has to be excellent. This is why we spend several hours every

341

Monday doing sound and lighting checks before the first show. We're dealing with a house sound system that's been used by various acts during the preceding week, with the leakage on stage from our different microphones, trying to address all the variables to make sure the person who pays to get in hears the very finest sound we can give them, and likewise for the lighting.

I know what it's like to try and make a living as a working musician, and sometimes a guy will take a job just because he needs the money. And maybe he doesn't care whether it sounds good, bad or indifferent because that's not the point. It's a job, and he's just there to get paid. But when they work for me, I try to make it as much a family affair as I can to consistently give people an unusually good show and an experience they'll be glad to remember. I believe all the members of my group take pride in being a part of it, and so do I.

To accomplish that, everything involved has to be the best it can be, and that's our basic thinking every Monday night. We try to make every performance the finest one we ever had. And that's the reason for the line around the block at the Iridium. And if you buy one of our records, you say the same thing. "My God, isn't that a wonderful sound." You don't see on a record, you only hear on a record, and what we're selling is sound.

The Iridium Band

I am very fortunate to be surrounded with such great talents.

Tommy Doyle has been doing the sound for me for twenty years, and Lou has been playing guitar with me just as long. Frank and Nicki came along about four years ago and it's like we've been playing together forever. John Colianni joined us last summer, and his piano has added another wonderful element to our sound.

All the people I work with are the best in the business at what they do, and I always compliment them when they're good. If Nicki or Frank or John plays a great solo, I'm waiting when they come off stage to

342

I play with this group every Monday night at the Iridium in New York City. That's Lou Pallo, Nicki Parrott, me, and Frank Vignola. My piano player, John Colianni, had not yet joined the group when this photo was made in 2002.

Tom Doyle

tell them how good it was. And that includes my son Rusty, who helps maintain the quality of my sound, and videotapes each performance. Do it now while he can hear you. And I try to do that with everybody involved. They're all great players, and any praise I give them is deserved.

Tom Doyle

Tom Doyle, an excellent guitarist in his own right, has been the Monday night audio engineer for Les since performances began at Fat Tuesday's in 1984. An avid LP fan since his early teens, Tom has known Les personally for over 40 years.

"In the '60s, my sister and I had an act based on duplicating the music of Les Paul and Mary Ford, complete with a sound engineer, Concert Tone recorder, 350 Ampex and a speaker system I built myself. We played our instruments live with pre-produced background tapes, and did everything we could to sound like Les and Mary. Someone sent Les a telegram telling him what we were doing, and he decided to come and see us."

"We were at the Silver Fountain in Montvale, New Jersey, doing *Bye-Bye Blues*, when Les walked in on us. When we finished the song, he walked up and said, "How you doing, kid?" You know, he's bigger than life, and we were speechless. He said, "You kids are great! Play!" I said, "Les, I can't. I'm rubber now." That was in 1965, and we've been friends ever since."

"In 1984, when Les was just getting into the Fat Tuesday's thing, he invited me to come see the show. The manager of the place was running the soundboard, and Les wanted me to hear it because he wasn't satisfied with the results. At Les' request, I became his Monday night soundman, and 20 years later I'm still honored to be doing it. He's a genius, an amazing entertainer, and what a wonderful legacy it is for me to be part of it."

Lou Pallo

Lou Pallo, Les' longtime musical associate, is a well-known session guitarist, having recorded with the Four Seasons, Dion and the Belmonts, and many others. More recently, he worked with Keith Richards on a recording project honoring Hank Williams, Sr., which won a Grammy award. Lou works steadily with his own group, but Monday nights are reserved for the Iridium and performing with Les.

"I've been working with Les for over 20 years, and it's still an honor to be on the bandstand with him because he is truly a genius. I've worked with many other people, but I've met more people in show business working with Les than I ever could with anybody else, and they all respect him, even the biggest names."

"After working together for so many years, I know where Les wants to go when I hear the first note, and whether he wants to slow the tempo down, or pick it up. If he wants to do *Long, Long Time*, he talks about Bing Crosby, and I know to start the song right away. Our whole show is like that, just automatic, and we've never needed to rehearse because the way it fits together comes naturally to us."

Lou Pallo

"I play engagements all over with my own group, and occasionally do things on my own, but working with Les is still the main thing for me. Les is just unique, and there will never be another like him. You listen to the records he made 50 years ago, and you listen to all the people since then who have tried to copy what he did, and no one comes near what Les Paul has done. And they never will because he's something special, a true genius."

Frank Vignola

Frank Vignola is a gifted guitarist and one of the world's most accomplished players in the Django Reinhardt tradition of jazz. He has worked with the Who's Who of jazz, including Hank Jones, Lionel Hampton, Tony Bennett and Bucky Pizzarelli, and travels all over the world performing as a soloist. Frank has been a member of Les' Monday night group since 2000.

"Les was one of my early guitar heroes, and still is because he plays so beautifully. His tone is amazing, and his selection and phrasing are just impeccable. It doesn't get any better than what I hear him do every Monday night."

Frank Vignola

"Since I started playing with Les regularly, which was in February 2000, I've learned how to listen to my guitar, always concentrating on what it sounds like, and what you can do to make it sound better. And I learned this because every week, Les is here three hours, four hours before the gig, working on the sound to get it right and make it the best it can be. I've learned the value of listening from Les because he's so tuned in to what's going on around him, and he never misses a thing."

"And there's a lesson there that goes beyond the music coming out of those efforts. It's the example of having the respect and dedication and love for what you're doing. If anybody can have that in life, with anything, they're going to be just fine. There are very few people I can say this about, but I've enjoyed every minute I've spent with him."

Nicki Parrott

A native of Australia now residing in Brooklyn, Nicki's musical education began at the age of five. Originally a student of piano and flute, she gravitated to bass in her mid-teens and discovered an affinity for the instrument. Comfortable with a wide variety of musical genres, she is now in demand as both an electric and acoustic bassist, working regularly in the New York area and traveling to other engagements around the country.

"I liked Les instantly the first time I sat in, and was thrilled when he asked me to join the group. I have learned so much being around him and working with him, and the fascinating people you get to meet through the Monday performances couldn't be found anywhere else. People from all walks of life, of all ages and career types from all over the

Nicky Parrott

world are in the audience every week. It's a unique situation, and an honor to be associated with him."

"The other thing I appreciate is the chemistry in the band. I play all the time, and not all groups have a great unity. But in this group, the rapport is complete because we all love Les, and that's what I really enjoy. The best way to make music is to be with friends and people you really respect, and all of us in the group realize how privileged we are to be a part of what he's doing."

John Colianni

Demonstrating an aptitude for piano at an early age, John Colianni became a serious student of the instrument at 14 and worked regularly with Lionel Hampton while still in his teens. For 4 1/2 years, he toured and recorded with Mel Torme, and has released several albums of his own work. Now considered among the elite of contemporary jazz pianists, John has been a member of the Iridium group since September 2003.

John Colianni

"I am very glad I was chosen to revive the piano as a solo and ensemble instrument in the Les Paul Quintet. Playing with Les is always fun and exciting because Les himself selects the material and creates our imaginative musical routines. Every show, we meet the challenge of numbers that move from R&B, jazz, country and blues to ballads, rock and show tunes, all of which reflect his unique musical concepts and skills as an arranger."

"Les' tonality and phrasing on the electric guitar are among the most recognizable sounds in all of music, and his sense of rhythm never falters. Altogether, he's an inspiring and magnetic musician to work with, and a great entertainer whose humorous stories and quips onstage are always an informative pleasure to hear."

"Musically, I consider it a rare privilege to be a member of Les Paul's group, and I enjoy his company tremendously offstage. In addition to his obvious talents, Les is a very pleasant and likeable person, and it's great to be a part of his world."

CHAPTER THIRTY-TWO

The Gift

I don't want to ever believe there's anything radically different between me and the next guy. Just because someone can't play steady rhythm or hear the right note doesn't make them bad. It just means they're gifted differently. We're all gifted in some way, so I don't see it as a big deal. I didn't do anything remarkable other than the fact that if I thought of something and it wasn't there, I tried to make it so it would be there. If I had an idea, I didn't just think about it, I built it. And if I hadn't done it, some other guy would've come along to get it done, sure as hell.

I have always, my whole life, been very active, following the impulse to carry forward to the next thing, and it's that drive and curiosity which has helped me get the most out of whatever gifts I was born with. It's the difference between just thinking and actually doing that has set me apart more than anything else. It's like it was bound to happen. Somebody had to do it, and that somebody was me.

The Seeds Are Planted

I'll tell you how this all came about. First, I think you have to be born with the persistent urge to become what's been planted in you. Plant a radish seed, and what you get is a radish; plant rhubarb, and you get rhubarb. And I believe these particular seeds, the genes that determine our make up, carry that impulse, that persuasion to the particular drive you have that pushes you along and keeps you going. When you're five, six or eight years old, you aren't conscious of it, but the curious kid who was poking holes in the piano roll and me at my age right now are still the same guy, with the same motivation.

I think Django had it born into him that way, and Eddie Lang. I was listening for Eddie Lang before I ever heard him because he was doing what I was going to be looking for. And it wasn't going to be the saxophone because if you hand one to me, I'll say, "Forget it." Hand me a drum and it's, "Forget that, too." It's a certain sound you're looking for, and you're naturally attracted to the instrument that makes the sound. After you locate your instrument, then it's the style you're attracted to. All these things add up and connect with your God-given sense of what's musically and rhythmically right; then your ego enters into it, and your personal style comes into being.

Here's an odd one from the early 1970s. We called it the Les Paul Jumbo, an acoustic flattop with a low-impedance single coil pickup plus a piezo under the bridge. I think Gibson made less than 100 of these, so they are quite rare today.

The Heart Of The Matter

I've been asked what was at the heart of everything I've done; was it music, was it recording or was it inventing? It was all of them together, but I've said many times, playing the guitar was important, but more than the guitar was the time consumed in building the stuff that wasn't there. So it wasn't just playing the guitar, it was building the guitar and getting it to sound right that really drove me.

I'm very proud of the Les Paul guitar. For one thing, we had the care and smarts to make it well and make it beautiful. Just recently, I was looking at a display of guitars, and I couldn't help thinking ours look better. And I asked myself, "Is this just because the guitar has my name on it, or is it the truth?" And, by God, the truth is our guitars *are* prettier, and classier.

Another thing I'm proud of is the fact that so many players who could have any guitar in the world choose the Les Paul. And not only do they choose it, they stay with it for keeps. And in the world of guitar players, that's something else. I'm very grateful to all the musicians who have made my guitar the standard by which others are measured. They didn't have to do it, but they did, and it was their honest preference that made the Les Paul guitar what it is today. And they're not playing it because of me personally. They're playing the

351

Les Paul guitar because they can sound better with it. They choose the sound they like best, the sound they love, and that makes me feel so good because it was the sound we were so focused on. That's what we did, and they're agreeing with me. It's one of the most satisfying things of my life.

And it was the same way with the recording machinery. It took a tremendous effort and help from a lot of people to build all the things that made such a difference, and without these inventions, the guitar would not be where it is now. Playing guitar, recording and inventing were separate areas I was involved in, but they were all in the same family. I think my guitar playing was pretty good, but without the inventions, the guitar and the records we made wouldn't have been as remarkable.

From the beginning, the guitar came easy to me. Everyone talked about how fast I played, but usually, I wasn't trying to play fast. I was just playing, and I was still in the process of learning that one right note is better than a bunch of half-right notes. And now the guy who could play so fast, who played all the licks that have been copied for generations, can't bend his fingers. But it's okay because I've compensated by learning the value of a single note.

These are the things that happen to a person that are the real challenge of carrying on with life. And it's these challenges that make you better and prove beneficial to you, if they don't break you. The good times are easy, but when you run into roadblock after

roadblock after roadblock, it becomes increasingly difficult to keep finding ways to make something of what you have left. I look at most of my buddies, and 99 percent of them have hung it up. They've said, "To hell with it. I can't do this like I used to, so I'm bagging it. I'm going hunting and fishing, I'm playing golf, forget it."

Walking away from the thing you love and have spent your whole life involved in, throwing it all away just because you've lost some of your ability, this is what I don't get. What bothers me is that you know you're not going to get it back, but you keep practicing anyway. This is amusing, and I laugh at myself for doing it, but it's true...you keep practicing knowing you're not going to get any better. Well, maybe a little.

Music For The People

After World War II was over, I attended a party for Capitol recording artists at Glen Wallich's home, where I had an interesting debate with Stan Kenton. He said, "I believe I was put here to educate the people as to what good music is." And I said, "That's a good point, but I don't believe the people coming to see me are wanting to be educated as much as they want to be entertained. They want to go out happy, and I want them to be satisfied." We had quite a discussion about it, and there was a big difference in the way we each regarded our audience. And just a short time later, Mary and I played an engagement where Stan Kenton's band backed us and we appeared on the same stage together.

During the performance, I was watching the dance floor and saw that Stan Kenton was not looking at the people and relating to them. Instead, he was looking at his band and getting knocked out by his own players. He's listening to his music and not looking at the people, and they're walking off the floor because they can't dance to the music. And this was a foolish thing because, for me, the whole idea of music is to fit the dance. The dance and the music have to come together, and the two have to marry. So you write the music to fit the dance, or the dance is created to fit the music, but either way, you have to be considerate of your audience. Otherwise, you may as well stay home and play for the goldfish.

Whether it is significant or just coincidence, I don't know, but the music changed after World War II. My small role in the war effort was to be involved on the front lines of what was happening with the music. And I played not only with Benny Goodman, Artie Shaw, Tommy Dorsey, Louie Armstrong and all the greats of jazz and swing, but also with Dizzy Gillespie and all the be-boppers who were coming in with this new, frantic music.

Be-bop somehow struck a nerve with certain people as the war ended, but your average Joe coming home from Europe or the Pacific didn't understand it. And it wasn't understood because be-bop was not intended for the public; it was for the musicians themselves who were constantly dueling it out. Bop was all about speed and riffing and never taking a breath. It was all 'go man go,' and very competitive. And in the wake of this, the familiar rhythms, arrangements and danceable tempos of swing were disappearing. So all the soldiers and gals came home to find this new music eliminating the old and leaving them nothing they could dance to.

All Those Licks

Back in the '40s, I told Gibson I wanted the biggest, fastest frets they had; jumbo frets like you now find on an electric bass. I wanted railroad tracks on my guitar because they gave me a better target for all the pull-offs and hammers I did. I got the basics of those licks from listening to Django and Eddie Lang, and then went my own way. I could play every note either of them ever recorded, but I wasn't doing it to copy them. I did it to figure out what they were doing so I could take it further.

All the jamming I did with great piano players and horn players had an influence on my guitar playing, too. When you listen to my earlier jazz stuff, such as the trio with Fred Waring, some of those licks you hear came from seeds planted by Art Tatum and Roy Eldridge and Benny Goodman, to name a few.

They would do something that grabbed me, and without even thinking about it, I'd take it to the guitar. All the influences from all the musicians I played with, from country to jazz to pop, came together with Django and Eddy to provide the basis for what I've done. Now the younger cats have done the same thing with me, and I say that's cool.

As a guitarist, I reached my peak in the '40s, when I was jamming every night with all the great jazz players. I loved to jam, and did a lot more of it than sleeping or eating in those days. So playing almost constantly in the clubs and on the radio, and coming up against so many gifted musicians night after night, I worked up some formidable chops. This period was really the highlight of my pure playing days because it was all me, with no layered tracks or special effects other than an amplifier. My hands were strong, the ideas were pouring out and the electric guitar was the greatest adventure in the world.

But once I reached a certain level on the guitar, I also became more and more interested in electronics and audio engineering and related technical things. The guitar then became an important tool in my recording experiments, and I was no longer pushing all the time to get better, as I had been. Also, making the decision to try and make commercially successful recordings, joining up with Mary and all that, took my attention away from guitar technique to some degree. Then came sound-on-sound, followed by magnetic tape and I was gone into that world for keeps.

I have never felt my guitar playing was all that great. I'm not ashamed of my playing, but I was never satisfied or greatly impressed with it. If I hit a lot of right notes, well, I was supposed to hit them. And the same goes for all the other guitar players I've listened to. I would hear what was good, and what wasn't, but I never heard everything in one guy. All of us have our limitations because, for starters, we're human. What comes naturally to me is hard for someone else, and a lot of things I wouldn't think of doing work great for the next guy. You can find something good in anyone's playing, no matter who it is, but there is no perfect guitar player, just as there is no perfect sound.

Chasing Perfection

No way has anybody, to my knowledge, ever achieved the perfect sound because there's no such thing. It doesn't exist except in the mind. And out in the actual world of magnetism and sound waves, with all the complexity and variables involved, it's very difficult to come out with a sound you can duplicate consistently. So many times, I would hear an idea that felt right, and lay it into a recording. Then I'd listen to it and say, "Well, that's pretty darn good. I'll do that again." And then the time comes to do it again, and you say, "Well, that isn't what I want to do at all."

Or I may spend half a day setting up one of my guitars in a particular way that seems exactly right at the time. Then I'm getting ready to play the gig, and I no more than walk into the room before I say, "Well, my action's too low now. I shouldn't have done that. What the hell was I thinking?" I think this same thing happens to everybody, in all areas of life, not just in music. But I'm also quite sure the guitar players, musicians and other artists who read this will be nodding their heads in agreement.

I can't understand why people have decided they like me, and love my music and the music Mary and I made. But when people bring me things, like a guitar, and want to give it to me or have me sign it, I realize what I've done has meaning to them. I'm humbled every time it happens, and sometimes, it's an emotional moment for both of us.

A doctor came to me at the club, handed me his card, and said, "I'm a brain surgeon, and I've been waiting 49 years to meet you. I'm a great admirer of your music, and I never do surgery without your records playing in the background. I listen for those certain moments that turn me on, and it helps me because it's just so great." And then, out of nowhere, with a group of people looking on, he broke down and cried. He said, "I feel so bad. I made such a fool of myself." And I said, "No, I understand. I understand."

I've had that kind of thing happen many times, in differing circumstances, with people who have been deeply touched by my music. The reasons vary from person to person, but the result is the same, and there's no way to explain it. It's strange. You'd like to know what is you've done that matters to people. But you can't name it. It's part of the mystery. And you don't ever want to solve it completely because if you do, there's nothing left to learn, or live for. As long as there's tomorrow, there's always going to be something new waiting when you wake up.

CHAPTER THIRTY-THREE

Encores And Echoes

I've dodged a lot of bullets from critics over the past 75 years, but I'm not at all concerned with any of that now. Ask me if I'm proud of what I've accomplished in my career, and I'll say, "You're damn right, I am." I've made many mistakes, I've stepped on some toes, but I got things done. And I know some of the things I've done, the recordings, the inventions, the influence I've had on the electric guitar, are going to be around for a long time.

And now I'm in the Rock and Roll Hall of Fame, the Country Music Hall of Fame, the Smithsonian Hall of Fame; and I'm in the history books for inventing multi-track recording, echo reverb and many other things. I can't begin to remember it all, and now I'm working with three different museums that will be preserving some of the things I've conceived and built. And I don't say this to brag, but to acknowledge how much I appreciate having my efforts recognized and acknowledged as being of some value. Am I also thumbing my nose at the critics? Yeah, maybe, just a little.

I've been asked how I want to be remembered, and my answer is, I doubt if I will be. And I'm speaking of me as a person now, as an individual. I think the things I've done with guitars and recording technology have some staying power, and some of the songs Mary and I recorded will still be knocking people out a hundred years from now, but Les Paul, Rhubarb Red, Lester Polfuss, those guys are going to fade. I've got great fans and friends all over the world, but most people now, when they hear "Les Paul," if it means anything to them they're thinking it's a guitar. They don't have any idea there's a person by that name behind it. And that's okay.

I haven't drummed up any list of final wishes for how I want this or that done when my time comes to move on. I just say, "By God Almighty, whatever the

deal is, it's no big deal. It's the same for everybody, and perfectly natural." And who but a few know where Sinatra is buried now, or where Bing is buried, or where anybody else is buried, and who cares? You're here and you do your thing, and maybe people love you for it, but when you make your exit, that's it. Your time is over, and it's time for somebody else to shine. And all I have to say to God is, "Thank you!"

Here's a quartet of Les Paul guitars leaning up against my old Lincoln Continental. All of the guitars I like to play have been fitted with low-impedance pickups because I prefer them.

A Friend At The End

One thing I do think about is that I don't want to go out alone, and I know I won't. I've got my family and the people close to me in my life, and I'm very fortunate to know the things I need will be provided when that time comes. And the most valuable thing of all is just to have a friend. Someone who knows you and knows where you came from and what you've been through, and you know the same about them.

And I keep going back to Wally because he was such a perfect friend. When he left with Carol, I missed him terribly. And then, in later years, he came back and nothing had been lost. He was immediately just as important to what I was doing, and just as dear a friend and pal. And he died in my arms because I made sure he didn't go out alone.

Chet and I became very close during the last ten years or so of his life. He had a tremendous ear for music and could hear things nobody else could hear, which is something we had in common. And I had the utmost respect for his talent as a guitarist. When he died, I was asked for my opinion of him as a guitar player. And I said, "Well, the thing about Chet is that he could do everything I can do, but I can't do everything he could do." And it was my way of tipping my hat to him, to say, "By God, Chet, for what you did, nobody could touch you."

We talked to each other regularly right up to the time when he couldn't talk anymore. And I know there were times when he was really hurting, but he always kept his sense of humor. The last time we talked, he said, "Les, we've got to get our act together. We're on the air in 15 minutes." And without missing a beat, I said, "Okay, Chet. I'm ready when you are. We're all set." And then the nurse took the phone, and said, "You know, he's a quart or two low." And I said, "That's okay, I understand."

But the nurse didn't understand. She thought Chet was out of it, talking nonsense, but we were where we needed to be in our conversation. And it wasn't nonsense because we were communicating with language we both understood. Chet got the phone back, and said, "What time you got there?" I told him, and he said, "You know we only got 15 minutes, Les. Are you ready?" And I said, "Yeah, Chet. I'm ready. We're all set. Let's get tuned up." And then he laughed that funny little laugh, and we said goodbye. And I'm so glad I was there for him in that small way, to be the one who listened to his mind holding on to what had always been so important, to be the friend who understood.

Set Your Sights

When I was a kid, I had my chores to do, and Mother wouldn't let me forget them. She was a drill sergeant barking out the orders, like, "Go up and do the garden, empty the garbage, burn the trash, do this, do that, and blah, blah, blah." And sometimes, like any other kid who would much rather be doing something else, it would just annoy the hell out of me. So I would walk up the hill with the radio blasting from inside the house, and I remember saying to myself so many times, "That radio station right there, I'm not only going to be on that station, but I'm going to play with that piano player right there." And you know, I did just that. I ended up at WBBM playing with Norm Shearer at the piano.

And that same determination to set a goal and just believe without a doubt I could do it led me to Fred Waring, Bing Crosby, the New Sound, *How High The Moon*, Gibson, and on and on. And now my new thing is that I'm going to have a hit record when I'm 90 years old. I tell people this and they laugh. They

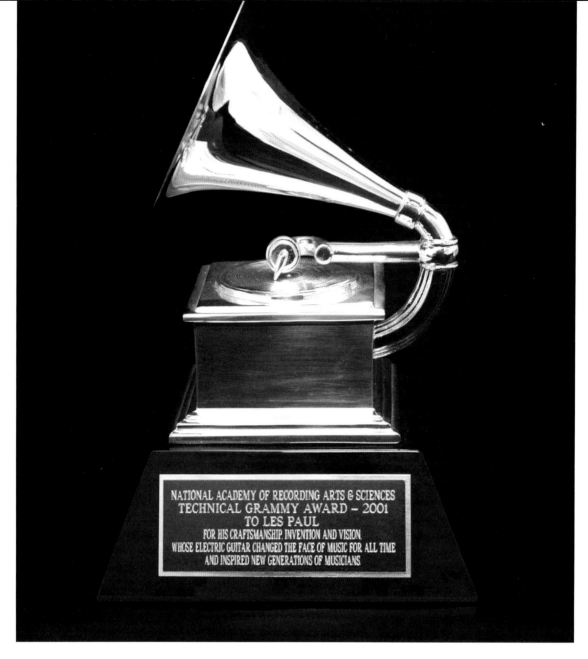

NATIONAL ACADEMY OF RECORDING ARTS & SCIENCES
TECHNICAL GRAMMY AWARD - 2001
TO LES PAUL
FOR HIS CRAFTSMANSHIP, INVENTION AND VISION,
WHOSE ELECTRIC GUITAR CHANGED THE FACE OF MUSIC FOR ALL TIME
AND INSPIRED NEW GENERATIONS OF MUSICIANS

think I'm kidding around, and I am to the extent that I understand why they're laughing, but I'm also serious about it. I don't see any reason in the world why it can't be done. I may not sing on it, or play guitar on it, but it will be a hit record I create, and I'll be 90 when it happens.

So I would say to anyone, set your sights on where you want to go in your life, make up your mind you're going to do it no matter what, and start digging. Give yourself a definite direction, stick to your purpose, and more often than not, you'll get there. The worst that can happen is you try but don't make it, and that's one hell of a lot better than not taking the shot. Whether it works out or not, it may lead to something wonderful you would've otherwise missed. Set your sights. Take the shot. Have a sense of humor, be willing to improvise, and something will work out.

Beyond The Sunset

I've never been one to spend much time looking back because I've never been headed in that direction. I love all the memories, and I've got a million great ones, but you can't live in the past if you want a future. I'm old now, and I've slowed down, but I'm still going, still pushing, still turning over rocks to see what's underneath. I've been quoted so many times saying I've spent my life looking for the perfect sound, trying to build the perfect guitar to play the perfect note. Well, it's good to try. It gets you out of bed, it keeps you interested in being alive, but you're never going to do it. And what if you did find the perfection you were looking for? Then what would you do? So, no, it's not finding perfection I want, it's the chance to keep looking for it. And when I no longer can, then I'm dead. I'm out of this world, and somebody else will have to pick up the chase.

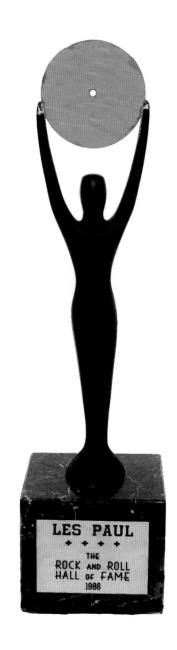

I've been asking questions all my life, but the biggest question of all is the one I've always sidestepped. When someone was about to put it in front of me, I could feel it coming and I'd go a different way before they got there because I didn't want to talk about it. And the question is, is there life after our mortal bodies give out? When the power goes off, does the music continue, and where does it go, and who hears it?

Mother was an atheist, so for her there was nothing to discuss. When you're dead, you're gone, and that's it. If my Dad ever thought much about it, I wouldn't know it because he never talked about it, not one time, and neither did my brother. My whole family, none of them ever really expressed themselves about it. So where most people in the beginning get a certain amount of their spiritual thinking from their family and the way they were raised, I didn't get that. And I don't think that's a bad thing because nobody was shoving anything down my throat, and it left the door open.

So my beliefs on the subject come directly from what I've experienced, from sitting on top of the world to being as far down as you can go. I've nearly died several times from injuries or sickness, and other times I've been in places mentally I wouldn't wish on anyone. And when those times came, I prayed. I asked God to help me get through it, and I did get through it. I've been saved so many times, I know there is a connection to something greater than us here in this one little world.

And I doubt very much if this Truth is a person in the sense that so many people want to believe, that He exists like we exist, that He's black or white or even a He, or that every move we make is being watched and judged, or any of that. I think if you get hung up on those things, you're missing the point.

The thing that really intrigues me is that life is such an awesome thing, and we've been here as far back as we can trace it and it just keeps going from there, in all directions forever. We know this and it's completely beyond us, so how are we ever going to know? It's the old question about the chicken or the egg, and it's the question all the others follow. Has man always been a man? This is something I really wonder about.

The Hard Rock Cafe presented me with this solid marble Les Paul guitar. It weighs a ton!

I once met Scott Carpenter, the astronaut, and I asked him, "When you're up there, and you take a moment to look down at this tiny little earth, does it change your mind or impress you in any way?" And he said, "Well, you look out and see a vast universe, and it's all in motion and somehow tied together, and our little home is part of it. When you see it from that perspective, you know there has to be some reason behind it."

The Big Rug

And this is the terribly interesting thing about being human; that we can know the Logic is there, the Reason, without being able to understand it. This is our condition, including the question every person carries around while they're acting like they'll never die: where do we go when we're dead? It's a tough one to handle, and to manage it, we sweep it under the rug. We've got the biggest rug in the world, and all these things we can't understand and don't want to see, we keep sweeping them under it. We all do it, and I'm not saying it's wrong. It's how we survive, and I understand it because here I am, pushing 90, and now Bing's gone, Mary and Mother and Wally are gone, Sunny Joe and Chet, everybody's gone, and one of

365

Our star on the Hollywood Walk of Fame.

these days, it'll be me. It could be ten years from now or next year or tomorrow when I pack it up. You don't know when it will be, and I've learned to be thankful for that.

And what comes then is only half the answer because it's not only where we go, but where the hell did we come from? Where were we before we got here? It's the greatest riddle of them all, and I know no one knows the answer. If there is an answer, I don't think we get it while we're here. We just go on to the next thing and we find out something when we get there.

As far into the past or the future as we can see, there's always uncertainty, and a lot of people have done a lot of things over the centuries to try and cope with that fact. We all have some way of dealing with it, but you can only think about it so much before you lift up the corner of that big rug and start sweeping. And then you understand how great it is just to wake up the next morning and find you're still here. Because for as much as we don't know, we do know this world is just such an awesome place to be, and you just want to be a part of it and appreciate it for as long as you can.

The Best Advice

And to all those who will be reading this from now on, don't expect to get through this thing without taking a fall. You're going to take a wrong turn and get lost, you're going to discover somebody lied to you, or have to live with the fact that you lied to somebody else. And you're not going to be alone because it's the same for everybody. It's called life. And maybe you can steer things a little bit this way or that way, but you can't control it. Nobody ever tried harder than I did to control it, and I'm telling you now, it can't be done. Some things are going to fall your way when you thought they wouldn't, and sometimes you're going to step on a rake and get a rotten deal when you thought you had it made. And it's the same odds for everybody. Life doesn't owe you a damn thing, but you owe life everything, so get off your ass and do something with it before they put you under the dogwood tree. And the best thing you can do for yourself, as an individual and for the world, is very simple. Try to be a good person, and have a good time doing it. And remember to forgive if you want to be forgiven. Stick with that, and you can't go wrong.

Photo Credits

Les Paul Archives: 8, 9, 11, 12, 13, 14, 16, 22, 23, 25, 26, 37, 38, 46, 48, 50, 51, 53, 58, 60, 61, 62, 64, 65, 69, 77, 79, 87, 88, 90, 104, 105, 106, 108, 116, 124, 133, 135, 137, 139, 143, 145, 146, 150, 152, 155, 157, 162, 165, 167, 168, 174, 175, 179, 180, 183, 191, 193, 194, 195, 196, 203, 215, 217, 219, 225, 250, 251, 252, 254, 255, 261, 265, 267, 269, 270, 271, 272, 275, 278, 309, 365

Wolf Hoffmann: 27, 30, 33, 49, 55, 56, 57, 59, 75, 102, 118, 119, 121, 163, 172, 173, 205, 207, 227, 230, 233, 237, 238, 240, 241, 242, 244, 281, 284, 285, 286, 291, 293, 299, 301, 302, 304, 305, 310, 311, 313, 315, 316, 323, 327, 330, 336, 338, 340, 343, 344, 345, 346, 349, 350, 351, 352, 353, 354, 359, 364, 367

Milwaukee Journal Stations. 1922-1980. Milwaukcc Manuscript Collection 203. Wisconsin Historical Society. Milwaukee Area Research Center.
UWM Libraries. University of Wisconsin-Milwaukee: 21, 34

Agence France Presse/Hulton Archive/Getty Images: 279

Michael Cochran: 7, 333, 335

Russ Cochran: 7, 280, 329, 337

Lou Pallo: 328

Rusty Paul: 6

Fred Waring's America (Pennsylvania State University): 93, 95, 97, 99, 100, 101

Waukesha County Historical Society and Museum: 15, 18, 29

Marty Winter: 295